PENGUIN BOOKS

A SCHOOL FOR MY VILLAGE

Twesigye Jackson Kaguri was raised in Uganda, graduated from Makerere University, and now lives in East Lansing, Michigan. He currently works full-time as the director of the Nyaka and Kutamba AIDS Orphans Schools in Uganda (www.nyakaschool.org).

Susan Urbanek Linville, a biologist and writer, lives in Pennsylvania.

Praise for *A School for My Village*

"Africa's *Three Cups of Tea* . . . A reminder of the boundlessness of human strength and the need to persevere."   —*The Daily Beast*

"This is a remarkable story about how Twesigye Jackson Kaguri transformed his suffering—the loss of several of his family members to AIDS—into action. If you've ever doubted your ability to impact the lives of others, read this story and it will change your mind and heart."
    —Ishmael Beah, author of *A Long Way Gone: Memoirs of a Boy Soldier*

"'Power of One': He started out just building a school. Then Twesigye Kaguri discovered it takes children to raise a village."   —*Time*

"An unforgettable memoir."   —*The Christian Science Monitor*

"Moving . . . Kaguri shows how much one person can do."   —*USA Today*

"This remarkable book is the best case study on the best practices in community-driven development in an African setting. Readers will be inspired by the book's stories as will anyone anywhere who is trying to make the world a better place."
    —Frank Byamugisha, operations adviser for Africa, World Bank, USA

"Many Americans feel disconnected from the AIDS pandemic occurring on a continent so far away. Twesigye Jackson Kaguri, in his inspirational book, shortens that distance, making the effects of this disease personal by giving names and faces to AIDS orphans. But more significantly, many of Uganda's discarded children have been given hope and, even more important, love as students at the Nyaka AIDS Orphans School. Twesigye Jackson's life illustrates beautifully that one person can make a difference."   —Ron Hall, coauthor of the *New York Times* bestselling *Same Kind of Different as Me*

"Twesigye Jackson Kaguri is a force to be reckoned with. He is a social entrepreneur who had a vision and made it a reality. [Here is an] amazing story of how, with courage and deep faith, he has brought the gift of education to children orphaned by AIDS in rural Uganda. I could not put the book down and cried through many parts of it."
    —Maya Ajmera, founder and president, the Global Fund for Children

"By creating a school for AIDS orphans in a remote region of southwestern Uganda, Twesigye Jackson Kaguri answered the question 'And who is my neighbor?' By telling his story with clarity and passion, he makes his neighbors ours as well."
             —Senator John C. Danforth, former U.S. ambassador
                 to the United Nations

"A uplifting read that will resonate with readers long after completion."
                                     —*Deseret News*

"This book shows that you can build a solid educational foundation for the future of Africa's children at the price of stones. Immensely inspiring."
             —Calestous Juma, professor of the practice of international
                 development, Harvard Kennedy School

"Too often we study poverty and disease as abstract phenomena in academic studies. Valuable as such studies are, Twesigye Jackson Kaguri brings us in this book face-to-face with the nature, culture, and response to poverty and the epidemic of HIV/AIDS in rural Uganda. It is also the story of one couple's determination to do something about one of the most moving crises in Uganda, the plight of HIV/AIDS orphans. Kaguri does not flinch from reporting the family arguments, the various manipulations of community and government officials, and the uphill struggle to get something even so fine as a school under way. But in the end it is a story of Africa's resilience, the courage of its peoples, and the ways in which even a small community in America can give hope to those who deserve it the most."

—Princeton N. Lyman, adjunct senior fellow for Africa Policy Studies, Council on Foreign Relations

"By page 23, I was hooked. By page 33, I had tears in my eyes, the first of many times as I read this impassioned account of one man's humble yet courageous efforts in confronting the grim legacy of the ruthless serial killer AIDS in his Ugandan village. If [Kaguri's story] doesn't break your heart over the plight of AIDS orphans in Africa, see a cardiologist immediately. You may need a transplant."

—Lynn Vincent, *New York Times* bestselling coauthor of *Same Kind of Different as Me* and *Going Rogue: An American Life*

"The book details not only the transformation of the young Kaguri, who became an international scholar, but also the seemingly impossible obstacles he overcame to build a school."   —*Lansing City Pulse*

"A reminder of the importance of education in the lives of children around the world."

—Rebecca Winthrop, Ph.D., fellow and codirector, Center for Universal Education, Brookings Institution

"Moved by the plight of more than one million AIDS orphans in a nation with a population of thirty million, Kaguri, a human rights advocate returning home after studying at Columbia University, decided to build a school for children who had lost one or both parents to the syndrome. . . . Anecdotes about the students, the author's family—his own brother and sister died from the disease—and his dealings with donors and corrupt officials, reveal Kaguri to be at once vulnerable and ferociously determined. . . . An affecting and accessible tribute to the difference one person can make in the world."   —*Publishers Weekly*

"A testament to the power of faith and the will to make a difference. A fantastic read—enlightening, enlivening, and inspiring."

—Allan R. Handysides, director, GC Health Ministries, Seventh-day Adventist Church

A
SCHOOL
FOR MY
VILLAGE

A PROMISE TO THE
ORPHANS OF NYAKA

Twesigye Jackson Kaguri

with

Susan Urbanek Linville

PENGUIN BOOKS

Previously published as *The Price of Stones*

PENGUIN BOOKS
Published by the Penguin Group
Penguin Group (USA) Inc., 375 Hudson Street, New York, New York 10014, U.S.A.
Penguin Group (Canada), 90 Eglinton Avenue East, Suite 700, Toronto, Ontario, Canada M4P 2Y3
(a division of Pearson Penguin Canada Inc.)
Penguin Books Ltd, 80 Strand, London WC2R 0RL, England
Penguin Ireland, 25 St. Stephen's Green, Dublin 2, Ireland (a division of Penguin Books Ltd)
Penguin Books Australia Ltd, 250 Camberwell Road, Camberwell, Victoria 3124, Australia
(a division of Pearson Australia Group Pty Ltd)
Penguin Books India Pvt Ltd, 11 Community Centre, Panchsheel Park, New Delhi – 110 017, India
Penguin Group (NZ), 67 Apollo Drive, Rosedale, North Shore 0632, New Zealand
(a division of Pearson New Zealand Ltd)
Penguin Books (South Africa) (Pty) Ltd, 24 Sturdee Avenue, Rosebank,
Johannesburg 2196, South Africa

Penguin Books Ltd, Registered Offices: 80 Strand, London WC2R 0RL, England

First published in the United States of America as *The Price of Stones*
by Viking Penguin, a member of Penguin Group (USA) Inc. 2010
This edition with an afterword by Ali Turro published in Penguin Books 2011

1   3   5   7   9   10   8   6   4   2

This work was previously published by Mr. Kaguri in different form under the title
Nyaka: Saving One Child at a Time.

Photographs courtesy of the Nyaka AIDS Orphans School

THE LIBRARY OF CONGRESS HAS CATALOGED THE HARDCOVER EDITION AS FOLLOWS:
Kaguri, Twesigye Jackson.
The price of stones : building a school in Africa / Twesigye Jackson Kaguri and Susan
Urbanek Linville.
p. cm.
ISBN 978-0-670-02184-0 (hc.)
ISBN 978-0-14-311912-8 (pbk.)
1. Nyaka AIDS Orphans School (Nyakagyezi, Uganda)   2. Children of AIDS patients—
Education—Uganda.   3. Orphans—Education—Uganda.   4. AIDS (Disease)—Uganda.
5. Linville, Susan U. (Susan Urbanek), 1956—Travel—Uganda.   I. Linville, Susan U.
(Susan Urbanek), 1956– II. Title.
LG422.N93K34 2010
372'.96761—dc22   2009049271

Printed in the United States of America
Map by Jeffrey L. Ward   Designed by Nancy Resnick

*Penguin is committed to publishing works of quality and integrity.
In that spirit, we are proud to offer this book to our readers;
however, the story, the experiences, and the words are the author's alone.
The names of some people in the book have been changed to protect their privacy.*

In loving memory of my brother, Frank, and sister, Mbabazi,

and in recognition of my mother and all the grandmothers who have

dedicated their lives to AIDS orphans throughout Africa

"The stone that the builders rejected has become the chief cornerstone."

—PSALMS 118:22

CONTENTS

A
SCHOOL
FOR MY
VILLAGE

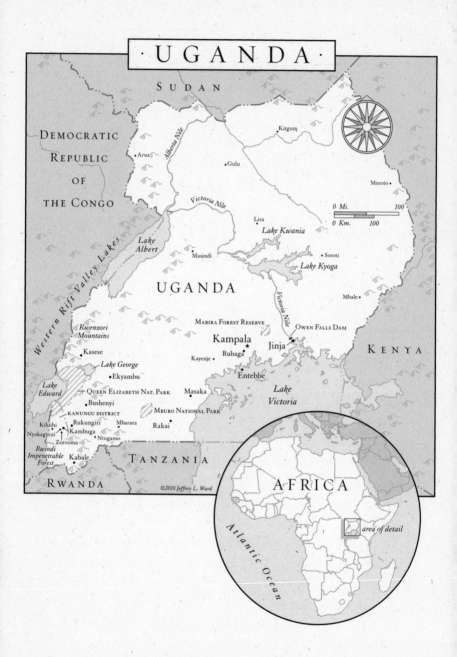

INTRODUCTION

From Uganda's capital, Kampala, it is a day-long journey by car to the village of Nyakagyezi. The main highway traverses a plateau along Lake Victoria's northern shore until it begins a gradual climb to the southwestern highlands. Bordered by the Democratic Republic of the Congo to the west and Rwanda to the south, the area is home to the Rwenzori Mountains, Western Rift Valley lakes, Ugandan national parks and some of the last remaining mountain gorillas. A region of awe-inspiring beauty, this is also home to a multitude of impoverished people, mostly subsistence farmers. Along with these stark contrasts of great beauty and great poverty is, amazingly, a sense of enduring hope.

Several years ago I traveled to Nyakagyezi with Twesigye Jackson, who had told me his inspiring story of building an AIDS orphans school there. I thought I was prepared to research the book we were to co-write. I had seen Africa on TV, hadn't I? The open dry savannas, the children with distended bellies, the grass shacks and primitive conditions.

I soon realized that I was a naïve *muzungu* (white person). This was not the simple Africa of my mind's eye, but a complex ecology of men in suits walking the highway's dusty edge, banana trees casually growing in front yards, long-legged storks nesting in trees as if they were sparrows or robins back home, and children, everywhere children, calling out to me, eager for attention.

Our last stop along the paved road was a café owned by one of Jackson's cousins in the city of Rukungiri, with its tiny shops, narrow restaurants, and open pubs. Jackson purchased a bottled Fanta for himself and a Coke for me, with straws. While he caught up on family news in Rukiga, the local dialect, I got my bearings. I hadn't expected culture shock, but there I was, a stranger in a strange land. It was the most discordant experience of my life. Suddenly, I was the minority, asking questions in a strange accent, not knowing where to find the toilet or when to shake hands. People showed nothing but kindness that day, yet it did not ease my sense of un-belonging.

From Rukungiri, the road turned west and became progressively more rutted. Jackson had told me about swimming with his boyhood friends in the gorge river. He had not prepared me for what I was about to see. *Enengo,* they call it, a spectacular canyon terraced with banana plantations and gardens fed by waterfalls that spewed rainbows. I was stunned. If ever there was an Eden on earth, this was it.

"We are almost there," Jackson said. "Nyakagyezi is just on the other side."

While I gawked, we made our precarious descent and Jackson spoke of family. I would soon meet the people he had been describing in our work sessions back home. Maama would greet us in bare feet, her wide smile lighting up the world. Taata would shake my hand, gruffly polite. Sister Faida would already have a feast prepared and encourage us to eat, eat, eat!

When we reached the metal bridge at the bottom of the *enengo,* the sun had set low enough that shadow obscured the river. I imagined its muddy churn dragging at my waist, pulling me down into darkness like so many lives in Africa since the HIV/AIDS crisis began. That rekindled my sense of purpose and made the drive up the *enengo*'s opposite face seem to take forever.

We crested the gorge as stars blinked into view. There was no electricity on this side. The hospital in Kambuga was lit only because it used diesel generators.

"It's so dark," I said, then smiled. Beronda, Jackson's wife, who was born and raised in America, had said those exact words, but they had been only words in my notes until this moment.

Jackson laughed. "I used to walk these roads at night all the time. My feet knew every stone and rock. I never got lost."

I wondered if it was that unerring sense of direction that had brought him full circle. Many Ugandans fortunate enough to obtain a college education did not return home. But Jackson was not like others. He had had role models, such as Professor Mondo Kagonyera, a local hero who never forgot his community, and Jackson's brother, Frank, a generous spirit who came back year after year to share his wealth with his home village. Jackson also had his faith.

We bumped along the narrow lane, and I noticed a light showing through the trees. At first I thought it was a star, for the stars in Africa were brighter than anywhere at home. But as we drew closer, I saw it was an electric light.

"That is the solar lamp at the school," Jackson said.

In the following weeks and years, this singular light became a symbol for Jackson's project, just as the school it adorns has become a beacon to a generation of village children who lost parents to a killer disease. It is also a beacon for me, this *muzungu* who went halfway around the world to document a moving story of determination and persistence, and came back inspired with Jackson's hope for a better future for these children and for us all.

Twesigye Jackson had told me stories of growing up in this

farming village, the loss of family members, his struggle to build the first two rooms of an unconventional school. As we drew closer, Nyaka AIDS Orphans School, six rooms at that time, became visible beyond the trees.

"We have one hundred sixteen students this year," Jackson said, smiling and nodding. I could see the mists of emotion gathering in his eyes. He always came across as a pragmatic man, but I knew this school and the children I would meet held a special place in his heart.

I spent one week in the village, working at the school and visiting the surrounding countryside. I shook more hands and met more gracious and welcoming people than I can remember. I spoke to chairpersons, ministers, chiefs, and teachers. I saw firsthand the basis for the reputation the school was already attaining. What I most remember, though, are students' smiling faces and inquisitive looks, their hunger as we practiced English one night in my lantern-lit apartment.

And I remember the words the choir sang to welcome me:

> *We are happy, very happy*
> *To receive you, our dear visitors,*
> *Who have come here on this occasion.*
> *Keep on, keep on, keep on coming*
> *And let us welcome you*
> *Welcome to Nyaka*

As I was welcomed, I welcome you, dear reader, to experience the adventure and the heartwarming story of Twesigye Jackson Kaguri's struggle to rescue a generation of children.

Welcome to Nyaka.

Susan Urbanek Linville

CHAPTER I

THE LINE AT OUR DOOR

It was the Christmas holiday in Uganda. The sun had barely risen when I followed my older brother, Frank Tumushabe, through the front door of my parents' mud daub house.

Already a line of people stretched from the door to the grassy lane leading to the village. A man in a button-front shirt with ragged shoulder seams stood with his head down at the line's front. Behind him, a distant relative wrapped in a flowered *gomesi* dress held hands with an undernourished boy. She was accompanied by two other young boys wearing only shorts and a teenage girl who stood behind her. Behind them, women clustered with small children, and three middle-aged men talked among themselves. Others stood alone, including one-eyed James, who spent most mornings drinking at the pub.

Life should not be this way, I thought. Western Uganda had many rich green banana plantations and terraced fields of beans and cassavas. To the west, tea shrubs covered the rolling landscape, producing a product that would be shipped all over the world. I could not understand why so few were wealthy while so many suffered. It was 1989 and we had no electricity, no clean water, minimal health care, and unaffordable education. Something was wrong here, something I wished desperately to fix.

"Sit with me, Twesi," Frank said, motioning to a three-legged stool.

"Really?"

"Yes."

My heart jumped. Every year, Frank's boss would let him borrow a company car to return to our home village for the holidays. In Uganda, Christmas is not a time of giving gifts, but Frank packed the back of the Land Cruiser with clothing, soda, bags of rice, and other food available only in the city. He would give these items to the family and then offer assistance to others in the village.

I had watched him perform this ritual for many years, but this was the first time he had asked me to join him.

"Take notes for me," Frank said, handing me a scrap of paper and a worn pencil. Ten years my senior, Frank was a lean, muscular man who always dressed smartly. He had trained as a military intelligence officer in Cuba when I was a boy. Now I had finished high school and he worked and lived in Jinja, a city on the opposite side of Uganda.

The first man straightened his frayed shirt. Despite his attempt to look professional, he had no shoes.

"*Nkuyambeki?*" Frank said.

"*Agandi.*" The man extended a hand. "I am Emmanuel Muhereza."

"What do you need, Muhereza?"

Muhereza stared at his feet. "My brother is dead and I care for his three children, plus two of my own. I promised him they would finish primary school, but I have no money for tuition and books."

Tuition and book fees were only a few thousand shillings, two or three American dollars. For many in Nyakagyezi, that was more than they earned in a month.

"Which school?" Frank asked.

"Nyakagyezi Primary."

"Don't worry," Frank said. "I'll take care of the fees for all five."
He motioned for me to write down the offer.

Muhereza's face lifted. He showed a half-toothed smile.

"*Webale,* Mr. Frank. *Webale.*" He shook Frank's hand firmly.

I was always amazed by Frank's generous spirit and his desire
to help others. In fact, I had tried to emulate his example that year
when I was at Kinkizi Boarding School. As Food Prefect, it was my
job to make sure meals were served on time and that every student
received a fair share. One evening, the cornmeal we call *posho* was
undercooked and the beans used to make the sauce so old they were
speckled with weevil eggs and larvae. The students refused to eat
and I felt it was my duty to support their demands for a better meal.

A small riot broke out and school property was damaged. My
conduct was reported to the headmaster and I was suspended. Afraid
to go home and face Taata, I spent two weeks at a friend's house and
asked a relative to vouch for my reinstatement.

My first attempt to help others had put me in more trouble than I
had imagined, but the students did get better meals. So, it was worth
it in the end.

The next woman in line was my relative. Her front teeth were
yellowed and the bottom half of her *gomesi* was stained with red-
dish dirt.

"*Agandi,* Namamya." I stood and clasped her hand.

"I could be better," she said. "But you, Twesigye, look at you.
Kaguri did not skimp on food when he raised you children."

Her boys were malnourished, their bellies distended with kwashi-
orkor, a condition of protein deficiency. We were fortunate that Taata
owned a large enough banana plantation to feed us and could raise
cash by selling cows, which we call *ente,* or goats, *embuzi,* when he
had to.

Taata was not so generous when it came to clothing. His philosophy was to wear clothes until they were thin and full of holes. Consequently, I relied on Frank for hand-me-downs. Coming from a stylish man, those clothes were often brand names. The students in my high school could not believe this poor kid from Nyakagyezi wore brand-name pants and leather shoes.

When I campaigned for the food prefect position, I wore a navy-colored safari suit Frank had given me. I won with many votes from boys who hoped to borrow that suit. Borrowing clothes is a common practice in the rural villages.

Namamya turned to Frank. "I do not wish to beg, but I have four children to feed. I have sold my *ente* and chickens. All I have left is a little spot of land and a house with a leaking roof." She wiped moisture from her eyes. "I would not ask if you were not family."

The money Frank gave her was enough to buy food for a month, but I feared what would happen after that. Her daughter had already been pulled from school to take care of the younger ones. When she reached puberty, she would likely be married and this would be her dowry.

Frank helped the next woman with money for food, school books, and tuition. He helped others with promises to speak to headmasters and public officials on their behalf. Frank did not hand out money to everyone who asked. Helping the most destitute, especially when children were involved, was most important to him. Able-bodied men like James were sent on their way with encouragement to find work. A man with one eye can work as hard as a man with two.

He spent the rest of the morning speaking with everyone in line and the afternoon talking to others who came to the house, taking a break only when Taata insisted we eat. By then, I was exhausted.

"I do not know how you have done this all these years," I said. "There are so many."

"You do what you can, little brother," he said, patting my shoulder. "God knows we can't provide for everyone."

When we entered the small living room, Maama was already sitting on woven banana-leaf mats with a grandchild on her lap. One of my young cousins brought a water basin around for everyone to wash their hands while the women placed steaming bowls of soup, *matooke* (steamed plantains), rice, and beans on a table pushed against the wall.

"Please, fill your plates," Maama said.

We were joined by other family members, my sisters and their husbands, Frank's family, aunts and uncles, and cousins. Some sat in the room. Others returned to the backyard to eat.

Christine entered the room with an empty plate. She was the middle of my three sisters, the third-born child. She had been an athlete, playing netball at the district level, an excellent student, a youth leader, and a singer. She should have gone to college, but Taata was not progressive enough to send her to high school. Instead she sought teachers' training, earning her certification and dedicating her life to students.

"Do you know your exam scores yet?" she asked, spooning *matooke*.

"Not yet," I said. Final exams for seniors and graduation took place in December in Uganda. My score would determine whether I was eligible to attend university at no cost the next year.

Faida, my youngest sister, sat next to me, balancing a plate on her knees.

"Do you have a girlfriend?" she asked.

"No."

"There must be someone who has caught your eye. A girl at Burema Girls High School?" Burema Girls High School was not far from the high school I attended. They would often invite the boys to school dances. Many budding romances started that way.

"I do not have time for girls," I said. If I wanted to escape the poverty of the village, education was my way out.

Faida laughed pleasantly. "Do not let Taata hear that."

Taata had taught me at an early age what was expected of boys and how to be a man. Gender roles were very specific. By the time I turned twelve, my paternal *mukaaka,* my grandmother, had already made plans.

"We will find you a hardworking woman. You will get married and she will stay home, till the land, and bear children while you continue school. I will take care of the children."

I always nodded in agreement when she said this, but inside I was terrified. At twelve, I was not ready to marry. I wanted to make something of my life and see the world, like my brother.

Now that I had graduated, my urge to avoid marriage and leave the village was even stronger. Faida was right about not telling Taata my plans. He had kept me in primary schools close to home to ensure that I had time for chores. When Frank suggested I go to the better-funded Bugema Adventist High School, Taata sent me to Kinkizi High School instead, insisting I come home on weekends to work.

Taata would not want me to pursue a university education. He would see that as an act of defiance and handle it the way he always dealt with such matters, with anger. He had beaten all of us in the past. In drunken rages, he had chased Maama with a stick around the village more times than I could count.

No, telling Taata was not a wise plan. If I was to leave, I would have to go without his blessing. And that is just what I did.

CHAPTER 2

THE DEVIL'S HAND

Five years later, I found myself on an overcrowded bus traveling to Nyakagyezi for the Christmas holidays. I sat near the bus's middle, squeezed to the window by a *mukaaka* in an immaculate red *gomesi* and her equally stylish husband in a black suit and tie. Passengers around me engaged in multiple conversations in multiple languages while we whizzed along the paved highway west of Kampala. I remained silent, listening to voices without interpreting them.

So much had changed since I left home. I had lived with Frank for a few months after graduating from high school, then moved to Kampala to attend Makerere University. For the next three years I studied for a degree in social sciences, but it was an extracurricular seminar that truly motivated me.

At that seminar I heard the United Nations Universal Declaration of Human Rights for the first time: *Everyone has the right to a standard of living adequate for the health and well-being of himself and of his family, including food, clothing, housing and medical care and necessary social services.*

No one had mentioned human rights in Nyakagyezi, where

farmers struggled to feed themselves and maintain their lands. They saw health and well-being as luxuries, not rights. What I heard at the seminar that day ignited my passion. I wanted every person to hear those important words and vowed to translate this information into our local language, Rukiga.

Upon graduating, I took an internship at Uganda Human Rights Activists. After that, I and two of my coworkers started our own organization, the Human Rights Concern. We became particularly interested in gender roles. At our events men would cook and serve a meal, or we would invite women engineers and male chefs to demonstrate principles of equality and encourage freedom in education and job choice. It was useful work, but it did not satisfy my desire to do something meaningful to fight poverty.

Even as the bus bumped along with gears grinding, I dozed off. Eventually, we came to Rakai, a town near the halfway point in my seven-hour journey to Nyakagyezi.

From the bus, one could see that Rakai was a devastated community. Abandoned shops stood alongside houses with crumbling iron roofs and peeling plaster. Land once cultivated into lush plantations was overgrown with weeds and unmarked burial mounds.

Rakai had once been a bustling highway stop where truckers traveling from the Mombasa coast in Kenya to the Congo and Rwanda would stop for the night. Sex workers had flocked to the area; some acted as second wives, cooking, laundering clothing, and pampering drivers.

This proved a perfect incubator for HIV/AIDS. *Slim,* our name for the disease, was detected in Uganda near Rakai in 1982. By 1991, 15 percent of Ugandan adults were thought to have the disease. In cities, 30 percent of pregnant women were infected. Thus, while I was crusading to advance issues of human rights and gender equality, my fellow Ugandans were fighting for their very lives.

People of Rakai had died by the hundreds from *slim.* To make matters worse, sex workers had fled the area, spreading the HIV/ AIDS virus to their home villages. What remained of the community depended on tourists. Orphans had been left behind to fend for themselves.

Brakes hissing, we parked behind a bus surrounded by teenage hucksters we call *batembeyi.* They waved bottled water and soda, roasted plantain, which we call *gonja,* and *muchomo,* or roasted chicken on a stick. I overcame the balky window latch and pushed the glass to the side.

"Would you like something to drink or eat?" I asked the woman beside me.

"This place is cursed," she said.

"HIV/AIDS is not a curse," I said. "It is a disease."

She scowled and turned away.

Superstition remained the biggest obstacle to treating *slim.* In 1994, effective drug regimens became available in parts of Africa, but many Ugandans relied on shamans and homemade remedies. Education could save us, but if the government did not recognize that fact soon, more were doomed to die.

The *abatembeyi* spotted my open window.

"Bottled drinks!" A tall boy raised his crate of water and soda above his head.

A second boy in a red shirt shoved a basket of yellow *gonja* in front of the first boy. "*Gonja!* Fresh!"

Four more boys were at the window by this time, two waving *muchomo* and two bearing drinks.

"How much for the *gonja?*" I asked.

"Three for a thousand shillings."

"Too much."

"Three *gonja* for seven hundred shillings," a shorter boy in a brown shirt said.

"I will take three."

I purchased *gonja,* water, and two *muchomo*. As quickly as they had descended upon us, the boys ran off to the next bus, waving their free arms and calling out. I said a prayer of thanks, pulled a piece of chicken from its stick, and chewed the stiff meat. The woman slid a brown paper package from her bag and unrolled it, revealing oven-baked bread and sweet bananas.

"Would you like some *muchomo*?" I offered.

"No!" She eyed me angrily. "I will not eat food from this place. It comes from the devil's hand."

I wanted to explain to her that *slim* could not be caught by eating food, but it would be fruitless. Many people avoided dealing with the HIV/AIDS problem by shunning those with the disease and ignoring its existence.

I turned toward the window and ate, thinking that HIV/AIDS was yet another struggle in Uganda's long history of struggle. From warring tribes of the nineteenth century to modern democracy in the twenty-first, nothing came without cost.

In 1958 and then again in 1961, Ugandans protested colonial rule with boycotts and violence against the British and Asians who held economic control of the country. On October 9, 1962, when they achieved independence from Britain, Kabaka Mutesa, head of the Buganda tribal group, was appointed president, while Apollo Milton Obote, who was not from Buganda, was elected executive prime minister. They were not a united front, being divided by both political and religious beliefs, and a struggle for power erupted between the two men.

In 1966, Obote exiled Kabaka Mutesa. Obote's reign did not last long. With support from the British, Israelis, other Western powers, and people from Buganda, he was overthrown by Idi Amin's coup in 1971. The eight years of tyrannical rule that followed saw the executions of several hundred thousand Ugandans. Israelis and Asians were expelled from the country, and Amin appropriated the property of British and Asian firms as part of his economic war. His soldiers ruled the countryside like warlords, ransacking homes and businesses, kidnapping, raping, and extorting, while Amin played genial host to the foreign media.

No place in Uganda, not even my home district, Kanungu, had remained free of Amin's bloody grasp. I was born the year before Amin took power, and as a child, learned to associate government soldiers with terror and cruelty. Anytime we saw an army vehicle, we would scatter and run for cover.

Like lions killing their rivals' offspring, Amin's people destroyed the roads that were constructed during Obote's time. Potholes, ruts, and frequent roadblocks turned the seven-hour journey from Nyakagyezi to Kampala into a twenty-four-hour trip of terror. At each roadblock, passengers were forced from their vehicles. Stone-faced military men demanded that people open their bags. *Kaa kiini,* they would shout in Swahili, "Lie down!" At some roadblocks, people were shot for asking questions. Women were often taken aside and raped. Amin himself ran over a bishop of the Anglican Church with his jeep because he refused to support the dictator. Firing squads were common, midnight curfews strictly enforced, and women never safe.

In 1986, the current president, Lieutenant General Yoweri Kaguta Museveni seized the government through guerrilla warfare. He was another military leader, but since he was from western Uganda, he was not consumed with the revenge killings of the previous administration. He also professionalized the army.

Even Museveni's military prowess could not protect his soldiers. After HIV/AIDS killed most of his officers, he was forced to confront the problem of *slim* publicly. Condom use was now encouraged, HIV/AIDS and its prevention publicized on billboards, and educational brochures passed out. Progress was being made, but it was much too slow.

No sooner had I finished my *muchomo* than the bus pulled onto the highway. The sky darkened to the west. Lightning flashed in the distance. Torrential rain suddenly poured down, and the driver switched the windshield wipers to high. Oncoming buses and trucks roared past, sending waves of water against us.

My neighbor slid a photograph from her purse. In the picture, a woman in a wedding dress stood next to a tall man in a suit. The *mukaaka*'s knotted index finger touched the bride's veil. I wondered if the bride had died from *slim* and that was the reason this woman cursed Rakai.

"Your family?" I asked.

"My daughter," she said. "We are going to visit her for the holiday."

I nodded. "I am traveling to see my parents."

She positioned her hand over the man's picture and whispered, "God rest his soul." She crossed herself in the Catholic tradition.

So, it was the woman's son-in-law who had died from *slim,* not the daughter. I took this moment of understanding to say a silent prayer, for I had been blessed. There was no HIV/AIDS in my family. My older brother, three older sisters, and their families remained healthy and thriving.

CHAPTER 3

THE CHICKEN IS FULL OF BONES

We arrived in Rukungiri just as light faded. The last town with electricity and paved roads on our journey, it bustled with pickup trucks and motorcycle taxis we call *boda bodas*. Narrow shops had closed their shutters and wooden doors for the evening, but restaurants and clubs remained alight with electric bulbs and neon beer signs.

After dropping off many of the passengers, including the elderly couple, the driver switched on the bus's headlights and we continued onto a dirt road leading toward the *enengo,* a deep mile-wide gorge cutting between the Rukungiri and Kanungu districts, carved by the Ekyambu River.

A man snored in the back of the bus. A woman sitting several rows in front of me clung to the smallest of her three children, knowing the long winding road ahead was dangerous.

Stars appeared as we started down. I braced myself against the seat ahead while the bus bounced, jounced, and groaned over the rutted, rocky surface. Parts of the road were always washed out. Local workers tried to keep it passable, but one heavy rain was likely to destroy an entire day's work. Vehicles had been known to bog down in mud or even roll over.

Brakes hissed as we rounded a curve and descended a steeper section. The woman whispered to her son.

By day, the *enengo* is an overwhelming sight. Its terraced cliffs form a patchwork of greens and browns, banana plantations and gardens bordered by hedges. Houses are built directly into the slope. Rains create temporary waterfalls that etch their way down rocky hillsides and spill into the wide, muddy Ekyambu far below.

By night, the *enengo* is a black maw that can swallow a vehicle whole.

"Do not worry," the driver said, glancing back. "I have not rolled a bus yet."

"Keep your eyes on the road!" the woman scolded.

He laughed. Water splattered down the cliff face to form muddy puddles.

Suddenly, the bus hit a deep hole and the entire vehicle tilted, goading my heartbeat to a sprint. Tires spun. The engine roared. The woman cried out and the man behind me stopped snoring.

"Jesus, please be with us," I prayed, squinting beyond the bus's lights. Several areas had been badly eroded, but the road had not fallen into the abyss.

Yet.

The driver downshifted. The bus lurched sideways, skidding away from the edge. He seemed unaffected by the event, but my worry did not recede until the black iron bridge crossing the river took shape in our headlights.

Thank God, I thought. Metal rungs vibrated beneath our tires, every revolution bringing me closer to Nyakagyezi.

We left the bridge and the driver stomped on the accelerator, urging the vehicle up the equally steep grade on the other side. Going up was not nearly as terrifying as descending.

After many minutes, we emerged from the ravine and entered Kambuga, where a few generator-powered electric lights marked Kambuga Hospital's wooded grounds. The town's main road was dark. Shops situated a few yards from the road hunched like blocky shadows, and houses winked with golden lantern light from behind closed shutters. The driver slowed, alert for pedestrians.

Brakes squealed and hissed as the bus came to a stop near my aunt Joseline's house, a whitewashed brick home at the edge of town. I was the only one to get off at Kambuga. The driver helped me unload four bags at the side of the road.

"You have someone to help you carry these?" he asked.

"Yes," I said, even though I had not made specific arrangements. It would not be long before help arrived. It never was.

I preferred to arrive after dark, so that people would not see how many bags I brought. Being one of only a few in this region to escape poverty, I had become a celebrity of sorts. This was good, for I represented a positive role model for many children in the village. But it was also bad in that it drew unwanted attention. People would gossip about what I had brought from the city. Did I bring baked bread or sweets? Maybe I had clothing and smoked fish. The old grandfathers, or *shwenkuru,* would no doubt sit outside the pub sipping their beer and speculating for days once they learned of my four bags.

Only seconds after the bus roared back onto the road, two boys approached. The shorter boy I did not recognize. The other was Julius, a lanky youth my father had adopted a few years earlier. Julius's father had been a polygamist with two wives and eight children before he died from a brain hemorrhage. Not long after, Julius's mother also died, and then the second wife. Consequently, the children had no remaining relatives in the area to care for them.

"It is our responsibility to help," Taata had said at the mother's burial, but I think his main goal was to have someone to help do chores. Nevertheless, and to his credit, Taata insisted Julius attend school.

"*Agandi,* Uncle Twesi," Julius greeted me. "Did you bring me gifts?"

"That depends," I said.

In unison, each boy hoisted a heavy bag to his head. I carried the smaller ones and we proceeded along the darkened dirt road to Nyakagyezi.

"Depends?" Julius reminded me.

"How were your exam scores this term?" Julius had failed primary-one three times, but the school eventually passed him to the primary-two class. I hoped he had become more motivated since I last saw him.

No answer. It was too dark to see his expression. Education is not often appreciated by poor farmers who need their children to help in the fields or at home. Julius was lucky to have that chance.

"Did you finish your exams?"

The shorter boy stumbled, but caught himself without tipping his burden.

"Are you still in school?" I asked.

"No," Julius said quietly.

I shook my head, dumbfounded. As a boy, I could not wait to go to school. Even now, I was making plans to travel to America to pursue my studies at Columbia University.

We walked in near darkness, following the road up a hill. Inside, I stewed, wishing I had a magical ability to bring boys like Julius to their senses. Without an education, he was doomed to a life of poverty. He would discover that all too soon.

Lantern light glowed from cracks in the window shutters of my parents' mud daub house, huddled behind a spiny hedge. A faint odor of chicken soup hung in the cool night. My mouth watered. *Muchomo* is nothing compared to Maama's soup! Adult voices chattered inside, while children giggled in the nearer darkness.

A Land Cruiser was parked beside the house, evidence that Frank had already arrived with his family. The boys carried my bags into the house and Maama hobbled outside. Her hair was covered by a pink scarf and her face showed the wrinkles of age, but her smile was what I longed to see. And it did not disappoint, as vivid and as wide as I remembered.

"Maama," I said, embracing her.

Taata strolled out, his permanent frown forming dark ravines across his face. He glared at me with his good eye. I did not attempt to shake his hand. Any greeting would start an argument, especially now that he knew I was leaving for America. His hair and mustache had grayed a bit since I'd last visited, but his hard stare told me he had not mellowed.

"*Webale kwiija*," Maama whispered in my ear, squeezing the air from my lungs. "God is good who protected you."

I noticed bare toes protruding below her green leaf-patterned skirt. The last time I visited, I had told her to keep her shoes on in order to protect her soles from the sharp stones that had scarred mine so badly. She often complained that shoes hurt her feet, but that was not the true reason she did not wear them. She worried about wearing them out. I do not know how many times I have told her I will buy her all the shoes she needs, but some worries never fade. Maama would never ask anything of me, while Taata was always making lists of things he wanted.

Excited greetings filled the air. "*Keije!*" "*Buhooro!*" "*Buhorogye!*" "*Agandi!*"

I was suddenly engulfed in hands and arms, as my brother's children and some of their cousins poured from the darkness, nearly squashing me with their hugs.

"Do you have sweeties for us?" Stephen asked. He was Frank's oldest, a tall boy with bright eyes and a big smile.

"I do not know," I said, checking my pocket.

"We have been good," the younger sister, Sharon, insisted.

"Have you been doing your chores?" I asked.

"Yes!"

"And you, Sandra, how are you doing in school?"

"I passed my exams, Uncle." She cast her eyes downward as is so often the custom with Ugandan girls when speaking to their elders.

I scooped a handful of hard candy from my pocket.

"*Webale,*" they thanked me. In a second, my hand was empty and the children had returned to the darkness.

Christine grasped my arm. I had not seen her since Michael, her third child, had been born earlier in the year. As always, she looked healthy and fit.

"Welcome," she said. "Come inside. We have lots of food."

"Yes," Maama said. "You must be starving after your long journey."

Christine led me inside. Window shutters had been closed to keep out bugs, but the door was open, shielded by a flowered curtain that reached to the floor.

The crowded sitting room was lit by a single lantern. The place resembled a nursery, with Christine's three children and Faida's toddler waddling at the room's center, while aunts and cousins congregated at the walls. Men's voices came from the backyard. No doubt they had gathered there to discuss politics and the recent war.

Before I could remove my shoes, my eldest sister, Mbabazi, approached with Faida's baby daughter asleep in her arms. Mbabazi had never formally married for fear she would end up with a man like my father. She had given birth to three boys over the years, but they had all died. At least she could gain some pleasure from all these nieces and nephews.

"Twesi," she said. "I should not have to come all the way to Nyak-agyezi to see my little brother."

"I am sorry," I said. Mbabazi owned and operated a small business in Kampala. When I first moved to the city to attend university, she had become a second mother, making sure I was well fed and staying out of trouble. Since I started working, I had neglected to visit her. "I have been very busy."

"Not too busy to go to America," she said.

"I plan to visit you before I leave."

"And what about me?" Faida appeared at my side. She lived in Kasese near Queen Elizabeth National Park with her family. From Kampala, it would take me a whole day to travel to her house.

"I am visiting you now," I said.

Christine pulled at my arm.

"Twesi," she said. "Come. The food is hot. You have all night to chat."

Behind the house, the glow from the hearth fire in the kitchen building cast orange light on the men gathered around the back stoop. Stones sparkled in the hard-packed dirt nearest the house. Grassy ground containing a few banana trees, *embuzi* pens, and the latrines lay beyond. The entire backyard was enclosed through a combination of barbed-wire fencing and prickly cactus hedge. *Embuzi* pulled hard at leashes as all goats will do, looking for fresh grass.

Within the kitchen building, just behind a dishwashing table made of lashed branches, a girl sat on the ground, feeding sticks into the fire one by one. Pots of milk and water boiled and *matooke,* steamed green bananas wrapped in banana leaves, occupied a shelf. Bags of *mugaati,* a special yeast bread baked in the city, had been opened. My stomach growled.

"*Agandi,*" I greeted the men. A few sat on a bench near the house, others on the ground. After shaking hands with brothers-in-law, uncles, cousins, and a few neighbors, I saw Frank sitting with a full plate. Even in near darkness I could see he had lost weight. His cheeks were thin and his suit coat hung loosely from his shoulders.

He smiled and patted the ground.

"Welcome home, Twesi," he said. "Come sit."

I lowered myself beside him. Christine handed me a plate over-flowing with *matooke,* pieces of chicken, potatoes, greens, and cassava. Faida followed with a cup of hot milk.

"Eat," Christine commanded in the same tone she used with me when I was a boy.

"Yes, dear sister," I said.

"*Yetegyereze!*" Frank warned me. "The chicken is full of bones."

I laughed and pointed to his almost full plate.

"Is the cassava full of bones too? You have barely touched yours."

"The food's good," he said. "It's this stomach of mine."

"Still bothering you?" He had been complaining for months about ulcers.

"Some days," he said. "I can deal with it."

"You should see a doctor," I said.

"It's nothing." He lifted a chicken leg from his plate and placed it on mine. "Tell me about this trip to America. Maama says you leave in January."

"Yes. I fly to New York. I have been accepted at Columbia University to their Human Rights Advocacy visiting scholars program."

"Excellent!" Frank said.

"It is a once-in-a-lifetime opportunity," I said. "I will develop my advocacy skills. I am very excited."

Frank nodded. "You must take every opportunity you are offered."

"I will," I said.

"Then eat." Frank moved his cassava onto my plate. "You'll need all your strength."

I laughed at the time, happy to enjoy my brother's joke. But if I had realized then what I know now, I would have given up those eighteen months in America to spend time with Frank during the last year and a half of his life. Even with all my education and training, I remained blind to the disease that was ripping our country apart one family at a time. *Slim.*

CHAPTER 4

MY BROTHER'S KEEPER

Eighteen months in America passed quickly. On the long flight back to Uganda, I recalled the initial incredible cold of New York City in January and the comforting warmth of the lifelong friendships made there.

I had found that Americans were quick to smile when they greeted you, but often that smile was only on the surface. I soon realized that I could not trust first impressions, but must wait to know someone before making judgments. I also discovered that many in New York considered Africa a country, not a continent. They thought all Africans were the same and did not know the names of the countries.

"Uganda. Where is that?" they would ask.

"East Africa," I would say.

"Oh, yes, Africa." They knew where Africa was.

Despite feeling far from home, I loved the freedom of expression I found in America. People could criticize the president and government without fear of retribution. I was amazed that primary through high school education was free, and the diversity of people in the city shocked me.

I also made many friends.

One of those friends was Beronda. At the time, she was working on her college degree. The first things that attracted me to her were her self-confidence, openness, and beautiful smile. She was every man's dream: smart, loving, kind, and independent. After only three dates, I knew she was the woman I wanted to marry and have children with. But how could that happen? She was an American and I was on my way back to Uganda. I might never see her again, but I prayed to God that somehow things would work out.

After twenty-four hours' travel on three flights, I was overjoyed to land in Uganda. That joy did not last long, however. When I rolled my bags into the terminal's main atrium, I found Edith and the three children waiting, but Frank was not with them. My brother was not the sort of person to miss engagements. Something was wrong.

"Welcome home, Twesigye," Edith said, hugging me as if I were a delicate vase. "How was your flight?"

"Long," I said. I glanced toward the parking lot, but Frank was not there either.

"Let us get you home." Edith was immaculately dressed as always and wore a single strand of pearls about her neck, but I could see by the circles beneath her eyes she was exhausted.

"Is Frank . . . ?"

"He is not feeling well."

I wanted to ask what was wrong, but it was not my place to raise the issue with Edith. Instead, I made conversation with the children during our two-hour car ride to Jinja.

When discussion turned to silence, I leaned back and gazed through the window. By moonlight, the tea plantations that covered the rolling hills on either side of the roadway resembled armies of shadow men. I could not keep my eyes from going to them again and again, watching for movement. The fields seemed alive with dread, as if at any moment those shadows might rise and rush onto the road.

Something is wrong, I kept worrying. My thoughts roamed to that last time I saw Frank, his thinness, the way his suit coat hung from his shoulders. Maybe the reason I had not asked Edith about him was that on some level I already knew what she would reply and did not want to face it.

No. Most likely Frank had had a flare-up of malaria. Or maybe it was the flu or a parasite. These things could be treated.

Gradually the land became less hilly and sugarcane replaced tea. I relaxed, for there was nothing deceptive about sugarcane. The plants stood at their full ten-foot height and the moonlight revealed individual stalks for the plants they were. These fields continued all the way to the sugarcane factory in Lugazi.

Beyond Lugazi, we entered Mabira Forest Reserve, one of several natural areas that the Ugandan government has set aside to preserve the diverse tropical environment. Stephen asked if America had such forests and we talked for a time about New York. I was glad for the distraction and happy to feed Stephen's hunger for knowledge in any way I could.

As we neared Jinja, my worry over Frank rushed back. The local name for Jinja is Ejjinja, which means "large stone" in Luganda. The name refers to a stone formation overlooking the Nile from the city side of the river. Frank was like that stone to me. If anything happened to him, it would be devastating.

We crossed Owen Falls Dam, which generates hydro-electricity for the entire country. Jinja was just beyond, a city of flat-roofed, whitewashed buildings with pillared porches and colorful painted trim. I remembered riding Frank's bike to all corners of this town when I visited as a boy. I knew every building and shop back then.

Edith parked on the street in front of their house; it looked exactly as I remembered. Two-tone walls, ocher brown below and yellow above, and sky blue paneled doors marked its front. Intricate wood trim along the eaves resembled white lace against the rusted iron roof.

We carried my bags inside, where what I dreaded most came to pass. The house had not changed, but Frank had. My once vibrant brother hunched on the couch, a shadow of himself. Clothes hung from his body like too-large hand-me-downs.

"Twesi," he said, patting the cushion beside him. "Welcome home. It has been too long."

"Frank." I could barely speak. Sitting, I took his hand in mine. "What has happened?"

Slim. He did not say the word, but I knew. I also knew that all my education and training could not save him.

"Tell me about America," he said.

As the weeks passed, Frank suffered with headaches and vomiting. I returned from my apartment in Kampala as often as I could. Each time I passed the tea and sugarcane fields along the highway I prayed for a miracle, that Frank would be spared the illness that was killing nearly 100,000 Ugandans a year. Each time I visited, I found less and less of my brother. Where once there was muscle, flesh now stretched across bone. His cheeks sank and his eyes lost their luster.

By the beginning of August, he was so emaciated that I could not even tell he was in bed when I entered his room. *Slim* was not a word to adequately describe him. *Skeletal, gaunt, wasted* were better descriptions.

"Sit beside me," Frank whispered, sucking in breath.

I sat in a chair beside the bed and leaned close.

"You must promise to be careful," he said. His face was like a mask at that point. His wide eyes blinked slowly. "Give yourself to one woman and remain faithful. It is the only way. You do not want this . . . this *slim*."

"I promise," I said. How could anyone witnessing such a death be anything but careful?

Frank rolled to his side and coughed up blood-laced phlegm. I patted his back in a feeble effort to help. He continued to cough and moan.

"I will get Edith," I said.

"No." Frank grasped my wrist until the coughing subsided. "She works too hard."

The sickness was taking its toll on Edith too. No longer did I see her soft smile or hear her encouraging words. Her eyes were always downcast and her expression twisted with worry. She tended to the children and the house as if walking in her sleep.

"I will stay with you," I said. It would be difficult to remain in Jinja and handle my professional obligations in Kampala, but my brother needed me.

Frank's lips pulled back from his teeth in a grim smile that exposed sores on his gums. "Thank you, brother," he sighed, before slipping into a restless doze.

From that point I stopped praying to God to make him well. It was selfish of me to pray to extend his misery. Instead, I asked God to end his torment and take him to heaven and eternal life.

Frank's last days were painful for us all. Maama, Taata, Christine, and Faida traveled by bus from southwestern Uganda to see him. He was admitted to Jinja's main hospital for a few days, but the doctors eventually sent him home to die. We tried our best to make him comfortable. We fed him spoonfuls of soft food, but even that was a struggle to swallow because his throat was inflamed with sores.

He did not speak often, but when he and I were alone, he would find the strength to tell me about his travels to Cuba, how he had been arrested and spent time at a maximum security prison in Uganda when the government changed hands. He confided personal feelings about his marriage, how he feared rather than respected our father, and his undying love for Maama.

Each day he took my hand and pulled me close. "My children," he whispered. "You must promise to take care of Stephen, Sandra, and Sharon."

"Of course," I said, blinking back tears. "They will be well supported." In Uganda, uncles accept responsibility for orphaned nieces and nephews. The problem by this time was that even uncles were dying from *slim*.

As I watched Frank settle back into sleep, my heart ached. Now that we had finally shared the intimacy all brothers should experience, Frank was being taken from me.

The final night, Edith, my cousin Herbert, and I took turns trying to keep Frank comfortable. When I was not at his bedside listening to the death rattle in his lungs, I sat in a chair nearby, praying. *Please, God. Please send your angels to guide Frank to heaven. He has suffered enough.*

The next day I planned to go to Kampala. I had not worked at Human Rights Concern in two weeks. There was business to attend to. At eight that morning, I was dressing in Frank's room, buttoning my shirt, when I caught movement from the corner of my eye. Frank's arm stretched out. Thinking he was about to fall, I leaned down and cradled his bony frame. He was so light it was like holding a child. With what muscle remained, he clutched my arm.

It is all right, I thought. *I will not let you fall.* In that moment, I was my brother's keeper.

Frank coughed twice, breath rushing past my cheek. I laid him back in the bed. He coughed again, but this time the air left his lungs forever. All was still. No sound. No pain. No suffering.

"Edith! Edith!" I heard myself call. "Maama!"

Edith called out, "My husband, why have you left me? How can you leave me alone in this world? Who will help me raise our kids?"

Stephen was only eleven. The girls were nine and seven. Edith was now a single mother, and her prospects for supporting her children were difficult at best. Frank had only a small pension, which would be given to her. It was more than most workers received, but not enough to raise a family.

Maama, always the strong one, sang, "When the roll is called up yonder I will be there."

Frank is dead, I told myself, hardly believing it. All those weeks to prepare for his passing had not prepared me. *My brother has died in my arms.*

CHAPTER 5

THROUGH THE VALLEY
OF THE SHADOW

The days that followed Frank's death were filled with grief. As is the custom in Uganda, the body remained in the house for viewing. Sempa Baker, an old friend working as an accountant in Kampala, was one of the first to arrive. It seemed so long ago since we attended secondary school together in Kanungu District. Both our lives had changed dramatically since then. I had been to America. He was dating a woman in his office, Marjorie, and would be marrying soon.

"I came as soon as I heard the announcement on the radio," he said.

Sempa was usually a happy man with a wide smile and kind words for everyone. This day there was sadness within him, as if his own brother had died. He stayed to comfort me while many people arrived to pay their respects. The family greeted Frank's coworkers, neighbors, and friends. Even people we did not know stopped by to offer condolences.

My family made plans to transport Frank's body to Nyakagyezi for burial. A few days later, I found myself in the back of the truck with my sisters and the plain wooden coffin. Silenced by grief, I had many hours to think of death. Thousands of families were going through the same experience, but that did not comfort me. Instead I found my thoughts returning to my first brush with death, the day after Christmas, long ago.

When I was seven years old, Maama grew sick of Taata's abusive language and traveled halfway across Uganda to live with Uncle David in Jinja. A few months later, the Tanzanians declared war on Idi Amin and invaded our beautiful country. Maama returned to her parents' house in Kambuga. No one knows how she managed to navigate through the center of the fighting in Kampala, but she arrived unhurt. I was happy to see her, of course, but disappointed that she refused to live with Taata. That was one battle she chose to avoid.

Christmas came without Maama's smile that year. At the time there were three of us children living at home, Christine, Faida, and me. Frank was away at secondary school. Mbabazi was living in Kampala.

The next morning, Taata assigned chores and joined the men at the pub for an afternoon of celebrating. Faida and I were sent to the *shamba,* the garden field, to harvest millet.

It was a sunny day, but I could see clouds building in the distance; rain would soon come. Birds sang in the eucalyptus trees surrounding the field and dived into the grassy millet, taking more than their share of the harvest. Even the *waringa,* the wooden scarecrow we had erected, did not stop them. That was not an acceptable situation to me.

Faida and I got to work snapping seed heads from stalks taller than us. The heads would be allowed to dry and then pounded to retrieve the small seeds. From these, the girls would make *akaro,* a doughy mix of ground seeds and cassava rolled into a ball and served in an *akeibo,* a small basket with a lid.

I looked forward to eating the tasty dough, but harvesting seed heads quickly became a chore. My mind was on those birds! I knew I could get a nest if I tried. Maybe it would contain eggs. Not large enough for breakfast, but something to look at just the same. The birds were stealing from our harvest. Why should we not take from theirs?

Yellow weavers no bigger than my hand flitted high in the trees. I soon spied a gray nest dangling from a limb twenty feet up. A short climb for me.

Leaving Faida to her work, I ran to the tree. At least a dozen previous trunks had been cut from the same root stock for use in building and as firewood, leaving jagged stumps surrounding the new trunk. I boosted myself over the stumps and shimmied up the rough brown bark. At first it was difficult, but climbing got easier higher up where I could grasp branches.

A bird peered cautiously from the nest. I looped my leg over a branch and slid out from the trunk, confident in my quest.

"Be careful," Faida called. "That limb is too small."

I had climbed a hundred trees. What did my sister know?

The bird darted out and up, perching above me and chattering. I reached for the nest. It was still a few inches beyond my grasp. The little birds were smarter than they looked, building their nests far out from the trunk.

I leaned forward and the branch bowed under my weight.

"Get back!" Faida said.

Just a little farther, I thought, scooting forward.

The branch broke with a crackling sound like lightning. I thought of rain.

"Twesi!"

The next thing I knew I lay on my back. I did not remember the fall or hitting the ground. My ears rang, but I remained calm. Boys can fall from trees without getting hurt. We are tough.

Faida arrived at my side, screaming. She dropped her basket and pressed her hands over her mouth, eyes wide.

I propped myself up on my elbows and saw that one of the stumps had impaled my left thigh, barely missing bone. Faida screamed again, but her voice seemed far away. I felt as if I moved in slow motion through thick air. In my painless dream, I stood and pulled a shard from my flesh. A gaping wound remained, but no blood.

Faida's distant voice commanded me. "We must return home, Twesi! Can you walk? Let me help you."

"I am fine." I felt no pain and there was very little blood. Refusing her help, I walked the two hundred yards home. Faida followed, crying the entire way.

The sitting room of our mud daub house was dark and quiet. No one was home. Not Taata. Not Maama. It was then that my dream left me. Maama had not been there for nearly a year.

"Sit down!" Faida's voice was suddenly clear and loud.

I sank onto a woven banana mat and stretched out my leg. Terror replaced numbness as blood gushed from the wound. I wanted to cry out, but I was a big boy, and big boys did not cry. Still, I was not so big that I did not need my mother at a time like this.

Faida left and returned with Taata's white church shirt. Fighting tears, she wrapped it tightly around my leg. "I am going for help!"

As soon as she went out, pain throbbed through my leg. Blood soaked the shirt and pooled on the mat. I tried to remember a prayer, any prayer, but my mind raced. I needed a doctor. I needed the hospital. Both were very far away.

What followed was a confusing jumble. Neighbor women rushed in and out, shouting commands and crying. Men were summoned from their celebration.

"*Nkakugambira!*" Taata grumbled, breath sour with beer. He leaned over to examine my leg with his straight eye. The other could not be trusted, especially when he drank. Now it inhabited the far corner of his eye socket, giving him the appearance of daydreaming.

Two neighbor women nudged him aside and rewrapped my wound with clean cloth, but blood continued to seep through. *Maama*. If only she were here. She would know how to care for me. Drunken men searched fruitlessly for a stretcher and returned empty-handed.

"We will carry him," Taata decided.

He scooped me up and pressed me to his chest. Pain tore through me. I clutched his shoulders.

Taata jostled me through the doorway, every movement torture. *I will not survive this. I am losing all my blood and the hospital is too far.* A dark cloud loomed on my horizon.

"Walk faster," Taata complained to his companions.

We did not travel far before his breath grew ragged and his arms trembled. "I have fed you too much," he said. "You are as heavy as a weaned calf."

He passed me to another drunken man. I do not know which was worse, the pain or the fear. Taata would protect me even if he had had a few drinks. The other might drop me or fall. I held tight and prayed for this journey to end.

The road descended to a crossroad bordered by hedges. Normally, I could run the distance from my house to here in five minutes, but it seemed we had taken hours. Every step stabbed and every exchange between hands was agony.

"We should have a stretcher," Taata grumbled. "We are too slow. Faster!"

I kept expecting to see the gravel road to Kambuga. Instead, I saw boys swatting their *ente* and *embuzi* to the side of the path, looking aghast at this troupe of drunken men with bloody shirts. Women and girls stared from gardens, eyes fixed on my red-soaked bandage. They knew I was dying. I knew they were right. My only wish was to hear Maama's comforting voice and hold her hand.

"Be careful with him!" Taata shouted.

By the time we reached the main road, Taata had run out of complaints, and something other than anger shaded his gaze. Had I not been so badly hurt, he surely would have given me a few swats with the *embuzi* switch to teach me a lesson about climbing trees. As it was, he held his tongue and that terrified me the most. Even Taata knew I was dying.

I faded in and out of consciousness.

Kambuga hospital was a low whitewashed brick building nestled beneath trees along the road to Rukungiri. We entered a gloomy lobby and I was passed to Taata. I felt relieved to be back in my father's arms, but the smells of antiseptic and vomit made my stomach clench.

I attempted to struggle but was too weak. "I do not want—"

"*Hassshhhi,*" Taata shushed.

We approached a girl in a blue-and-white uniform reading through a stack of papers at the reception table. Beyond her, half a dozen people sat on benches along the wall.

"May I help you?" The girl looked barely older than Christine.

"He needs his leg sewn up!" Taata said. "Do you not see all this blood?"

"The doctor is not here," she said. "It is the holiday. Everyone is celebrating."

"Go find him!"

"But he is—"

"Find him!"

The girl nodded submissively and stood. "Just one minute." Clutching the side of her skirt, she hurried down the women's wing corridor.

"No doctor!" Taata's hand gripped me tight. "What sort of hospital is this?"

The girl returned with an older nurse in a matching uniform, hair tied back with a white scarf. As soon as she saw my bloody bandages she pressed a hand to my forehead.

"My God in heaven," she said. "We must get this boy to a bed."

Without delay, she led us through the overcrowded men's ward, a long room that also stank of alcohol, to a bed by an open window. Some men watched me from their cots, including one with yellow-tinted eyes, a characteristic of those who have seen many bouts of malaria. Most were sleeping.

Taata laid me on the hard mattress, causing a fresh jolt of pain. I cried out.

"Everything will be fine," the nurse assured. She unwrapped the makeshift bandage. Clotted blood formed a black jelly at the base of a jagged wooden shaft. I had not removed the entire shard, not even close. I wanted to run away from that place and leave that ugly wound behind.

"Maama!" I cried. "I want my *maama*."

Taata held me down while the nurse used forceps to remove some of the debris. I screamed even louder.

"This will have to wait," she said, frowning. "The doctor will clean this out and sew him tomorrow."

"Tomorrow!" Taata yelled. His voice echoed through the ward.

"It must wait until tomorrow." The nurse's voice remained calm and strict, as if she were a teacher instructing a student.

Taata glared. The nurse stood her ground, forceps in hand.

Taata released me and stepped back.

"I will rinse it and put on a new dressing," the nurse explained. "But this wound requires surgery. All this wood must come out or it will start an infection. Both muscle and skin have been damaged."

I squeezed my eyes closed.

Taata's fingers tapped nervously on the bed frame. "I am not happy with this treatment," he said. "We have carried the boy all the way from Nyakagyezi only to be told he must wait until tomorrow?"

"Everything will be fine," the nurse assured him.

Everything is *not* fine, I thought desperately. I had seen all that blood on the mat at my house, on the shirts of the men who carried me.

The nurse applied a new dressing and pain filled my leg with fire. The dark cloud overtook me.

"Twesi?" A hand took mine. "Hear, O Lord, when I cry aloud, be gracious to me and answer me."

When I opened my eyes, I saw a miracle. Maama stood beside the bed, a wide smile stretching across her prominent cheeks. Her hair was pulled back and tucked under a red scarf that matched the sash tying her *gomesi* at the waist.

"I am here," she said.

My body relaxed. Maama always knew the right words and the right prayers. The pain subsided just because she was there with me. She was my strength and so long as she was with me, there remained a chance I would live.

I needed that strength and prayer the next day. I was given penicillin shots to reduce my fever and taken into the surgical theater, already weak from blood loss. They used anesthesia, but I felt each cut and every tug as slivers of wood were pulled out one by one. By the time a nurse washed out the remaining debris and the doctor stitched the wound, I had run out of tears. There was nothing more anyone could do. If I wanted to live, I must fight.

That evening after Maama left, her mother, my *mukaaka,* came to the men's ward, back bent by age, but head held high. A bright green scarf set off her weathered face in the golden glow of a bedside lantern.

With the aid of a rough-hewn eucalyptus stick, she walked slowly to my bedside. Taking a deep breath, she gathered her *gomesi* and sank onto a wooden chair. Sad brown eyes searched my face. She nodded.

"You are in God's hands now." She slid a Bible from a pocket hidden within the folds of her garment and opened it. "'He that dwelleth in the secret place of the most High shall abide under the shadow of the Almighty. I will say of the Lord, He is my refuge and my fortress: my God; in him will I trust.'"

I tried to pay attention to the words, but mainly it was her voice that comforted me through that long night.

Maama spent her days with me, holding my hand while the doctor opened the wound, drained pus, and trimmed dying tissue. I worried that he had not removed all the splinters. Would they remain buried in my thigh only to become infected over and over, someday killing me? How unfair it would be to die because of a single mistake.

I was afraid. I was angry. The infection continued.

Night after night, Mukaaka returned. From Psalms, she read, "'Even though I walk through the valley of the shadow of death, I will fear no evil, for you are with me. Your rod and your staff, they comfort me,'" and "'The Lord is my light and my salvation; whom shall I fear? The Lord is the strength of my life; of whom shall I be afraid?'"

I found that I was not afraid when I listened to her voice.

"'Teach me thy way, O Lord, and lead me in a plain path, because of mine enemies.'"

It occurred to me that Mukaaka had to ford two streams, bracing her stick against the shifting stony beds to reach the hospital. Each night she returned.

"'Thou shalt not be afraid for the terror by night; nor for the arrow that flieth by day.'"

I started to see my suffering not as a punishment but as a lesson. Each night Mukaaka walked in darkness to comfort me. During those three months, only at the end of each month when the moon was full did she have light to guide her.

"'For He shall give His angels charge over thee, to keep thee in all thy ways.'"

Mukaaka was my angel, bringing God's light into my young life. It was that light that guided me through the shadow of death.

A jolt brought me back to the wooden slats of the truck bearing Frank's casket. Nothing brings the reality of death home like the feel of a coffin against one's palms. A sob shook me to my core.

Why had God taken Frank? He was a kind and generous man who would be missed by more than his family. There were many people in the village who depended on his annual generosity. Who would help them now?

CHAPTER 6

THE PROSPECT OF MARRIAGE

After Frank's death, I struggled to continue with my life. Work kept me busy, and I was even offered a position in America with a human rights organization. My friend Beronda wrote letters of comfort. Mbabazi gave birth to a healthy boy, a happy baby named Gaddafi with fat little thighs and a contagious laugh. I visited them as often as I could manage in order to keep up my spirits and remind myself that life continues. But in the quiet of the evening or in the middle of the night, I would find myself crying. When I saw two men walking along the street hand in hand, I would think, *That could be me and Frank.* A terrible emptiness was left inside me.

And then another shock. Mbabazi received devastating news. She too had *slim.*

By November 1996, my oldest sister was bedridden. Since she was unable to care for herself in the city, we brought her to the village, where my faithful Mukaaka nursed her and my parents cared for Gaddafi. I returned regularly, bringing money to help cover expenses. Little Gaddafi was always happy to see me.

Each time I visited, I prayed Mbabazi would be better, but she grew weaker and thinner. It was Frank all over again.

"Why, Lord?" I remember praying one dark night. "How much loss must one family endure? You have already taken my brother. Must you take my sister too?"

I was in Gambia, West Africa, attending a human rights seminar when Mbabazi's condition became grave. I planned to visit her when I returned to Kampala, but news of her death greeted me instead. Mbabazi had passed away the previous night.

Alone in my apartment, I shed no tears, having none left to shed. I had cried enough to fill the Nile while Frank and Mbabazi wasted away. Overburdened with grief, I went to my knees.

"What is it you wish from me?" I asked. "What can I do to end this suffering caused by HIV/AIDS? Tell me and I will do it."

Of course, I heard no magical voice and encountered no burning bush, for that is not how our Lord typically works. Instead, depression set in and I was soon questioning the direction of my life. I briefly considered quitting my job and returning to the village. At least I would be closer to my kin as they died one by one.

When we learned that Gaddafi also had *slim,* it was too much. I wanted to curl into a ball and never rise again.

Taata had other thoughts.

Not long after Mbabazi's death, he met with other men in the village, and when I went home for a visit, he asked me to help him move the *ente* to the upper pasture. As we guided the mooing animals with switches, he suddenly announced, "It is time for you to marry."

I did not say anything, shocked that he would suggest such a thing with Mbabazi's grave still fresh.

"Did you hear me?"

"Yes," I said.

"I have spoken with Kyakwera's father, He thinks you will make a good husband and is happy for you to marry his daughter."

I had not mentioned Beronda for fear it would spark Taata's anger. He would not understand how her letters had comforted me over the previous year. Now that Taata had made plans, I could hide my thoughts no longer.

"I cannot marry Kyakwera," I said. She was a fine woman. If I had never left the village, I would have been happy to marry her.

Taata's wayward eye passed over me. "You are my son and you will do what I say."

I stood my ground. "I will not."

"You think because you have attended university and gone to America that you are better than the rest of us? You think you may disgrace this family? Is my one remaining son too stupid to listen to his father?"

"I cannot marry Kyakwera," I said. My stomach burned with pent-up resentment. "I have found a woman in America. Her name is Beronda."

"America!" Taata's eyes narrowed. For a moment I thought he would strike me. "America. I should never have permitted you to go there."

"I am not a boy to be *permitted* this or not *permitted* that!" He had been able to threaten me when I was young, but no longer.

"You are still my son."

"Beronda is a good woman." I did not mention that I had not asked her to marry me and doubted very much she would agree if I did. I knew only that I could not marry Kyakwera while there remained even a chance that Beronda could be my wife.

"A good woman," Taata snorted. "What do you know of choosing a woman?"

"She is—"

"Is she from our clan?"

"No," I said.

"Then what clan? The Bakimbiri or the Bazigaba?"

"I do not know," I said. It would be difficult to explain the situation in America to him.

"You do not know her clan!" Taata stormed. "What of her family? Do they work hard? Do they own land?"

I shrugged.

"Do they possess *embuzi*? *Ente*? Do they farm?"

"I met her at the university," I said. "I have not met her family."

"You do not even know her family and you are planning to marry her?"

"I love her," I blurted.

"Love!" Taata threw his hands high. "Bah!"

"You will see. She is—"

"People do not marry for love," Taata said. He tapped his forehead. "You are not thinking with your brain."

"She is intelligent. She is hardworking."

"And will she come here to care for you and your children?"

I realized I had not thought things through. If I married Beronda, I would be moving to America. She would obtain her Ph.D. and find a job at a university. How could I explain this to Taata? Life in America was nothing like here in Nyakagyezi.

"I will return to America," I said, watching Taata's face. I had been considering taking a job as a programs assistant with People's Decade for Human Rights Education (PDHRE). I would be working with Shula Koenig on human rights education in Africa, Latin America, and Asia.

"I forbid it," Taata said without much fire. I saw something in his expression I had not seen before. Something like fear, but not quite.

"I have already decided," I said. Did I want to hurt him as he had hurt me so many times? I did not know.

He shook his head wearily. "I have already lost one son. Now you tell me you are leaving for another world. Must I lose a second son?" His mouth formed a tight line.

"No," I said, relenting. "It will be as if I am living in Kampala, just a longer journey."

Taata removed his hat and rubbed his forehead. "This will only lead to trouble."

"I can take care of myself." It was not the first time I had been in conflict with Taata's will. I did not expect it to be the last.

Taata glared, but said nothing further. He did not have to. I knew what he would say later if I failed with this idea: *Nkakugambira*. I told you so.

Taata never got to say that. I took the job in America and married Beronda on October 23, 1998. Upon receiving her master's degree she was accepted into a Ph.D. program in California. We made the cross-country move and Shula Koenig allowed me to continue working for PDHRE until I got another job, at California Federal Bank in Sacramento.

Three years after leaving Nyakagyezi, my life was going well, but I found myself missing Maama and my family. I longed for fresh Nile perch and *matooke* steamed over an open fire. I wanted to walk the *enengo*'s steep slopes and enjoy the quiet darkness of night in the village. Finally, in 2001, I suggested to Beronda that we visit Uganda.

"Do you think they will accept me?" she asked. I had told her of Taata's plans for me to marry. I could not blame her for being nervous.

After some encouragement, Beronda accompanied me to the village in April 2001. I expected Taata to start complaining the moment we arrived at the new house I had had built for my parents, a plastered brick building with a corrugated iron roof. *It is fortunate Beronda does not understand Rukiga,* I thought. She would not comprehend Taata's insults.

I could not have been more surprised when Taata greeted us at the door.

"*Agandi*," he said, shaking Beronda's hand. "Welcome to the family."

"Please, come in and sit," Maama added. "We have food ready."

Beronda followed me inside.

"She is a very beautiful woman," Maama said.

Taata was on his best behavior and liked Beronda immediately. Maama was overjoyed to have another daughter. All that worry over nothing. What a welcome change.

News travels fast in the village. The morning after Beronda and I arrived, we woke to find a long line of people waiting outside. Where once mothers and fathers had waited, now *mukaakas* in faded dresses stood patiently with one, two, or more orphaned grandchildren ranging from toddlers to young teens. Men in everything from worn suits to stained T-shirts escorted nieces and nephews.

Beronda peered past me. "Who are these people?"

"Some of the families I told you about." I stepped outside. "Now that I am a rich American, they think I can support everyone in Nyakagyezi."

I had been financially helping my brother's three children since his death. I had also helped a girl named Rebecca attend nursing school, and a boy named Dixon finish school to become a teacher. Unfortunately, that was but a ripple in a big ocean. So many people were dying by this time that even Ugandan optimism could not shield my heart.

Beronda surveyed the crowd. I had told her about the HIV/AIDS crisis in Africa. She understood it intellectually and supported my helping the orphans, but it was not until that day that she fully understood the scope of the problem.

I stooped down to greet a girl who held a young man's hand. Her face was dirty and her dress torn at the hem.

"What is your name?" I asked.

"Tukamushaba," she said, looking away shyly.

"This is my sister," the man said. "Our mother died two years ago. Our father died this year. My wife and I are trying to care for the children, but we cannot afford food."

I reached into my pocket, removed a ten-thousand-shilling bill, and handed it to him.

"*Webale,*" he said.

Next, a *mukaaka* approached with a boy.

"*Agandi,* Mr. Twesigye. This is my grandson, Natukunda."

"*Agandi,* Mr. Natukunda." I shook the boy's hand.

"Natukunda's mother died when he was one year old," the *mukaaka* said. "It came to me to suckle him. Now I have no money for tuition and school fees."

"I will provide that," I said.

I turned to Beronda. "Tuition is only a couple of dollars in American money, but many need food and clothing as well."

"What about all the international aid coming from America?"

"They focus on short-term aid," I said. "They send food for a while or educational supplies for a year. But these children must be cared for for the next ten to fifteen years." My throat tightened. "Frank and I tried to help people over the years, but now there are too many."

I saw that fiery spark in Beronda's eyes that appears when she prepares herself for a challenge. She grasped my hand tightly.

"We must do something," she said.

"Amen," I said quietly, turning back to the line of people.

After listening to villagers' pleas all morning, and helping as many as we could, Beronda and I were both exhausted. We sat on a bench behind the house enjoying the cool shade. Faida washed dishes in a plastic tub near the kitchen, while Taata busied himself in the pasture repairing barbed-wire fence.

One family had given us a box of limes. I fished a couple from my pants pocket, split one open, and bit into the sour pulp.

"How many orphans do you think there are in the village?" Beronda asked.

"I do not know," I said. "There are probably thousands in the surrounding area."

"Thousands!"

"There are almost two million orphans in Uganda," I said. For a country no larger than the state of Oregon, it was a mind-numbing figure. If a tragedy of this proportion happened in America, people would demonstrate in the streets. But here amid the peaceful rolling hills and quiet farms, death crept silently from house to house, taking a mother here and a father there. No news crews splashed the story across the television. No drugs were available to stop the disease. Frail bodies fought to stay alive in tiny mud daub houses, unseen and uncounted, dying in silence. In surrounding hospitals, mothers sobbed as their HIV-positive children were snatched away. Coffin makers collected higher and higher profits, and grandmothers spent their life savings burying their children.

"There must be a better way," Beronda said.

I nodded. The children we had seen at the house that morning were the lucky ones. They had family who cared about their welfare and education. Because of the stigma of AIDS, many children are abandoned, people assuming they will soon die from the disease. In other instances, families take the parents' property and use the orphans as household servants or hire them out as prostitutes. These orphans we saw that morning required more than single payments for books or tuition fees, or even a month's worth of food. They needed consistent education, a supportive family, and good nutrition.

"I have been thinking about building a school," I said.

"A school?"

"With free tuition."

"What kind of a school?"

"Primary." I split open a lime and handed it to her. "Classes one through seven."

Her lips puckered as she sucked on the green fruit.

"Can you just buy land and build a school?" she asked.

"Yes," I said. In Uganda, there were some government-run schools, but many were run by private organizations and churches.

Beronda tossed the fruit rind into the yard and gazed up at the cloudless sky. I could not tell if she was upset by the idea or considering it. This was really not the time to be thinking about building a school. Beronda had just received her Ph.D. and we were getting ready to move from California to Indiana, where she would start her postdoctoral work. We had a little money saved for a down payment on a house. After years of renting we were ready for a home of our own.

"We need more than a building," she said. "There will be books and supplies and teachers' salaries."

"I know," I said, wishing I had not brought the issue up. Beronda had enough to worry about without me adding to her burden. "It is a big project. Maybe in a few years—"

"The kids will require nutritious food," Beronda said firmly. "Health care. That means at least a lunch program."

"Yes," I said. "We cannot afford it now. But maybe in time—"

Beronda's jaw set with determination. "These children don't have time," she said. "They need a school *now*."

"What?"

"You're right," she said. "These orphans need a school."

It took a heartbeat for her words to sink in, but when they did, joy blossomed through me with such radiance I nearly cried. I had not truly realized the extent of the darkness Frank's and Mbabazi's and little Gaddafi's deaths had left within me until that moment lifted it out.

Eyes tearing, I took Beronda's hand in mine and kissed her. We had been living halfway around the world from each other, but God in His mysterious way brought us together. Taata was right in a way about marriage. This marriage was more than love. This marriage had become a mission.

When I finally released Beronda, she smiled and touched my face.

"Will we need an orphanage too?" she asked.

I had to laugh. It is not for my Beronda to be swept away by emotions when there is a problem to be solved.

I wanted to kiss her again. But, of course, she had raised an important point. Many of these children were double orphans with no parents or relatives to support them. In some cases they lived alone without adult supervision. Still, the thought of institutionalizing children did not sit well with me. Most people in the village were related through clan or tribal ties.

"Maybe we can find sponsor families," I suggested.

"Can families afford to be sponsors?"

"I do not know." Building a school had been in the back of my mind for a long time, but I had not thought through these details. Paying for a child's tuition was easy. I had only to count out the cash. Building a school was another matter. There were permissions and building costs to think about, construction workers and teachers to hire, land and supplies to purchase. The thought was both exhilarating and terrifying.

"We'll pray to God for guidance," Beronda said. "He'll show us the way."

CHAPTER 7

THE GREAT ESCAPE

Taata was not in the house the next morning when I mentioned the school idea to Maama, but I think he had birds spying for him. News of our plan reached him before I was even ready for my morning run. I stepped outside and there was Taata, hoe in hand.

"What do I hear about building a school?" he said.

I sat to tie my shoes.

"Beronda and I have discussed it," I said.

"Why do you want a school? There are plenty of schools. There is a school just up the road."

"We want to build a school for orphans."

"Orphans! Ha! How are orphans going to afford this school of yours?"

"The school will be free. Free tuition. Free uniforms. Free school supplies."

"How are you going to do that?"

"We will find the money," I said.

He slammed the hoe's wide blade into the grassy ground. "Well, if you have too much money and have nothing to do with it, give it to me."

I expected as much from my father. When I paid for their brick house so that Maama would not have to continually patch mud daub, Taata barely thanked me. I gave them plenty of gifts and they lived well in the village. Still, Taata was not happy. He always wanted more.

I leaned forward to stretch my hamstring. "There are hundreds of children in Kanungu District who lack education," I said. "Someone should help them and the people of Nyakagyezi."

"Bah," Taata said. "Building a school will not help Nyakagyezi."

"Education helped me." I stood and put my hands on my hips and leaned to each side.

Taata grumbled. "I suppose you will do what you want. You have always been a stubborn *embuzi*."

I was surprised he backed down so quickly.

"An orphans' school will help," I said. "You will see."

Taata walked away.

After one last stretch, I trotted to the road and turned uphill from my parents' house. A smile came to me. Taata was right. I have been a stubborn *embuzi* all my life.

When I was a child, Maama closed the wooden shutters tight each night to keep out mosquitoes. She was vigilant about preventing malaria, stuffing scraps of material into cracks around sills and keeping the doors tightly closed.

Even so, tiny streams of light would filter through the thatched roof, announcing morning. I was usually awakened by the rustling and hushed whispers of Christine and Faida returning from collecting water and dressing for school. Most of the time I rose with them, but on one particular day when I was no more than four or five years old, I had other plans in mind. Feigning sleep on my woven banana mat and tucked under the many folds of Maama's green-and-yellow *gomesi,* I waited.

"That is *my* belt," Faida protested.

"It is not," Christine answered with the authority of an older sister.

"Stop it!"

A struggle ensued. Faida crashed down on the mat next to me, but I did not react. Christine always won these battles and Faida would take out her frustration on me if I were awake. Normally I would have pushed her away, but this morning I remained still. I was going to the school, and this time, I was going inside a classroom.

"Breakfast," Maama called. "Come wash your hands."

My sisters rushed from the room, leaving the bedroom door ajar. Through slit eyes, I watched as they dashed out the back door and returned with hot milk and plates with steaming potatoes and cassava. Adjusting their uniforms, short-sleeved aqua dresses trimmed across the chest with a white cord, they sat cross-legged on brown floor mats and started eating with their fingers. The starchy sweetness of their cassava tempted me to give up my plans, but only for a moment.

"Hurry," Maama said, peering through the doorway. "You will be late."

"It is Faida's fault," Christine said at once.

"It is not," Faida said.

Christine slid a leg from beneath her and nudged Faida. Milk spilled over the edge of Faida's cup.

"Stop it!"

"Enough!" Maama said. "*Ruhanga wangye.* How did I end up with two girls such as these?"

The meal finished in silence, but I could tell by Faida's fierce expression that she was thinking revenge. Maama returned and handed each of them a packed lunch wrapped in banana leaves. I could almost taste that leftover cassava as they shoved the green bundles into carry sacks and left with Maama through the front door. But I had no time to worry about food. Not if I wanted to make good on my escape. Before Maama returned, I scooted out the back, scattering chickens near the door.

"Hush!" I said to them, but they did not listen. Chickens seldom do.

The square backyard, with a cooking shed to the left, *embuzi* pen at one corner, and a latrine at the other, was bordered by a prickly cactus hedge. *Embuzi* tugged at their rope leashes and bleated. I leaped over a mud puddle, ran to their pen, and grabbed the black-and-white female's soft ears.

"Be silent!" I scolded. Maama might hear and they would ruin my entire plan. She butted my head gently and nosed my hand when I pulled it away. I yanked a tuft of grass for her to chew, mainly to keep her quiet. Where *embuzi* are concerned, the old mother is usually the ringleader.

Squeezing between the woven branches of the pen, I crawled to a narrow opening in the hedge and surveyed the banana plantation beyond. There was no sign of Taata, but I saw a switch propped against the hedge. He had been training me to take the *embuzi* out to graze, to herd them by smacking their legs and sides with a switch. Soon I would be a big boy and able to do it on my own, just like I would be able to go to school. Only, I could not wait for school.

Thorns raked my arms as I pushed through the hedge and inched along the yard's outer edge. A sudden gust of smoke from the kitchen shed stung my eyes. I pinched my nose and closed my mouth. Maama would surely hear me if I coughed this close to the house. Without further thought, I ran to the road, a rutted path in the grass that saw mainly foot traffic and the rare pickup truck.

My sisters were far ahead, talking and laughing about things they would never share with me, having already forgotten their argument, as sisters do. I could just make out the white stripes on their uniform belts. One day I would have a uniform too, black shorts and an aqua shirt like the other boys. I would get to count numbers and learn to spell words.

I followed them, trying to keep to the road's edge where I could duck into a hedge or behind a tree. I had been caught many times before sneaking off to school, usually by Christine. On other occasions, neighboring farmers had noticed me and escorted me home. That would not happen today. I would pretend I was *embuzi* and they would not see Twesigye Jackson at all.

Excitement kept me warm at first, but this morning, like all mornings in the hills of Kanungu District, was cool. Rain had soaked the area the previous evening. Before long my legs and shorts were wet and I was shivering.

I am *embuzi,* I reminded myself. *Embuzi* cared nothing about wet and cold. With a mighty bleat, I pranced along the path and pulled handfuls of fresh grass. It smelled sweet, but the taste was nothing to write home about.

I could barely see a brick house on the right, the yard was so full of fruit trees. Avocados and mangoes dangled. A man slouched over his hoe, tilling soil between two of the larger trees. Even this close to the road, he did not notice me. My plan was working!

Emboldened, I jumped for an avocado hanging over the road, but missed. My stomach grumbled. I tried a second time without luck. The man straightened.

Giggling, I ran to the end of the orchard, where thick-leaved brush sprinkled with small orange flowers and spindly trees bordered the road on both sides. By now, Christine and Faida were gone.

No matter. I had been to the school before. It was at the end of the road.

"Get along," a boy's voice said. I heard the grumbling snorts of *ente* moving toward me.

Hide. Someone was coming!

I crawled into the brush, concealing myself in leathery, round leaves. If the boy was one of my cousins, he would recognize me and take me home. Taata would be angry and use the *embuzi* switch. I held my breath. A brown *ente* sauntered by so close I could smell its wet hide. A second *ente* passed, followed by the boy's bare feet, within inches of my hiding spot.

"Keep moving," he said. A curious calf thrust its wet nose into mine. I covered my mouth with both hands to keep from laughing and curled into a ball.

After the fourth *ente,* I waited until I could no longer hear the long grass rustling. Then I peered from my hiding place. The road was clear.

I ran to the bottom of the hill where a stream, brown with soil and congested with branches and grassy debris from the hillside, rushed across the road. I did not remember that being there before, but I did remember Taata's warnings: *Your sisters are big enough to balance on limbs to cross streams. You are too small and will certainly be whisked all the way to the bottom of the* enengo.

A limb arched across the swirling water. It had several stubby branches, but the main part was barely wide enough for my feet. From the footprints in the mud, however, I saw that other children had used it to cross. As a boy, I might be unsteady, but as *embuzi,* my balance would be razor sharp.

I stepped onto the limb, using an upturned branch for balance, and it bowed, submerging my already cold feet in the colder flow. The force of the stream was more than I anticipated, and I struggled to grip the slippery wood with my toes.

Nkakugambira, Taata's voice echoed in my mind.

Fear quickly overtaking confidence, I held tight, fighting the force of the water, but making no progress along the branch. My feet slipped, dropping me to my knees in the rushing water.

I slid farther into the stream. The stinking water, brown with soil and animal waste, was now up to my armpits.

"Help!" I shrieked, heart pounding. "Save me!" The boy with the *ente* was gone and the houses were too far away.

A white-breasted crow flapped to a nearby tree.

"Caw! Caw!" it laughed at me.

"Stop it!" I yelled.

Thrashing against the murky current, I managed to pull my way a little closer.

"Caught. Caught," the crow accused.

"We will see about that." My heart beat like a drum as I looped a leg around the limb. I grabbed a second branch. Pulling and pushing, I gradually worked my way back onto the limb. Then ever so slowly, I scooted the rest of the way across and flopped onto the muddy ground. My fear suddenly vanished.

"I am *embuzi*!" I was sure of it now. Leaping up, I bleated at the crow. Nothing could stop me.

I scampered, sopping wet, along the winding road through thickets and farm hedges, expecting the school to appear at any moment. I crossed two more streams, much shallower than the first, and climbed a grade to a copse of eucalyptus trees.

Still I did not reach the school.

"Lost. Lost," the crow teased. I looked up to see him flapping atop a banana tree.

"This is the right direction," I said, but could not stop doubt from seeping into me. Maybe the hard rain had changed the road overnight. Maybe a stream had washed the school into the *enengo*. I slowed to a stop and looked back. The road would take me home. I was sure of that, but I had *so* wanted to see the school again.

Also, my shorts and shirt were stained brown. If I returned home,

Taata would know I had been up to no good. I could not go back. But how was I to find the school? I trudged forward, slower with each step.

The singing was low at first and I thought it was the pestering crow. But as I stood shivering on the road, clothes dripping wet and teeth chattering, I recognized a few words.

"'. . . may you live and shine forever more.'" It was a song I had heard my sisters sing, the school's song! Without another thought, I took off running, splashing through puddles.

The singing became louder, charging me with anticipation. The school must be just ahead, beyond the banana trees.

"'. . . we shall always progress with utility, discipline and democracy . . .'"

A faded aqua sign marked the entrance road to the school. I could not read it, but had seen it before. I hurried along the stony track, out of the plantation and up a small slope.

The school! I laughed and danced with excitement.

Two red brick buildings with rusted corrugated roofs faced a central yard that held a single tree with gnarled limbs and dark green leaves. Aqua shutters had been thrown open to greet the morning sun. Matching doors gaped, welcoming all students. *And me.*

I made a beeline to the nearest building and rested beneath the window, back pressed against rough brick still cold from the night. I had imagined myself walking straight into the classroom, but now that I was only a few steps from the door, I was afraid. Would the teacher let me stay? Would I be chased away with an *embuzi* switch? My pulse raced as I tried to find my courage. My wide eyes searched the tree for the pesky crow. If it could see me now, it would certainly be laughing.

"You will practice addition this morning," a woman teacher said from the other side of the wall. *Just a few steps and I will be inside.*

Wood slid against gravel, paper shuffled. Someone coughed. I could not get my feet to move.

Chalk clicking on the blackboard finally sparked my curiosity into such a frenzy, I had to peek. Grabbing the windowsill, I scrabbled up the wall with my toes until I could see inside. The students sat four to a bench, each bench connected to a narrow table. Their uniforms were clean and crisp and glowed as if they possessed an aqua light of their own. Gray unlined paper and stubby pencils were laid neatly on the tables. The front wall held a blackboard covered with white symbols.

A smile stretched my face tight. It could not be any more exciting. This was where I wanted to be, a student at school.

"Twesigye Jackson!" Taata's voice boomed behind me. "*Nkakugam-bira . . .*"

I am not Jackson, I thought instantly, dropping from the sill. I am *embuzi*. But I knew from his stern expression that Taata saw me for who I truly was, a little boy in big trouble.

I jogged along a grassy path and thought of Taata. That was not the last time I was in trouble. Taata and I disagreed on a regular basis. I would always be the disobedient son. He would always be the belligerent father. I just had to accept that as part of my life, pray to God for the patience to deal with him, and continue doing what I thought was right. He had stopped my great escape but he would not stop me from building this school.

CHAPTER 8

ONLY ONE ACRE

The morning Beronda and I were to leave the village I tried to get Taata to donate a piece of land for the school.

"Only one acre," I said in Rukiga.

"No." Taata stared across the table.

"You have plenty of land," I said. Beronda was in the bedroom packing the suitcases, and she could not understand our conversation in any case. "You have acres that you do not even use."

My *shwenkuru* had been a wealthy man, and even though he had several wives and many children, he had helped Taata pay for his land.

"I use all my land for grazing," he said. "I will not have you building a school on top of good grass."

"One acre," I said. "That is all I ask."

"How much will you pay?"

"Never mind," I said, angered at his selfish attitude. "I will find land elsewhere."

I stood and walked to the bedroom to help Beronda.

"No one will give you free land," Taata said, getting the last word in. He was probably right, but I would rather buy from a stranger than from my selfish father.

"What are you talking about?" Beronda asked.

"Nothing." I set my attention on packing our bags and allowed my anger to subside.

By the time we were ready to leave, all Nyakagyezi was abuzz with rumors of my building a school. Mr. Arineitwe stopped by the house as I carried bags out the front door.

"*Agandi,* Twesigye!" he said, shaking my hand. "I heard you were leaving and came to wish you farewell."

I shook his hand but did not smile. Maama had told me that Mr. Arineitwe and another neighbor, Mr. Niwamanya, had been spreading rumors like a couple of old women with too much time on their hands. Mr. Arineitwe was telling everyone I wanted to build a school in order to run for political office. Mr. Niwamanya insisted I was starting a personal business because my wife was leaving me and I needed something to do in Uganda.

"I leave today," I said.

Mr. Arineitwe nodded. "Going back to America with your wife?"

"Yes," I said.

"When are you returning to Nyakagyezi?"

"Maybe next year," I said.

Mr. Arineitwe hesitated. "I hear you will build an Adventist school."

No doubt some members of the Anglican Church were unhappy at the prospect of a new school, thinking it would be open only to members of my church, the Seventh-day Adventists. There were other church-run schools in the area, but people divided along religious lines. Catholics would not send their children to Anglican schools and Adventists would not send theirs to Catholic schools. I had not planned it all out, but one thing I wanted to do with this school was overcome such division. The last thing I would want was a school open only to Adventists.

"I will build a school for HIV/AIDS orphans," I said.

"Orphans," he repeated with a faraway gaze. I suspected he was trying to work through my diversion to whatever devious scheme I was truly hatching. I nodded and continued carrying bags to the SUV we had rented in Kampala.

A man approached with a hoe propped over one shoulder. He flashed a missing-tooth smile, and I recognized Twebaze, an old classmate from primary school.

"*Agandi,* Twesigye," he said. Twebaze was a smart man, but he had lacked the patience for school. While I finished my studies and went on to university, he married and had children.

"*Nigye,* Twebaze," I said.

He shrugged. "Things are difficult. We all suffer."

I could tell by his threadbare clothes that he was not doing well. I separated a twenty-thousand-shilling bill from my remaining money and placed it in his palm. "This is to feed your family."

"You are most generous," he said, eyes lowered. "How may I repay you?"

"Keep your children well fed," I said. "And send them to school."

By the time Beronda and I finished packing the vehicle, the front yard was filled with people wishing us farewell. Maama hugged me tight and asked God to keep us safe on our journey. Taata watched with a scowl on his face. I did not mention the land again.

While we drove to Kambuga and down into the *enengo,* I had doubts about building a school. Maybe this was not the right time. People of the village did not appreciate what I was trying to do. Perhaps it would be wiser to expand on the help I was already giving the poorest families in the area.

"You look angry," Beronda said.

We crested the *enengo* and followed the road toward Rukungiri.

I shook my head. "I am worried about the school."

"I thought we had decided."

"I cannot get my own father to support the idea," I said, explaining how Taata had refused to give us any land. "How will we build a school?"

Beronda nodded encouragingly. "When in doubt, think of all the grandmothers and uncles and brothers standing outside your parents' house. Think of the children they bring."

"Yes, but it is difficult to imagine how—"

"Isn't that a beautiful goat?" Beronda said, changing the subject. "You say 'embuzi,' right?"

I nodded distractedly.

"You see?" she said. "I am learning a few words already."

I stared straight ahead, still replaying the argument with Taata in my head.

"Trust in God," Beronda said, taking my hand. "He will show you the way."

I pulled the SUV to the roadside to give room for a produce truck to pass in the opposite direction. Instead of being loaded with bananas or melons, it carried a family and a casket. *Slim*. Soon the country would overflow with orphans. Beronda was right. I had to trust that God would show us the way.

On the long flight back to America, we made plans. I became optimistic about the idea again. We would build despite what the people of the village and my own father thought. I only had to raise the money required.

That optimism was dashed when I started telling our friends in America about our idea. "No one trusts sending money to Africa," several told me. There was worry about corruption. Once a week people were receiving e-mail scams from Nigeria seeking to steal their money in various creative manners. "People will think your school is a swindle too."

Frustration haunted my days and nights. No one was going to trust me. Where was the school? Where were the children? I had nothing to show them.

An immigrant friend from Ghana shook his head when I explained the idea to him.

"This is America," he said. "You work hard, buy a nice car, and pay to bring your family here. Forget your village."

Others echoed the same sentiment, telling me I should look forward, not back.

At the same time, our apartment filled with boxes as we made moving plans and found a place to live in Bloomington, Indiana.

My daily prayers became a steady appeal to God.

"Lord God, show me the way," I asked. One afternoon, Beronda found me praying amid the boxes in the living room.

"What is wrong, Twesi?" She sat on the floor and put her arm around me.

"No one will give money to build a school," I said.

"Then we'll do it ourselves," she said.

"How?"

"We'll use our savings."

"But that is for our house."

Beronda sighed. "Those children need a school more than I need a house."

"Are you sure?"

She nodded.

Tears welled in my eyes. I had married an angel. I was sure of it then.

A few days later, as I walked back from a soccer game, my good Australian friend, Dale Val, noticed my distraction.

"Oy, mate," he said. "Where was your mind today? Not on the

footy match." Dale and I had met at the Woodland Seventh-day Adventist Church and found that we had more in common than soccer. Both of us had come to America to continue our education, had met the loves of our lives, and decided to stay. Since that time, we had played on a soccer team every Sunday morning.

"My mind is on the move," I said. "We have many friends here. I do not look forward to starting over again. We must find a new place, get settled in a new church, and meet new friends."

"I hear Indiana's nice," Dale said, "but basketball's their game, not soccer. And housing's cheap. You can buy a house for a fraction of what you'll pay here."

"We will be renting," I said.

"Oh." Dale looked surprised. "I thought you and Beronda were saving for a house."

"Beronda and I are planning to build a school for AIDS orphans in Uganda instead. Since we have no way to raise money, we will do it on our own."

"A school? When'd you decide on this?"

"On our flight home from Uganda." I explained our plan in more detail.

Dale laughed. "That is a bonzer idea," he said. "Count me in."

"Really?"

"Of course. Why not?"

"People have told us it will not work, that many projects have been started and died in the second year and some even in the first. They warned us we would invest our money and it would be stolen or misused and nothing would be built. In Africa, that is a real concern. So much depends on bribing public officials to get things done."

"But you know the system there, mate. You've an advantage over some foreigner coming in from the outside."

"You are right about that," I said, feeling a bit more hopeful.

"Is there no international group to help you?"

"No," I said. "Large organizations choose location over need, making social services available in cities and towns. Rural areas get left behind."

"Yeah, mate. The back blocks always suffer. And no one supports a school that hasn't been built yet, right?"

"Yes," I said.

"How much to get you started?"

It took me a moment to realize he was talking about money.

"We must purchase land," I said. "Then we will start small, a two-room building for primary grades one and two."

"Jacinth and I are happy to help, mate. Once the school's up and running, I'm sure plenty of blokes'll kick in."

Thank you, Lord, I thought.

Beronda's parents, Earnestine and Willie, also supported the idea. This was not surprising to me. Earnestine had become my second mother in America, being there for me no matter what the circumstance. They brought our idea to their church in Little Rock, Arkansas, a few weeks later. Even though we had no tax-exempt status at the time, the church promised to support the school on a monthly basis.

We were going to build!

CHAPTER 9

PLANS

After getting settled in Indiana, I returned to Uganda to purchase two acres of land from a man named Rucumu and obtain permission to build the school. In Rubaga, I was invited to a traditional lunch by an old friend, Polly Mugisha, and his wife, Emma. We caught up on news and our conversation eventually led to the school.

"A school?" Emma asked, surprised.

"Twesi is building a school for orphans," Polly said.

"In the village," I said. "We are going to name it Nyaka AIDS Orphans School."

"You must be kidding!" Emma had just received her MBA in the Netherlands and knew more about business and financial matters than I did.

I braced for her objections. "We have the money for the first two rooms of a primary school."

She slapped the table so hard the plates rattled. "I cannot believe it."

I winced, expecting her to say I was wasting my time.

Instead, she laughed. "I designed a community school plan as part of my degree requirements. I have research on everything, building plans, supply costs, the cost to hire local Ugandan workers."

"A plan?" After all the mistrust and negative responses, I could not believe what I was hearing.

"Everything," she said. "Two classmates helped me. One from America and one from Sweden. They asked me to please make sure someone used our plans one day. I would be happy to share them with you."

Thank you, God, I thought. Just when I must make plans to build a school, there they are, delivered with a good meal and satisfying company.

"Bless you," I said. The Lord works in mysterious ways.

After lunch, we downloaded a copy of the project from her home computer to a floppy disk.

With a happy heart, I boarded a crowded bus for Nyakagyezi.

That happiness lasted until I walked through the front door of my parents' house. The sitting room was dimly lit with a paraffin lantern. Taata sat alone, brow wrinkled in concentration. He did not greet me or call out to Maama that I was home.

"The land you purchased for the school is no good," he said. "It is not close enough. The students will have to walk too far."

I had not seen him in six months and this was my greeting? I prayed to God for patience.

"Where is Maama?" I asked.

"It is better for pasture than for building."

I moved by him and looked out the back door. I saw only *embuzi* and chickens milling about the yard. The kitchen fire had nearly burned out.

"Did you hear me?" he said. "The land is no good."

"Yes, I heard you!" I snapped. "But it is the only land we have. It will have to do."

"The land here is much better," he said. "It is flatter, better to build on."

"You did not want to give us land for the school."

"That was a long time ago." His wandering eye swept past me. "That cliff-side pasture you bought is useless for a school."

"We will build on the land we have," I said. I was not sure what Taata was up to, but refused to give in. Experience had shown me I could outlast the man.

It was 1982 and I was only twelve years old, but in our village it was not unusual for a boy just shy of his teen years to want some independence from his family. In those days, my parents lived in a two-bedroom mud daub house. They used one bedroom, and my sisters and I shared the other windowless room. By the time my sisters were teens, the room had become too small for the three of us. Christine and Faida wanted their privacy and I was tired of getting kicked during the night and waking up in a bad mood because of the poor air circulation. Maama suggested I sleep in the sitting room near the back door.

That seemed a workable solution at first. I would wait until everyone was in the house for the night and lay *bishansha,* dried banana leaves, and my mats on the floor by the door. But it was not unusual in those days for Taata to be out as late as midnight talking and drinking with local men at the pub. I would be under Maama's warm *gomesi* sleeping when he came barging inside, insisting the lantern be lit and that he needed warm water to wash his feet and food to fill his belly. Some nights, he was so agitated, he would wake everyone.

"Out!" he would yell. "I want you all out!"

On those nights he forced the entire family into the chill. We would walk along darkened roads until we found a neighbor or relative who would let us sleep with them. Unfortunately, Maama always returned home. Taata would be apologetic the next day, but as I grew older, the apologies became meaningless.

Eventually, I could take this routine no longer. I hatched a plan. I would build my own house. The first thing I needed was wooden poles for framing.

Each afternoon, it was my chore to take the *embuzi* and *ente* to graze in fresh pastures. I always took a machete to cut undergrowth, so it was easy to start collecting wooden poles. I would select small trees and cut them to size while I tended the animals. Dragging one pole back each day, it took more than a month to collect enough to start building.

"What is all this?" Taata asked when he found some of my pole collection. He did not know that I had other support poles, and also reeds to be used as cross supports in the walls, hidden beneath banana leaves and dirt on the plantation.

"I am building my own house," I said.

"We have a house. If you have extra time, I will give you more chores."

"I am tired of sleeping by the door!"

"Then sleep in the kitchen."

I did not want to sleep curled up on the dirt floor in front of the hearth. I wanted my own room and my own place to sleep. I could barely contain my urge to argue, but it would be fruitless. Taata always had the last word.

It seemed for a while that I would not get my house started. Even though I had collected poles and reeds, time was never available to build. Monday through Friday, I attended school and had chores at five in the morning and more chores after school that lasted until after dark. Saturday was the Sabbath, so I could not work on that day, and on Sunday Taata always found additional chores to keep me busy.

I hatched a second plan.

My father was never home in the evening, so I decided that was the time to start. After milking, while my sisters helped Maama make dinner, I dug post holes on the north side of my parents' house. Building there was not easy because the land was hilly, but I did my best to level the ground with a hoe and my feet. Taata did not notice the first few nights because I covered up my work when I was finished, but one morning he came into the house angry.

"What do you think you are doing?" He held up the hoe I had left near my construction site.

"Nothing," I said.

"If you think you are going to build a house, think again," he said. "I will tear it down."

"Other boys have houses." Could he not see I was growing up? I would be a man soon. He could not keep me here forever.

"You are not other boys!" he said, brow wrinkling. Even his wayward eye focused on me, and I knew he was too angry for me to challenge. I was not too old to take a switch to, and there were plenty of switches close at hand, thanks to my collecting.

I lowered my eyes and did not speak. He was worried that once I had my own place, I would have the freedom to go places, like dances, while he slept. God forbid that I should have fun. It already angered me that I was not allowed to play soccer after school, though I did stake the *embuzi* and sneak off to the games many times.

I stopped construction, but it did not take long to come up with a third plan. To build a house quickly requires help. And the person to help me would be my best friend, Emmanuel Tiyeitu.

Emmanuel and I had very different backgrounds. My family was not destitute, but Taata struggled to pay our school tuition and we lived in a small house. Emmanuel was the son of a reverend and member of the Anglican Church. They owned large tracts of land and several animal farms and lived in a six-room home. I had to share pencils with Faida by breaking them in half; we would always fight over who got the end with the eraser. Emmanuel had plenty of school supplies. I spent my evenings watching the stars and listening to crickets, while Emmanuel listened to music from the city on his own radio. Still, despite our differences, we were the best of friends, and I could always count on him.

"We must build the house in one night," I told him.

"One night!" He shot me a questioning glance. I am sure he thought I was playing a joke on him.

"Yes," I said. "Taata will tear the thing down. So we must get the support corner posts and some of the walls packed with mud, so that they are dry and hard by morning."

Emmanuel's eyes sparkled. "You think we can do it?"

I nodded. "I will find more help."

Two nights later, we were ready. The poles and reeds were lined up. I had invited two other boys to help fetch water and mix mud.

As if he suspected something, Taata lingered at home that afternoon, questioning me about the *embuzi* and asking about school. He gave me extra chores and even made me break up some of the reeds for firewood.

The sun was low in the sky and the others would be arriving soon, and still he remained. I tried not to seem anxious, but it was hard to hide. Finally, I went and sat in the latrine until it was pitch-black outside.

"Are you in there?" Emmanuel said, knocking on the side wall.

"Is Taata gone?" I asked.

"Yes."

"I think he knows something is going on." I peered around the latrine edge.

"We need to hurry. Hudson and Geoffrey are here."

Taata always liked his privacy, so the homestead was fenced with a dense prickly hedge and restricted by a wire gate. Any building on the property was to face toward the inside of the compound. Taata had indicated as much a few days before, as if reading my mind. *I will not let you build your silly house,* he seemed to say, *but if some responsible person did build a house on this property, the door must face the inside of the compound.*

I decided to face the door toward the outside of the property. Taata had kept me trapped behind his gate my whole life. He would not keep me trapped any longer.

I uncovered the hidden post holes and we mixed *obudongo,* mud cement used to hold the four corner posts in place. We lashed cross-beams together for support and added additional vertical posts to the wall frame. Then we wove reeds around the support beams to give the walls their structure. Once the *obudongo* was packed into the reeds, the walls would be solid.

Even though nights in Uganda are much cooler than days, we were all sweating hard by the time we heard Taata singing in the distance. The house was far from finished.

"Stop!" I rasped. "Taata's coming. We must hide."

We bolted into the banana plantation and hid among the broad leaves littering the ground. From beneath dried fronds, I watched lantern light flicker inside the house. I heard Taata's gruff voice complaining. Maama came out the back door and hesitated. She knew we were building, but had not told Taata. Without a word, she walked to the kitchen and retrieved his dinner.

I held my breath for what seemed like hours, hoping Taata would not come outside and see our construction. Conversation inside finally quieted and the lantern light extinguished. We waited until I heard Taata's familiar snoring before climbing from our hiding place.

"Back to work," I said.

We worked well into the night, squeezing fistfuls of mud between the reeds at the corners of the building. Taata would not be able to destroy the house so easily now. By morning the mud would set and it would take a sledgehammer to loosen.

"We did it," Emmanuel said.

"Let us see who Taata hires in the morning to destroy it," I said. We high-fived like NBA players after winning a championship. I felt proud and invincible at that moment. Let Taata do his worst.

When the morning sun rose and light filtered across my mat in the sitting room, I expected Taata to come charging into the house screaming and yelling. But as luck would have it, he was not home.

"God is watching out for you and your house," Maama said. "Taata was called to a burial forty miles from here. He will be gone for one night."

I could not believe it. I skipped school that day and we finished the walls and constructed a roof with wood we had stolen a few nights before from three local tree plantations. One of the plantations was owned by Emmanuel's family.

If God was watching over us, for some reason He had decided not to punish us for stealing the wood. That would come later, I suspected, and Taata would probably be the one doling out justice.

Anger is not the word for Taata's reaction when he saw the finished house two days later. Pacing back and forth before the front door he shook his head and mumbled.

"Am I raising a son or *embuzi*?" He snatched the hat from his head and threw it to the ground. "I cannot let this stubbornness continue."

Maama and Faida peered around a corner of the house.

"It is bad enough you build this thing in my yard, but you build it with the door facing outside?" Taata glared at the roof. We had done a good job. The building was strong and would last many seasons.

"You show me no respect!" he shouted.

"I am sorry, Taata," I whispered. I was not really sorry, but did not know what else to say.

Taata looked me directly in the eye. "Nothing else can be done. I must burn the place to the ground!"

I was sick to my stomach the rest of the day. After all our hard work, Taata was still going to destroy the house. He sent me off to graze the *embuzi,* and I grudgingly guided them to the far pasture, expecting to see smoke rising into the sky at any time.

When I returned, the house was still standing. Taata had gone off to the pub for the evening. I breathed a sigh of relief.

Taata never did make good on his threat to destroy my house. I built a bed with poles and reeds and covered it with banana-leaf mats. Mukaaka gave me a little money to buy a door and I covered the one window with woven reeds. I even had enough nerve to plan a party to celebrate the first day in my new home, but Maama warned me against the idea.

"You have already defied so many orders," she said. "Do not embarrass yourself. Your *taata* will come home and beat everyone at the party."

Maama was always the peacekeeper. I decided to heed her warning. Instead of having a party, I waited until my parents were asleep and went to Emmanuel's house where we listened to music on the radio late into the night.

Our conversation about school property ended when Maama came into the room. Taata left in a huff. The next day, he approached me with a deal. He would trade the land I bought for a good spot near

the road at the back of his property. I did not want to agree, but the
new location was better. In the end I decided it was in the best interest of the orphans to agree to his offer. It was not the first time I
would have to swallow my pride for the orphans' sake. Even a stubborn *embuzi* can learn, it seems.

CHAPTER 10

THE PRICE OF STONES

I spent the next few days meeting with government officials about the school. Locally, I met with the sub-county chief and the council of chiefs. I also met with education officials in Kanungu. Finally, I spoke with officials at the Non-Governmental Organizations Co-ordination Board. Before I returned to the United States, everything was in place to build the school.

Since I could not be in Nyakagyezi to supervise the building process, Taata took on the job of foreman. All things considered, he was the best man for it. He kept his good eye on every part of the construction, making sure we were not cheated. In many ways, I pitied the poor men who worked for him.

I heard about all his problems over the phone. The foundation stones were too large and he had the men break them up. Some bricks were not of good quality and he made the supplier take them back. A local man had tried to swindle him on the price of sand. The price he had quoted was two thousand shillings more than the agreed-upon amount. That was only a dollar in American money, but Taata would not put up with dishonesty. The man would never work for us again.

As the building progressed, I learned that not all villagers were against the school. Tibihika Silver donated bricks and Charles Kambamu donated his construction services. Mr. Ndazororera gave us stones and bricks. It was nice to know that we were not alone in this project.

In October 2001, not long after construction began, we discovered Beronda was pregnant. I was overjoyed at the prospect. I prayed every day for a healthy child and promised to be a good father.

While the school's first two rooms were being completed in Nyakagyezi, our son, Nicolas, was born in Bloomington, Indiana. It was June 25, 2002, and that event filled my heart with more joy than I ever thought I could have in one day. I called my sisters to tell them the good news. I called all our friends in the United States. I was the most blessed man on earth.

But now I realized my responsibilities had doubled. The prospect seemed overwhelming.

I think it was this that allowed me to speak up about the school at our church one day. When we first moved to Bloomington, I had not felt it appropriate as new members of a church to bring up our project or ask for contributions. Now, as a new father struggling with more responsibilities, I found the boldness to mention the school to one of our church elders, Mike Riley, during a church dinner. Impressed that we had nearly completed a two-room school building with so little funding, Mike replaced one of his sermons with an interview with Beronda and me. I was nervous at first, for in those days I was not used to speaking in front of crowds.

We answered Mike's questions, giving him details about the HIV/AIDS epidemic in Uganda, the plight of orphans in Kanungu District, and the purpose and goals of our school. Church members responded, some giving single contributions, others sending monthly support. One woman, Emogene, sent us a contribution with a note saying, "I got my Social Security check and wanted to share with the orphaned children at your school." Terry Self and Marilyn Morgan published updates in the church's monthly newsletter.

In this way I discovered that my worries had been unfounded. God was watching over the school and it would be a success.

In late December 2002, Dale Val traveled with me to Nyakagyezi for the school's grand opening, set for January 2. I was excited to have Dale with me, but my Ugandan family was at their wit's end over this white visitor from the United States.

"A *muzungu* in my house!" Taata exclaimed after Christine had told him.

"What will I feed him?" Maama added. "*Ruhanga wangye,* Twesi! What have you done to me? Now you have gone too far."

That concern passed quickly once they met Dale. Before long, Taata was bragging about his *muzungu* visitor and Maama was taking everything in stride.

We spent Friday evening in fasting and prayer in preparation for church services the following morning. Although I did not enjoy public speaking, Dale and I had been chosen to address the local congregation. I could have refused, but the original church had been built by my *shwenkuru*. If he could teach the word of God under threat of imprisonment and death from the Amin regime, I could surely gather courage enough to speak to the congregation. In the end, faith overcame nervousness, and our dual sermon was a success.

Sunday, the day of the school's grand opening, I awoke to light filtering into the bedroom through wooden shutters. Being on the equator, Ugandan day lengths are always the same; the sun rises around seven in the morning and sets about seven each night. I sat up in bed and prayed, for praying is something we do every morning and evening, and often many times in between. "Good morning," Dale said, pushing aside the mosquito net covering his bed.

"Good morning," I said. "Are you ready for the big event?"

"Can't wait, mate."

Maama insisted we sit at the table for breakfast. After milking, Taata took a few moments to join us, but he did not relax. I could tell he was pondering the day's events.

"Are you ready to work?" he asked. He stood and pulled his floppy hat over his balding head. "We must dig the foundation trench." Rather than waiting until after the ceremony we had decided to start a trench for the next classroom foundation.

"We are both ready to work," I said. Now that the school building was up, Taata was taking credit for it, as if it had been his idea all along.

"Good," he said. "It is a big job."

"First, we finish eating," I said.

Taata would not wait. By the time we finished breakfast and walked to the building site, he was sitting in a plastic chair, ready to watch us work. The new school was bare brick with no plaster finish. Wooden doors and window shutters had been hung, but the floors were still gravel. It was not yet a finished product, but a wonderful start. New rooms would be added at a right angle to the first two rooms, giving the school an L-shape.

It was nearly noon when the school's headmistress, Freda Byaburakirya, in a dark blue dress and heels, approached with a purposeful walk. Her brow was wrinkled.

Months before, I had asked her if she would come out of retirement and work at the school. She said that I should talk to her husband. He was excited about the prospect of her teaching at the school and agreed that she should volunteer.

"What is wrong?" I asked.

"We need to build another school," she said. "The classes are full and still people come to register their children."

"I feared this would be the case," I said. Mr. Agaba, the second teacher, who also had offered to work for free, had been working with the local management committee to interview and recruit orphans. Each class would hold thirty students.

"Are we to reject the rest?" Freda asked.

"We do what we can," I said to Freda. "God knows we cannot help everyone."

"But there are so many," Freda said.

"Yes," I said. "This will not be easy for any of us." I squeezed her hand. It would be hardest for Freda. I knew from personal experience that she would be not only headmistress, but a second mother to our orphans.

When my parents separated in 1979, it was Freda who kept watch over me. One day she cornered me and said, "Twesigye, I realize you are sad these days and I do not blame you. You miss your mother. But I know she thinks of you every day and misses you as well. This situation should not be an end for you, but motivation to work harder and prove your father's rage cannot defeat the love of others."

Whenever Taata got angry at me he would say, "You are stupid like your mother." Nearly everyone in the village had heard him at one time or another and it had made me cry more than once.

"I encourage you to study hard," Freda told me. "Get your education, then one day you will build a house for your mother and bring her here to live happily forever."

It was Freda's encouragement that gave me the strength to prove Taata wrong. I was not stupid. He would see.

Freda read Bible verses to inspire me. I still remember fascinating stories of David killing the gigantic Goliath, of Samuel being dedicated to God at an early age, and of Joseph being sold by his brothers, later to return and save the tribe.

No wonder I pushed myself to study and do well in school. With a *maama* who loved me, a *mukaaka* who saved me from death's door, and a teacher who believed I could move mountains, how could I not do my best?

Eventually, Freda's prophecy came true. I got a good education and returned to build my mother a new house. Now we were opening a school.

While Dale and I worked on the trenches, people arrived to erect an open-sided tent in the school yard. Once the tent was up, they moved benches and chairs from the classrooms into the shade of a nearby tree. Women tied balloons to the tent poles and set up a table with refreshments. We even had a cake for the children. In Uganda birthday cakes are not a tradition, but this cake was to symbolize their passage from orphans to students.

We had invited local church leaders, teachers, community leaders, fellow citizens, and guardians of all the registered orphans. I also had invited the Honorable Minister Professor Mondo Kagonyera from Kampala.

Maama used to tell stories about how Mondo had grown up in the same poverty as many in the village, but through his own efforts excelled in school and worked hard to pay his own school fees. He had been a hero and role model in the Nyakagyezi area. We all wanted to grow up to be like him, but none of us children ever suspected what he had lived through.

Mondo had managed to survive through the turbulent years of Idi Amin's tyranny from 1971 to 1979, when public officials, including the archbishop, chief justice, vice chancellor of Makerere University, and even Amin's own wife were murdered. He witnessed Amin's overthrow and the upheaval that followed: rigged elections, the return of the Obote regime, and economic chaos. At a time when the military barracks became killing centers and there was no protection for property or life, he endured. And when a civil war erupted in 1986, resulting in the overthrow of the Uganda National Liberation Army and putting the country into the hands of Yoweri Museveni and the National Resistance Movement, he continued on.

The village doubters were already talking about Mondo's visit. "A government minister will not show up in a small village like this," they said. Of course, they had also doubted there would be a free school for orphans in the first place.

Mondo not only showed up, he arrived early with his escorts in his government Land Cruiser. Dale and I were dirty and sweaty from digging our trench. Mondo, casually but neatly dressed in a short-sleeved shirt and dress pants, greeted us as if we wore immaculate suits.

"*Agandi,*" Mondo said as he approached.

I climbed from the trench and wiped my hand on my pants.

"*Nigye,*" I said, shaking his hand. "I am sorry, but I am unprepared to greet you. The celebration is not for a couple of hours."

"Oh, yes, I know," he said. "I was so excited and happy about what you have done I could not wait. I had to come early to get a tour before the function."

I introduced him to Dale and we walked him through the classrooms. They were simple brick-walled rooms with gravel floors and few furnishings. I told him we were continuing to raise money and would soon begin the next two classrooms.

"I am amazed at how much work you have accomplished in such a short time," he said. "I do not know how you manage to live in America and get this completed here."

Mondo knew as well as I that it was not easy. Among his other accomplishments, he had attended the University of California at Davis. Of course, it had been many years since he lived in the United States, but the experience must have provided him a broader view of Uganda and the problems our country faced. I suspect that was why he so adamantly supported education and worked to stem corruption.

Nearly five hundred people gathered that afternoon to witness a revolutionary event, the opening of a school that offered not only free education but also free books and uniforms. At the beginning of the ceremony, our students, all orphans, gathered before the crowd in their purple-and-white uniforms. We had chosen purple because it symbolizes happiness.

I recognized some of the students. Olivia's father died when she was nine years old. Onesmus lived with his aunt, where he harvested coffee, tomatoes, and eggplants to sell. Denis had been chastised and beaten by people who knew his parents had died of *slim*. Both Moreen and Hillary's parents had died when they were very young.

The orphans sang first. The choir from the local Seventh-day Adventist Church followed. Then local students sang, danced, and recited poems about their life experiences. District officials made speeches using a portable microphone, one announcing that there were now more than four thousand AIDS orphans in the area around Kambuga.

That put things into perspective, and my happiness dimmed. Giving sixty orphans a chance to go to school had seemed a staggering achievement only a moment earlier. Now it left a sour taste. Only sixty out of four thousand!

When Professor Mondo took the microphone, everyone applauded, even those who had doubted he would arrive. Taata puffed out his chest like this was all his doing.

"I would not have normally been here in this busy time of year," Mondo said. "But given what Twesigye has done, I had to come. I only came to say thank you, because so many people in the world are selfish, and even those who have much money have not done what this young man is doing. We need more people like him, and today all I want to say is thank you to him, his wife, and his parents who raised a responsible man."

That changed my mood again. In fact, as he continued his inspiring speech, my heart soared. It had been two and a half years since Beronda and I had first made plans for the school in spite of facing tremendous odds. Yet, here it stood before me, two small rooms offering hope to children who had nothing.

I thought of Taata watching over the building process, rejecting inferior stones, haggling down the price of sand. Then I thought of Dale coming to Uganda to dig a trench, Mondo coming from the city to give a speech, Mike Riley changing his sermon to promote the school, Emogene pledging from her Social Security check, and hundreds of other donors. *This is the true price of stones,* I thought.

On January 2, 2003, a purple ribbon was cut to officially open Nyaka AIDS Orphans School, with its motto: "For Our Children's Sake." The crowd burst into applause.

AN ARTICLE OF FAITH

I returned to Bloomington with pictures and a video, and the members of our church were able to see the results of their support. I received even more encouragement. In June 2003, with the help of my friend Samuel Carpenter, I was invited to speak to Sacred Heart Church in Farmington, New Mexico. After learning about Nyaka, the parishioners decided to raise money for a rainwater tank for the school. Safe drinking water is a precious commodity in much of Africa, not due to a shortage of rainfall in most places, but due to contamination and parasites.

Terry Self suggested we take advantage of an HIV/AIDS-related trip President Bush was taking to Africa, and call the *Bloomington Herald Times* with our story. A few days later, I was interviewed by a writer named Dann Denny, and a photographer came to take pictures of my son, Nicolas, and me. I thought nothing further of it.

The morning of July 17, 2003, Beronda walked from our apartment to the gas station to pick up a paper. When she returned, she held it up, stretched tight between her hands, and a big smile spread over her face. There on the front page was a bold headline: SCHOOL SERVING

AIDS ORPHANS: BLOOMINGTON COUPLE LEADING EFFORT TO HELP UGAN-
DAN CHILDREN WHO HAVE LOST PARENTS TO AIDS. I could not believe it.
What were we doing on the front page of a newspaper?

Beronda and I read the article together. It was a long feature and
included photos of us giving out seeds from Seed and Light International of New Mexico, as well as the Kanungu District speaker,
Peter Mugisha, standing before hundreds of people at our opening.
My stomach tingled with excitement. Each word was a morsel to be
tasted and treasured.

The *Herald Times* article attracted many contributors, including ninety-year-old Mary from Worthington, Indiana, who still sends
monthly donations with inspiring notes typed on her manual typewriter.
An anonymous supporter and his family paid to build an entire classroom, which we named Bethel. Harriet Lewis, an elderly woman from
New York, who had offered her support before the school was built, created a scholarship in the name of her deceased daughter, Nancy Lewis.

I was so inspired by this support that I decided to send mailings
to other Bloomington churches. I typed a letter explaining the goals
of Nyaka School and made one hundred copies of the letter and
Dann Denny's article. A week after sending the mailings my spirits
remained high. When two weeks passed without a single reply, and
then three, my high hopes faded.

One morning I returned from the mailbox to find Beronda sitting in a chair with Nicolas sleeping in her arms. The scene brought
joy to my heart, but even that was tainted by my increasing concerns
for the school. It was all well and good to build schoolrooms, but if
Nyaka School was going to survive, I would have to start paying the
teachers, buying books and supplies, and feeding students. I worried constantly that my friends in California had been right. What
if Nyaka withered on the vine in its second year? Would that not be
crueler than never having built the school at all? False hope is poison
to a community mired in death and poverty.

"Nothing in the mail," I said, leaning over to kiss Nicolas's forehead.

"These things take time," Beronda said, with a quick smile. "It may be the pastors are waiting to meet with their committees before responding."

I nodded. She was right, of course. Sometimes decisions take a long time when they go through committees. I was just being impatient. Surely, God had not helped us this far only to abandon us. That is what faith is about, I reminded myself.

Another week passed and still no response. I tried to estimate the amount of money we would need for the school over the coming years. We had several more classrooms to finish if we wanted an official primary school with seven grades. If we added thirty students each year, we would have to buy books, uniforms, and supplies for each, and add a teacher to teach them. At eighty-five dollars a month per teacher for a low-end salary, these expenses alone were more than the donations I had coming in.

I must have prayed fifty times each day, asking God to help. Was this school meant to be? Was I doing the right thing?

One morning as I was changing Nicolas's diaper, the phone rang. I laid him on the bed and reached for the receiver, assuming Beronda was calling me from work.

"Hello," a man on the other end said. "This is David Bremer from the United Presbyterian Church over here on Second Street."

David Bremer. The name was not familiar to me. I tried to recall if I had met him.

"I received your letter in the mail a couple of weeks ago," he continued.

My mind went numb. After all this time, someone was responding to my letter!

"I am glad to hear from you," I said. I was more than glad. I was overjoyed.

"I would like to talk to you about your school," he said. "Do you have some free time?"

"Yes." I was ready to go right then and there, but tried to hold back my excitement. We made an appointment for later in the week. I did not sleep for days.

The church was in a residential neighborhood near campus. As I parked the car, I was filled with anxiety. I checked my tie in the mirror and straightened my suit. I *must* make a good impression. This minister might have doubts and suspect I was trying to swindle him. I would have to show him I was a man of truth.

I entered the church, walked up the steps, and stopped at the sanctuary entrance. Gold and blue light reflected through stained-glass windows.

"Please let Reverend Bremer know I tell the truth," I prayed. "Let him see the good this school is doing and understand the suffering of these children."

The main office was at the end of the hall. Inside I was greeted by a smiling older man with glasses. His name was Allen Pease. He showed me into the adjoining office, which featured a large desk and bookshelves along two walls.

Reverend Bremer stood up behind the desk.

"Welcome, Mr. Kaguri." He was of average height and build, but what stood out at once was his sincere face. I knew immediately I could trust him. "I'm sorry I didn't respond to your letter sooner, but I have been busy."

"Thank you," I said. "I am happy to meet you."

"Please, have a seat."

We had a pleasant conversation, in which he told me that many people were suspicious of projects in foreign countries because the funds were often misused. He had faith in our school because the story had been published in the *Herald Times* and he had been assured they investigated our legitimacy.

In turn, I told him about the Nyaka children, future goals, and our ongoing financial needs.

"We are a small congregation here," David said. "But I think you can get some support from other organizations in the community. Have you attended any of the area service clubs?"

I shook my head. "No."

"I am a member of the Bloomington North Rotary," he said. "We have a noon meeting next week. You can come as my guest and meet a few people."

"I would be happy to," I said.

I left feeling better than I had in weeks, but also nervous about meeting even more new people. As it turned out, my worry would have been much better spent on other matters.

At the Rotary I met many local business people, including Otto Ray, a gregarious and genuine man who would give the shirt off his back to help someone in trouble. David and Otto not only became instrumental in promoting Nyaka School in the Bloomington area, they became two of my dearest friends. Otto invited me to become a Rotarian and through him I met Brad Pontius of Sherwood Oaks Christian Church of Bloomington and Bill Humphrey of Faith Missionary Church in Martinsville.

David introduced the Nyaka program and our wonderful Ugandan children to his church and we began to receive a steady flow of donations. It was not enough to support the school for the long term, but it was a tremendous start and energized me to spread word of Nyaka far and wide.

In the next year we were able to raise enough money for basic construction of four more classrooms, bringing the total to six. These new rooms had yet to be finished and furnished, but the shell and roofing were now in place. We also began paying our teachers, though not as much as we would have liked. The problem with relying on individual donations is that they can vary widely from month to month. We had a base of monthly contributors by this time, but with a new classroom to staff and support each year for the next several years, the pressure was mounting to find additional income.

Someone, perhaps it was David or Otto, suggested I begin applying for grants. Of course I leaped at this suggestion and began researching immediately. With God's blessing, we would find the money we needed.

CHAPTER 12

CONSTRUCTIVE SOLUTIONS

In August 2004, we moved to East Lansing, Michigan, for Beronda's job. We purchased a home, which put a strain on our personal finances. Since I had no income, I would have to obtain a full-time job. Somehow I had to find time to work, keep Nyaka School going, and help Beronda care for our new son.

The American dream was ours at last.

In the next few months, I applied for grants from many prominent groups and funding organizations dealing with AIDS and Africa, without luck. Eventually, I applied to a group in Canada called the Stephen Lewis Foundation, whose mission is to "help to ease the pain of HIV/AIDS in Africa at the grassroots level." Surely Nyaka fit that objective.

In October, I traveled back to Nyakagyezi to check on the school's progress. Earlier that year, we had hosted the first of our student interns. Ashley Pushkarewicz from Smith College taught the students English and drama. Stephen Kerns, a pre-med major, was so inspired by his month-and-a-half visit, he planned to return when he was a doctor. We were serving eighty-six students and had one totally furnished classroom. There was much more to do.

The morning after my arrival in the village, Taata was his usual impatient self and left me alone to eat my breakfast of hot milk, bananas, pineapple, avocados, and some *mugaati* I had brought from Kampala. Maama was busy in the backyard preparing for my welcoming celebration that afternoon. I was pleased to see Freda and a young girl helping. Maama had been increasingly bothered by an injury to her back from when a cow kicked her years ago. Now the pain sometimes forced her to stop what she was doing in mid-task and lie on the ground until it passed. Taata, I found out later, had arranged for Fortunate, an orphan girl attending Nyaka, to live with them so that Maama would have help.

Strict gender roles prevented him from helping her with her work, though. In America, I was a stay-at-home dad who cared for Nicolas and did housework, but at home in rural Uganda this was unheard of.

Wanting to stretch my legs and get some exercise, I left my parents' house from the front instead of taking the shortcut to the school through the banana plantation in back. Even before I reached the road I was greeted by neighbors. There must have been at least ten people loitering in or near the yard.

"*Agandi.*"

"*Nigye.*" I shook hands and greeted everyone. As I strolled, others joined the procession: schoolmates who had not continued their education, former teachers, my parents' friends, relatives from the village.

A thin elderly woman with tired eyes approached. I stopped, recognizing her as my parents' neighbor Matrinda. She always made sure to see me whenever I visited.

"Twesigye," she said, taking my hand into her bony fingers. "God is good who has brought you back safely. How is that far place where you live? Are your wife and son with you?"

"I came alone on this trip," I said. "I see God has kept you well."

"Bless the Lord, who is good and great," she said. Tears formed in her eyes. "But I am so weary. I raised my children, and now I must raise my grandchildren. Sometimes I cannot find the energy to rise from my mat. It is easier to sit in one position and sleep until morning."

I smiled as best I could. "God knows and sees your suffering, Matrinda."

Matrinda nodded. "Where would we be without you, Twesigye?" She squeezed my hand tight. "My grandchildren not only attend your school, they bring home food and have a nurse to watch their health. I feel as if part of my burden has been lifted."

"*Webale,*" I said.

"God knows and God will pay you back." After a final squeeze, Matrinda released my hand and let me continue my walk. I felt energized for a few steps, before the problem she represented seeped into my thoughts like a building storm.

Matrinda was just one of many heroic grannies in the village and across Africa. At a time in their lives when they should receive care from their children, they must take on the burden of raising another family. Without grandmothers like Matrinda, Harriet, Einidi, Margaret, and countless others who had opened their homes to children and volunteered at the school, Nyaka School could not have been a success.

So far, I reminded myself. The job is barely begun. I continued along the narrow roadway, leaving most of my companions behind. Soon, the others dispersed as well and I walked alone.

At the top of a grassy hill, sitting well back from the road, was the L-shaped school, its upper section holding three classrooms and what would soon become the teachers' offices. Finished rooms had purple shutters and doors installed, while the four classrooms in the lower section were unfinished shells, built in step-wise fashion to follow the sloping topography. The room nearest the finished section, which would become primary four in a few months, had window openings and a floor, but no shutters. Floors and window openings would be added for the other rooms the following year as long as generous people kept contributing. I prayed that by the end of 2005, we would finish construction and the school would be complete, with enough rooms for the seven primary grades.

At the north end of the building, the new ten-thousand-liter cement water tank stood, a tribute to our generous donors from New Mexico. Now we had relatively clean water available at the school, which was certainly a godsend. Unfortunately, the rest of the community lacked clean water. Our children would continue to suffer so long as we sent them home to drink water contaminated with disease and animal and human waste.

Dennis Mwebaze, the Kanungu District water engineer, had suggested we build a gravity-fed water system for Nyakagyezi. Before obtaining his position with the district, he had voluntarily created building plans for such a system. I was impressed with his passion and design skill, but was forced to tell him we did not have the twelve thousand dollars it would cost to construct the system.

"You found someone to buy a water system for the school," Dennis had reassured me. "You will find someone else to help the village."

I prayed he was right. Waterborne illness remained a serious problem for school attendance. If solving that problem also helped the community, that was all the better.

I saw children gathering in the school yard. It was not even eight in the morning, but students had already arrived for the celebration to welcome me that afternoon. A group of boys played soccer in the open field. Girls stood in the doorway to one of the classrooms, watching the boys and chatting. Most wore their purple school uniforms, for in many instances, the uniforms were the only good clothing they owned. Some wore the new black shoes and white socks they had just received, but many had bare feet, no doubt to keep their shoes and socks clean.

I had barely passed through the gate onto school property when they spotted me.

"Director!" someone yelled. Faces peered out windows. The soccer boys stopped in mid-rush. Children ran toward me from all directions, waves of purple and white uniforms and smiling faces.

"Welcome, Director! Welcome, Director!"

Eighty-six students. I reached out and tried to touch them all. Seeing those beaming faces and healthy bodies, it was hard to imagine what their lives would be like without Nyaka. I had seen them grow from quiet, unwanted children under the stigma of AIDS to confident students with a future of promise and possibilities.

And each had a story to tell.

I noticed Jane in the crowd, a delicate girl with a round face and sparkling eyes. When her father died from AIDS in 1998, her family was forced to move from Kampala to the village. Unable to cope, Jane's mother committed suicide, and Jane and her two brothers were taken in by her uncle, who already had four children of his own to support. The combined family of nine occupied a two-room house with dirt floors and a leaking roof. Jane was given chores such as cooking, cleaning, and washing dishes, and was not permitted to go to school because her uncle could not even afford uniforms and books for his own children. Under the burden of caring for so many, he had planned to marry Jane to an older man when she turned twelve, until one of the Nyaka School teachers stepped in to register Jane and her brothers for free classes. After that, the family received seeds, extra food grown at the school, and the benefit of a visiting nurse.

Thank you, God, for giving me this opportunity to help Jane and all these children. Thank you for blessing me with the chance to save these kids.

One of the teachers, Agaba Innocent, strolled up the hill, his thin frame supporting a tan dress shirt and black pants. Agaba, who had worked at the school since its inception, taught primary two and was also choir director. As he approached, his round face broke into a smile beneath large eyes and a sculpted nose.

"Welcome back," he said, wading through the purple sea. He shook my hand. "The children have missed you."

"And I have missed them," I said.

"But we have much work to do this morning." Agaba clapped his hands. "Choir members! It is time for practice. Clear the benches from the classroom. The director will be here all week. You will have plenty of time to see him."

The students seemed reluctant to leave.

"Now!" Agaba said.

Almost as one, the children ran back toward the building, rushing past Freda Byaburakirya like river water around a stone.

"Welcome back," she said. "The students are excited to see you."

Lydia strode up the hill to join us. She was a thin woman with prominent cheeks and a gap-toothed smile, who kept her hair combed back and gathered in a short ponytail. Singing had proved so popular with the students that we now had two choirs, and Lydia had taken on the position of second choir director as well as teaching the primary-three class.

Together, we strolled toward the classrooms, the teachers outlining accomplishments and setbacks they had encountered so far that year. I inspected the classrooms, making sure that the reports and photographs I had received reflected actual conditions at the school. I was happy to see that much progress had been made. Primary four would begin in January. That classroom was almost barren compared with the others, but I hoped to obtain funding from the Stephen Lewis

Foundation to pay for school supplies. Of all the grants I applied for, it seemed the most likely to succeed. That money would go a long way toward relieving the stress of trying to pay for construction as well as teacher salaries, supplies, and lunches for the students.

The night watchman met us outside. Wearing a threadbare T-shirt and armed with a sharp *panga* and a flashlight, he stood stiffly and saluted before shaking my hand.

"I must speak with you later, sir," he said. "I will soon need a gun for protecting all the good stuff you keep at Nyaka." His lips pressed tightly together and his brow creased as if he were discussing national security. I tried not to let him see my amusement. It seemed Taata had been nothing short of a genius when he hired the man. "If you want to protect the school," Taata had argued, "who would be the best man to hire? The man most inclined to break in to the place."

By hiring him, we had not only given him a steady means of employment and income, we had instilled in him a sense of pride in protecting a valuable part of the community.

I pictured Taata tapping his finger to his temple near his good eye. "Two birds killed with the one stone," he would say. I preferred to think of it as one life redeemed and a potential problem averted through a constructive solution. It is not as catchy a saying, I admit, but it appeals to me.

CHAPTER 13

BEING THE MAN

One day after classes were over, I decided to play soccer with the children. The school did not have an official field or goals yet, instead using trees and bricks to mark boundaries, but I sauntered across the grassy field like a professional soccer player entering an arena. These boys did not stand a chance. I played regularly as a member of an over-thirty league in Okemos, Michigan, was twice their size, and had been kicking soccer balls since I was their age. *Maybe I should tie my shoelaces together to even the odds.*

Soccer after school was another thing Taata was dead set against. "School is for book learning," he would say. "You have chores. I want you to come home right after school." When I lingered to play for a few minutes, he would come storming up the path and practically drag me home. It did not take long for me to change tactics. Instead of delaying at school, I would rush home to do chores. Tending *embuzi* took me far enough away from the house that I could set my plan into motion.

Embuzi are not the brightest animals; one will lead and the others follow. Therefore, I roped the lead *embuzi* to a stick anchored in the ground. With enough slack for it to forage, the lead animal ate its fill, the others did not wander far, and I was free to sneak back to school.

I was a good runner and dribbler, one of the best in primary school. During practice games, my friends Emmanuel and Sempa played forward while I defended. Mukasa Kelesi, now the volunteer coach for Nyaka, was our midfielder. We made a good team, so good in fact that one day I could not resist playing in a real game.

"We need you," Emmanuel said. "Stay and play."

"If Taata catches me," I said, "he will take a switch to my backside."

"He will never know."

I had to agree. After all, I was watching *embuzi* at the time.

I did stay and play the game. Our team won, thanks to great teamwork and my winning goal through a penalty kick. It was one of the best moments of my childhood, that kick.

Unfortunately, news spread fast in Nyakagyezi. The next day a neighbor bragged to Taata about what a good player I was. At first, Taata insisted it was not me at the game, but after hearing the news from a second person, he realized my deception. Thank God I had done so well, for his pride as the father of the winning player got in the way of his anger. I escaped punishment that time, but I did not sneak off to soccer practice for a while.

I approached the players gathered at midfield and we chose sides. Agaba joined my team, which made two adults on each side.

"This will be an easy win," I told my group. The boys jumped with excitement, but Agaba did not look so certain.

Our team got the first kickoff and the boys quickly dribbled the ball downfield until Coach Mukasa intercepted it. I stayed on his heels, but Mukasa was in good shape and I could not stop him. Fortunately, he missed the goal.

Girls cheered from the sideline.

On our second possession, I passed to Izidol, a student. He and three others dribbled around my nephew Stephen and even managed to outmaneuver Mukasa, but missed the goal by a long shot.

The girls cheered. They were rooting for both sides.

As the other team dribbled toward our goal, I was confident I would stop them. I used my best moves, but even in bare feet those boys dribbled around me as if I were standing still. When I tried to intercept a crisp pass, my foot slipped and I fell hard on my hip. The other team scored the first point.

The girls jumped up and down and screamed. I got up and hobbled back to my group.

"This time *we* score," I said gravely.

Being the stubborn *embuzi* I am, I insisted on taking the ball for the next play. I passed to Izidol, who returned the ball quickly, and we zigzagged downfield. *This is it,* I thought. Only Onesmus, one of the smaller boys, stood between me and the goal. Faking right, I kicked for the gap between his legs and waited for the ball to cross the goal line. It was not there. Onesmus had blocked my move and the other team had the ball.

The girls cheered, "Director! Director! Show them style!"

Their cheering did not help. As the game continued, I gradually swallowed my pride. These boys were good! Their ball handling and passing were crisp and they even held their positions along the length of the field. It was apparent they had practiced together a great deal. It dawned on me that the best players were the same boys who excelled academically. They were using their minds as well as their bodies, not just passing to an open player, but calculating all sorts of scoring options.

By game's end, I was exhausted and a little disappointed that we had lost and I had not shown them a thing or two. But it was also exciting to see these boys doing so well. They had the makings of a good team. I hoped we would soon have money to create a real soccer field and buy uniforms. Nyaka was already becoming known for its academic achievements. If this team also became the talk of the district, it would be one more blow against the stigma surrounding AIDS orphans.

Afterward, most of the boys headed home, but Bruno, a thirteen-year-old in primary three, lingered near the field. Bruno's father had been a relatively wealthy farmer, owning a banana plantation, land supporting several crops, many cattle and goats, and a sturdy house. But his father's wealth could not protect him from AIDS; he died when Bruno was eight, and Bruno's mother died two years later. One tragedy followed another. Bruno and his two older brothers then lost their only guardians, a grandfather and aunt, and Bruno's brothers had to leave home to work.

Now Bruno lived alone.

"I could use some additional exercise," I said. "Do you mind if I walk home with you?"

Bruno's eyes brightened. "It is a long way, Director."

"I like walking," I said, rubbing my sore hip.

Bruno's house was nearly seven miles away over rough, undulating terrain. The sun was setting by the time we reached it. Bruno did not say much, but I could tell he liked having some companionship. His brothers lived close enough to visit regularly, but he was alone most of the time as master of the house. It was not surprising that he lingered at school as long as possible. The students were his new siblings and the teachers his new parents during the day.

Of the four buildings on Bruno's compound, three were in disrepair. The banana plantation required maintenance and the garden, although tended, needed additional work. Inside the house, a film of dirt covered everything. The lanterns were empty of paraffin, and the only food in the kitchen was some bananas and a few mangoes.

Bruno opened up a little once we were inside. He told me nights were hardest for him. He would often wake with bad dreams in the pitch blackness. I asked if he lay awake a long time.

"When I can't sleep, I recite homework in my head," he assured me. "That forces the fear from my mind." He said this as if it were a typical topic of conversation.

My heart cried out. At twelve, I had constructed my own house, thinking myself a man, but I had had family and friends close by, and was far from able to care for myself. At thirteen, manhood was expected of Bruno; he was responsible for a house, property, and animals. I thanked God that Nyaka School was there for him during the day. He deserved whatever opportunities we could provide.

During the walk back, darkness wrapped the trail and stars winked into view. I thanked God that He had created stars to cast light into the darkest night.

CHAPTER 14

IT IS NOT ENOUGH TO BE SORRY

The next morning, my daily run took me past Zorooma Primary School. It was typical of many of the schools in the district, composed of brick buildings with plaster finish and corrugated iron roofs. Zorooma was also typical in that there had been little upkeep of the infrastructure. Part of one building had been demolished, leaving a blackboard exposed on the outer wall. Shutters were missing from one window and a hole in the wall functioned as a doorway. Some of the students arriving for class wore blue uniforms, but at least half were dressed in tattered, unwashed clothing.

The headmistress, standing near the hole-in-the-wall doorway, waved.

"*Agandi,*" she said.

"*Nigye.*" I jogged over to shake her hand.

"Are you not the director of Nyaka Orphans School?" Children gathered around us, curious.

"Yes," I said. "Twesigye Jackson."

"Hush," she told the children. "Go to your classrooms." The mob dissipated at once.

"I am curious about how you get money from America," she said. "This school has four times the number of children it can handle. The Universal Primary Education plan did not provide us additional teachers, buildings, or even supplies, only more children to educate."

I nodded. In 1997, the Museveni government had decided to make primary education available to everyone without tuition.

Unfortunately there was very little money available to make this plan a reality. Enrollment increased rapidly, leading to pupil-to-teacher ratios exceeding 100:1 in many places, but funding for teacher training, school supplies, and infrastructure was lacking. American politicians would have derided the plan as an unfunded mandate if it had been instituted in the United States, because no mechanism existed to provide additional funding to implement the program. In Uganda we called it politics as usual.

"It is not easy to raise money," I said. "Even in America."

She frowned. "I am desperate. Many have to stand because we lack desks and benches."

"I understand." It would be difficult to explain the problems of fund-raising. Even with Nyaka up and running, it was hard to persuade people to donate.

"Can you help us?" she asked.

"I will see what I can do." I doubted I could find aid for government schools, but did not want her to lose hope. Hope was all many in the village had to keep them going.

Leaving the school grounds, I continued my jog along a narrow path. I soon encountered a woman balancing a yellow jerry can atop her head. When she spied me, she smiled, forcing the deep wrinkles in her face into a new pattern. I noticed a baby bundled in the flowered material wrapped across her back.

"*Agandi,*" she said.

"*Nigye,*" I said, stopping. "A new little one?"

"Yes. I am on my way to get water to bathe him."

"He is looking forward to it," I said, smiling down at the wriggling baby.

The woman laughed. "Heavy is what he is. I am not as young as I used to be. Carrying a baby and water is almost too much for me. At least there is clean water at the Nyaka School. Did you know that?"

"Yes," I said with a grin. "I have heard good things about that school."

"I used to have to walk to the spring."

A *mukaaka* in a tattered gray dress limped toward us. In one hand she grasped a walking stick, in the other a smaller jerry can.

"You are Kaguri's son, are you not?"

"Yes," I said. The first woman looked more closely at my face.

"I hear you are building us a water system," the *mukaaka* said.

"There are plans," I said. "But we are not—"

"Even with the tank at the school, I walk two hours for clean water. Two hours with little ones alone at home. Two hours! And God help me if I arrive home late."

"I—"

She thumped the can down, cutting me off. "My husband is a jealous man. If I walk farther because the tank is dry or have to wait in line for water, my husband will be waiting for me. He will accuse me of being with another man. He will beat me with his hands until my face is bruised."

I gaped, not knowing what to say. We had all heard stories of girls being raped and women beaten on their way to obtain water, but it was rare for someone to be so open.

"I am sorry, *Mukaaka,*" I finally managed. I touched her shoulder.

"It is not enough to be sorry," she said, pulling away. She lifted the jerry can and continued on her way.

The first woman stared after her, shaking her head. "That woman is craz—"

"Right," I said firmly. "That woman is right. It is *not* enough to be sorry." I had been paying so much attention to Nyaka School that I had neglected the larger community.

CHAPTER 15

TWO GIRLS

After a busy day meeting with board members and townspeople, I looked forward to a quiet evening. But as is usual when I visit the village, my time with family was interrupted. Shortly after dinner, Maama came into the backyard to inform me that "one of my girls" was in the sitting room.

"Thank you, Maama." In the crush of events I had forgotten that I had arranged for two girls to stop by for interviews today.

I peeked inside. Eva sat quietly on the flowered sofa in the sitting room, hands clasped in her lap, eyes gazing absently at the floor. Her three little brothers had tagged along and now sat at the table across the room, peering around the backs of the chairs. Since Nyaka School was not able to take older orphans, Beronda and I had decided to pay school expenses for several girls who would otherwise have dropped out.

"Welcome," I said in English when I entered the room. "How are you?"

The boys giggled.

"I am fine," Eva said, glancing up. Now twelve years old, she had matured since I last saw her. Her face was thinner and her legs longer.

I sat beside her.

"Are you working hard in school?" Eva would graduate from primary seven the following December and would need additional support to go on to secondary school.

Eva shrugged. Like most girls her age, she was shy.

"How have you done on your placement exams?"

"Seventeen," she said softly.

"Only seventeenth out of thirty-five?" I knew she could do better. Her father had been a classmate of mine and one of the brightest in school. Unfortunately, he had chosen to drop out, marry early, and take a fishing job near Lake Albert, forty miles from the village. Had he continued his education, I have no doubt he would have gone on to Makerere University. As it was, he took a second wife, adopting the polygamous tradition so common in Uganda before Christianity changed many people's lives. His second wife had contracted HIV/AIDS from her first husband, who had died from the disease. HIV spread from the second wife to Eva's father and from Eva's father to her mother. Before long, both of Eva's parents were gone, dying one month apart. An uncle adopted her and her three brothers, but he also supported a wife and two children of his own.

"Is the material too difficult for you?" I asked. "Is there a problem at home?"

"Home," she barely whispered.

This was not a surprise. In a subsistence culture without electricity, running water, ovens, microwaves, dishwashers, clothes washers, or vacuum cleaners, everything must be done by hand. Everyone must do their share of the work, including children. Boys tend animals, fetch water, and do other light chores. As long as the cows are in good pasture, a boy can sit in the shade and even nap; he has plenty of time to read and study. Girls, however, are responsible for gathering and transporting wood, starting and keeping the cooking fires burning, cleaning and preparing food for cooking, boiling water and milk, serving meals, washing dishes, sweeping floors, making beds, fetching water, and washing clothes. They rise with the sun and often there is no stopping until they drop onto their mat at the end of the day.

"Not enough time to study?" I asked.

Eva nodded.

"What do you do when you arrive home from school?"

"I have to cook supper."

"And after that? Can you study then?"

"Sometimes there is not enough paraffin for the lamp."

"And in the morning before school?"

"I must fetch water."

Her eyes filled with tears. Her brothers slid from their perches and joined her, one climbing onto her lap. She probably thought I was going to end my support because of her poor test scores. Many girls are pulled out of school when they become young teens. Others drop out when they start menstruating because of lack of sanitary supplies and embarrassment. Many families will pool resources to educate boys because they know a boy will stay with the family. But girls get married and support the husband's family, so educating them is considered a waste of resources.

Eva had already lost her parents; I was here to make sure she did not lose her education.

"I had a similar problem with study time," I said.

She wiped her eyes.

"It is true," I said. "My *taata* did not think I needed to study. When I was home he kept me busy with chores."

"He did?"

"The solution is to bring your reading with you wherever you go. Take your book when you fetch water and read it there. Study whenever you can. A minute here. A minute there. Soon enough you have created an hour."

Eva sighed and hugged her brother.

"I will tell you something," I said. "I am willing to send you to Ishaka Secondary School, but it is your responsibility to improve your standing."

Eva sat straight. "Yes, Director."

"You understand that your grades must improve?"

"Yes." I saw the hint of a smile.

"And you know that if your scores decline at secondary school, I will bring you back here?"

She nodded.

"What about boys? Are you fooling around with them?"

"No." She looked down, embarrassed.

"No letters saying 'I love you'?"

"No."

"I do not want you fooling around with them. They only start trouble. You understand?" I found myself sounding more and more like Taata, but sometimes I had to be authoritarian so that the children would understand the seriousness of the situation.

"I understand," she said.

Maama pushed through the back door curtain, holding a bunch of tiny sweet bananas we call *kabalagala*. The boys ran to her and she handed each a piece of fruit.

"Thank you, Director," Eva said, glancing at me before herding her brothers outside.

Fiona, another student we were supporting, peered through the doorway. "I am here, Director."

"Come in."

She strode inside, proudly displaying the new pink dress and matching secondhand shoes I had given her. She knelt before me and took my hand.

"I want to thank you and the Nyaka donors for everything you have given me," she said.

"Please, do not kneel," I said, directing her to the sofa. Kneeling is a traditional sign of respect, but it made me uncomfortable.

"Thank you, Director," she said. As soon as she sat, she began fidgeting, hands twisting, feet tapping. Her gaze flitted from place to place too. She reminded me a bit of myself as a child, impatient, eager to experience whatever the world could offer.

"How is your *mukaaka*?" I asked, sitting beside her.

"She is well."

Fiona lived with her brother, Hillary, one of our Nyaka students, and their *mukaaka* not far from the school. Her grandmother had lost all five of her children and their spouses to AIDS. "How are you doing in school?"

"Fine," she answered.

When Nyaka opened, Fiona was already in primary five, but she had been so excited to attend the school she begged to start over in primary one. When pressed, she confided to me that she was desperate for a clean uniform and books to read. She lived with her *mukaaka*, who had sold most of her land to pay for medical care. Now they owned only the land under a small shack, one *embuzi*, and a few chickens. They had no choice but to graze their animals and pour their waste water on another person's property.

Fiona was too old for Nyaka, but I promised we would help support her while she attended another school.

When Hillary was accepted as a Nyaka student, her *mukaaka* cornered me and handed me a folded paper. Inside, a few lines of scribbled words read:

When the Lord takes me, I will die a happy woman knowing that my grandchildren will be taken care of by Nyaka School. Please make sure this small house and the one embuzi *and three chickens are not taken away from my kids. It is all they have and I want them to keep it.*

The note was signed with a thumbprint.

Tears welled in my eyes. "This is not necessary," I said, taking her hand.

"Yes, it is," she said, squeezing. "I entrust what I have left to the school to make sure my grandchildren receive what little I have. Death has taken too much already."

"Your grandchildren are part of the Nyaka family now," I assured her. "We will watch over them." Even if the school ran short on funding, I would personally make sure her children were cared for.

Fiona's eyes sparkled.

"Some of the girls tease me because I like books," she said.

"They are just jealous. What do you do when they tease you?"

"I ignore them," she said.

"Good."

Her fingers curled and uncurled. She seemed to be trying to find something to say to keep our conversation from ending. But it was already getting dark outside and I wanted to make sure she would get home safely.

"I have news for you," I said.

She looked up, her expression tense.

"I have decided to send you to Ishaka School in Bushenyi District."

Her eyes widened slightly, but she said nothing.

"You will live in a dormitory with other girls," I said. "There will be three meals a day and in the evening you will study instead of doing chores. You will even be able to read books at night."

Her worry dissolved. "You mean there is *electricity* at the school?"

"Yes," I said.

"Will I have a bed and a good roof?"

"Of course." Her grandmother's shack was prone to leaks. They had no bedding, and when the rain came they would all stand in a corner until it stopped.

"Oh, Director," she practically shouted. "It is a miracle from God!" She slid from the sofa onto her knees, and then bounced to her feet, an apology flashing in her eyes.

"You will need high test scores at the end of this term," I said. But I knew she would accomplish that.

"I will!" she said. "Oh, Director! Thank you, Director." Her whole body seemed to tremble. I stood, ready to catch her if her legs gave out. Instead, she grasped my hand and pressed it to her cheek.

"You will not regret this," she said.

"I know," I said, gently pulling my hand away. I nodded toward the door.

Before I could bid her good night, the door curtain pulled back and Olivia, a local woman, looked in.

"Good evening, Twesigye," she said. "Do you have a few moments?"

"Of course," I said. I had hoped to spend the rest of the evening listening to the radio and relaxing with the family, but I always made time for Olivia. Many in the village thought she was deranged, but Olivia represented a new direction for women in Uganda. With two children at home, at the age of thirty-two she had gone back to school.

"Come in." I sat on the sofa and indicated that Fiona should sit beside me.

Olivia entered the room, eyes shifting from the lantern to Fiona. Olivia had always been a thin woman, but she looked as if she had lost weight. Her prominent cheekbones stood out more than I remembered. I assumed it was simply malnutrition and not AIDS, because she was married to a good man.

"I do not want to interrupt," she said.

"Please join us," I said, gesturing toward a chair beside the sofa. "Fiona and I were discussing her education."

Olivia sat.

"Olivia is in high school," I said to Fiona.

"High school?" Fiona's eyes widened.

"She knows how important an education is," I said.

"I will finish my studies soon," Olivia said.

"I am going to Ishaka School next year," Fiona said proudly, and suddenly they were conversing so intently I felt like a forgotten man. There is nothing quite like witnessing a shared passion between two people. Watching sparks spew from a bonfire on a chilly night is the closest I can come.

I could not help but smile. Olivia gave me hope that any girl we lost because of family commitments, early marriage, or even prostitution was not lost for good. There was always the possibility that as they matured they would see the value of education. Starting a school is like planting seeds. A green shoot sprouts here, another there. Soon enough you have a garden.

CHAPTER 16

THERE ARE NO STREETLIGHTS

On November 10, 2004, David Bremer, Otto Ray, and Allen Pease sponsored the first Nyaka benefit at Chapman's Restaurant in Bloomington, Indiana. The event attracted about twenty people and raised more than two thousand dollars through contributions and sales from a silent auction of African crafts. I planned to use this money to increase teacher salaries to a competitive rate, about eighty-five dollars per month. I was also invited to give a talk at Faith Missionary Church in Martinsville, north of Bloomington, which resulted in several additional contributions.

Shortly after that we received word that a one-year grant from the Stephen Lewis Foundation to support teachers and purchase supplies had come through. The Rockefeller Foundation also approved a one-time $3,000 matching grant. Then, in February 2005, two professors visited Nyaka School with Dr. Deborah Delmer of the Rockefeller Foundation and took an interest in Dennis's gravity-fed water system. When they returned home, they raised enough money to put his plans into action.

It was the beginning of a very busy period, which required me to put my personal job hunt on pause. More money was coming in for the school, but our personal finances suffered. We were managing on our low income, but only barely.

In the next couple of months, I gave a talk at the East Lansing Rotary, traveled to Davis, California, for the Global Philanthropy Forum and Global Giving Marketplace, talked at churches in Fremont, Michigan, gave another talk at the Bloomington Rotary, led a church service at Beronda's parents' church in Little Rock, Arkansas, and made formal presentations in Texarkana and Nashville, Arkansas.

Over the summer I spoke at more churches. Contributions grew, and some people were inspired to visit Nyaka School that year. My parents took in visitors from America, Canada, Japan, and Namibia. It seemed we had turned an important corner in the school's development.

And then I returned to Nyaka.

As the plane's seat-belt sign blinked on and the attendant told us to take our seats, my old worries returned. I had believed that once funds started coming in, things would get easier, but as the building progressed, so did my responsibility. Yes, we had raised enough money to get us through 2005 without major problems, but 2006 was quickly approaching. Soon there would be 120 students to educate and feed, four teachers to pay, another room to finish, and more school supplies to buy. There was a good chance the Stephen Lewis grant would be renewed, but it was far from certain.

I thought of all the places I had visited and spoken at to raise the money for this year. How could I possibly increase the number of talks in 2006 *and* hold a full-time job? It seemed an impossible dilemma.

The plane landed with a thump and decelerated. I relaxed my grip on the armrests.

Almost home, I thought, forcing my worries into the background. Soon I would enjoy late-night chats with my family under the stars and kick back to have a local brew with some of my friends in the city. And the food! I had been craving fresh Nile perch for months.

We deplaned onto a poorly lit tarmac, and I headed for the terminal beneath a sky brimming with stars. In the east, Venus glowed like a beacon. I breathed the warm night air, ripe with moist sweetness from Lake Victoria, a blue jewel set in the green landscape of East Africa. After experiencing Michigan's cool autumn and its inevitable march to a cold, dead winter, the heat was welcome. No matter what problems I and my home country faced, Uganda would always be warm, always bright, and always green with life, the *Pearl of Africa,* as British colonizers had so aptly nicknamed it.

Even so, a pang of homesickness hit me. I slid my cell phone from the pocket on the side of my pants leg and flipped it open. Nicolas's wide-eyed face smiled back.

"Where are you going?" Nicolas asked from his car seat while I unloaded suitcases from the back of our Rover. He and I had spent an entertaining half hour weighing and repacking them several times to make sure they were within the airline's weight restrictions. Only now that we had arrived at the airport had it dawned on him that I was traveling somewhere far away.

"I am going to see Mukaaka and Shwenkuru," I said. Nicolas had visited his grandparents two years before, but he was only eighteen months old at the time. I did not know how much he remembered of the village, but he had photos to remind him. "You must be the man of the house and take care of your mother while I am gone."

"Okay," Nicolas agreed.

But when I closed the rear hatch, his bravery subsided and he began to sob.

"I will be back soon," I said through the driver's side window.

"Don't go!" Nicolas cried.

"How are you going to take care of Mommy if you are crying?"
I reminded him. That settled the tears temporarily, and I turned to
Beronda.

"I will phone you when I arrive in Kampala," I said.

"God will keep you safe," she said.

"Take me!" Nicolas demanded, jaw set with determination.

"I do not have a ticket for you."

"I fit inside a bag."

"I am sure you do," I said, recalling the adventures of my own
stubborn childhood. "But how would you breathe?"

"I will hold my breath."

"Keep a close eye on him," I told Beronda, only half-joking. "He
will have a plan."

"Oh, I cannot watch over him," Beronda said. She reached over
the seat to rub his head. "He is supposed to watch over me."

"That's right, Daddy. Did you forget?"

Waiting in the customs line, I wished I had brought Nicolas, but
there was much work to be done, and our finances were not strong
enough to afford extra tickets this time.

At the baggage carousel I found one suitcase, but the other was
not there. For a split second, I envisioned the baggage handlers dis-
covering Nicolas inside and trying to figure out what to do with this
little boy from the cargo hold. That brought a smile to my tired face.
More realistically, I hoped the old bag had survived the trip. For even
with tape and extra care, several trips to Uganda with loads of gifts
had not been kind to it. The zipper was coming apart at one corner
and the seam was starting to break.

That bag contained the school's annual allocation of seed from
Seed and Light International, an organization in Albuquerque that
included us among the many groups it supports around the globe.

Some of the seed was to be planted at the school for food to use in lunches and to provide the children food to take home. Other seed would be given to sponsoring families, grandmothers, and other relatives or even unrelated families in the village who volunteered a home for our students. It was a small thank-you for those willing to take in orphaned children. An unusual plant, like yellow tomatoes, helped them make ends meet and signaled our appreciation.

The bag finally arrived, still in one piece. I hoisted it onto a cart and rolled it out of the baggage area. Around the corner, a crowd of people waited in the passenger area.

Before I knew what was happening, I was shaking hands with my old friend Sempa Baker.

"*Webale kwiija!*" he said, welcoming me home.

"Sempa," I said. "It is good to see you." A shy, soft-spoken man, Sempa possessed a heart of compassion and a head for numbers. He had been keeping Nyaka's books for free since the school's inception. It had been important, especially in the beginning, to make certain that all donor money went to the school, and Sempa was someone I could trust completely; he would not skim money from our accounts or use it for personal gain.

"It has been too long." Sempa's round face contained a huge smile.

"How are you, my friend?"

"I am fine," he said.

I tried to read his tone. Though Sempa had come from a polygamous family and had a chaotic childhood, changing households and religions, he had settled down in a monogamous relationship with Marjorie, the kind, loving woman he had met at work. They now had three beautiful little girls.

But Sempa was not fine. Even though he had been too shy to approach girls during his teen years, and his wife was the only woman he had dated, Sempa had tested positive for the HIV virus. I had known this for a few years and knew he preferred not to dwell on it. He was an optimistic man who tried to make the best of everything.

"How are Beronda and Nicolas?" he asked.

"Well."

"I am parked nearby." Sempa pointed across the poorly lit parking lot. He took the cart in hand and pushed.

I followed, feeling a nagging sadness. Sempa was not the only one infected; his wife and two of his girls were also HIV positive. Because their firstborn remained free of the virus, they believed the family had become infected through unsafe medical procedures. In order to make more money per delivery and save time, doctors in Kampala gave Cesarean sections to most women during childbirth. Equipment sterilization was not always adequate, and the HIV virus was sometimes spread from one woman to another at the hospitals.

In Kampala, access to anti-AIDS drugs was possible, and so far Sempa's family showed no signs of *slim*. For his part, Sempa had taken the news of the disease in stride. "No wonder God has impressed me with a heart for helping AIDS victims," he told me after he discovered he had the disease. "God knew mine would soon enough be among the numbers counted in Uganda. For this, I will continue to serve forever."

We stopped at the rear of Sempa's old white Land Cruiser. He unlocked the back door and pulled hard to open it. Buying a vehicle, even a used one, was prohibitively expensive for most people in Uganda, where the average income was about two dollars per day. I remembered growing up not even knowing what a car was. We saw Toyota pickup trucks carrying people and coffee once in a while, but I never even dreamed of one day owning one. Even today, in Nyakagyezi there is no public transport and hardly anyone owns a car.

"These are gifts for the school?" Sempa asked as he helped me hoist the heavy bags into the back.

"Yes," I said. "Seeds and shoes." We already had uniforms for the students, but most needed shoes. This year was the forty-second anniversary of Uganda's independence, and the school would take part in the celebration. The students would be thrilled to have matching white socks and black shoes.

"And I have other good news," I said after Sempa slammed the back door. "We have received two more grants for the school." I opened the passenger door and slid onto the seat.

"That *is* good news," Sempa said. The vehicle started with a rumble, and he backed out of the parking space. "The grants make such a difference in our ability to grow." Our first Stephen Lewis Foundation grant had not been large by American standards but had been a godsend for the school.

"The new funds come from Marcy Corps and the Global Fund for Children, a U.S.-based funder," I said. I had been very pleased to be pursued by this funder, which invests in innovative, community-based organizations supporting vulnerable children and youth throughout the world.

"Well, I hope the grants will be enough to build a health center," Sempa said.

"A health center?" I was shocked at the suggestion. Sempa was the most frugal man I knew. I swear he squeezed coins from paper bills to make change for his coffee.

"We are building a school, not a hospital," I said. We had hired a nurse earlier that year to come to the school twice a week and monitor the children's health. Malaria remained a problem in the village and students became infected despite the mosquito nets we had provided. Many host parents, unable to afford nets, had used the gifts for themselves. With our new funding we might afford the nurse full-time to make home visits and educate families in disease prevention, but we certainly could not build a health center.

Sempa turned onto Entebbe Road, the main highway to Kampala. "Then we must decide what we are going to do about the babies." He glanced sideways at me.

"What are you talking about?"

The Cruiser sped along the dark highway, passing dangerously close to people making their way by motorbike and on foot. Entebbe was a small resort town on the shores of Lake Victoria that formerly housed state administration buildings, and the Ministry of Health building was still located there. Even though the town had electricity, it lacked streetlights.

Sempa tapped the brakes. "In July, while Gloria was working at the school, a new mother arrived looking for help. It seems she had given birth, but the placenta had not come out for two days. After six hours, Gloria managed to deliver it."

Lord help us, I thought. Gloria Mutesi was trained as a nurse, not a midwife. But in an area where there is no midwife available one must make do.

"I suppose we cannot turn away emergencies," I said.

We sped past a beachfront restaurant, windows lit with dim yellow light, then the empty market and nearly deserted bus station.

Sempa tapped the horn and the vehicle veered left. "While Gloria tends to the children," he said without blinking an eye, "pregnant women wait outside to see her. The baby she delivered last month was named Bethel after that classroom's name painted on the wall."

"We do not have facilities to birth babies or run a clinic," I muttered.

"Precisely," he said. "Which is why I brought the matter up." He flashed his smile. "We had better think of some way to solve the problem." He swerved to miss a man on a bicycle. "And speaking of emergencies, there is another problem."

"What is that?"

"We have had no luck dealing with the Kambuga police. The men who hurt Milton have not been punished."

I took a deep breath. Milton was a college student attending Makerere University who volunteered at Nyaka School. He was mistakenly accused of theft by a bus driver, which led to his arrest and beating.

"I will see if I can get an appointment with Professor Mondo," I said. "Maybe he will have some sway with them." My bright day was quickly turning dark. *There are no streetlights on this path I have chosen,* I thought, letting my heavy eyelids close.

CHAPTER 17

MY MEETING WITH MONDO

Every time I visit Uganda, I must force a year's worth of activities into two weeks. This time was no different. Before going to bed, I managed to schedule a short appointment with Professor Mondo at nine in the morning. He could not meet later because of a cabinet assembly he had to attend.

After visiting with Sempa until the wee hours of the night, it was hard to pull myself out of bed. Jet lag or no, I had best get used to a busy schedule.

Sempa's wife had prepared a breakfast of steamed *matooke,* cassava, and fresh fruit.

"Good morning," she greeted me. "Would you like coffee?"

"No, thank you," I said. I had been living in America for a long time, but had no interest in coffee.

The morning's radio news covered local and world events, but the biggest story was about the recently deceased former president Milton Obote. Obote, a dictator who controlled the country before and after the more infamous Idi Amin, was forced from power by a military coup in 1985. He escaped to political asylum in Zambia.

Now his family wanted to bring his body back to Uganda for burial. The country was divided over the prospect, some wanting his body returned, others wanting him exiled forever.

Sempa entered the room wearing a suit and tie.

"You are up early," he said. "Going to the forex bureau?"

"Yes." I could have had the school's money transferred via Western Union, but exchange rates were much better at foreign exchange bureaus on the streets. Corporations could afford the difference in exchange rates, but I wanted to make the most of our money. When forty-five dollars paid for a student's books for an entire year, saving a few dollars was worth the extra effort.

"I will also meet with Professor Mondo this morning."

He nodded. "I hope he can help. This incident is a bad mark on our reputation."

After breakfast, I caught a taxi, a fifteen-passenger minivan, to Kampala Road and walked from there. Engines rumbled and horns blared. I kept my hand on my backpack. This area of Kampala was not dangerous, and I was not at risk of having my bag stolen, but I knew how much cash I had and was uncomfortable carrying it around.

At the main intersection to Kampala Road I crossed the churning river of pedestrians, cars, taxis, and *boda bodas,* recalling the first time I visited Kampala with my high school class. Riding on the back of the truck through the city, I had been amazed at the numbers of people. Back in the village, we rarely saw crowds. One of my friends remarked, "I am glad we arrived on market day." Little did we know that every day in Kampala was market day!

The best rate I found at the forex bureau was 1,850 shillings for a dollar. It was not as good a rate as I would have liked, but I would have to accept it. I told myself it was at least better than I would get at the bank. I glanced at my watch as I hurried to my meeting.

Professor Mondo's office was in the NRM Secretariat building, an old high-rise probably built during the Amin regime. Amin might have been a brutal dictator, but he had done one good thing for the country in leaving behind many sturdy buildings.

A ten-foot-high cement wall surrounded the Secretariat building. I crossed the street and approached an iron gate opening onto a parking area crowded with expensive government cars and SUVs. To the gate's left stood a kiosk with two guards inside. One carried a rifle, the other sat behind a counter looking official.

The one with the gun asked for my identification. I handed him my Ugandan passport and he examined it closely, looking up repeatedly to verify that my face matched the picture. After some time, he handed the passport to the second man, who looked it over as well.

"We will return this to you on your way out," he said.

I thanked them and walked a short distance across the parking area. Glass doors led into a small lobby. From there it was a short ride to the sixth floor on an elevator that creaked and groaned. I stepped out and nearly bumped into another guard with a rifle.

I expected to be questioned, but he only nodded for me to pass and I gladly complied. The hall was plain, with none of the paintings or green plants that usually adorn American buildings. Professor Mondo's office was two doors down on the left. A sign on the door read MINISTER OF GENERAL DUTIES.

Inside, a male secretary greeted me warmly while another man in a business suit waited in a chair looking annoyed.

What neither the secretary nor the man knew was that I had a blood advantage. Professor Mondo was related to me on my mother's side and was a member of Parliament for Rubabo, not far from the school. I did not like the whole process of bribes and favors that went on in our government. I refused to pay officials for aiding Nyaka School, but did not have anyone else to turn to about the police incident and did not have time to go through regular channels.

Professor Mondo's office provided a welcome contrast to the sterile outer office. Velvet-upholstered mahogany chairs that matched the lush burgundy carpet surrounded a glass-topped coffee table. A Uganda map covered one wall above a long couch. An oversize desk bearing stacks of folders and overflowing inboxes took up another. A miniature Ugandan flag rose from the midst of the clutter.

From behind the desk Professor Mondo stood. He was sharply dressed in a gray suit with a burgundy tie that matched the décor.

"*Webale kwijja!*" he said, shaking my hand and smiling.

The man seemed ageless, with only a few fine lines to testify to his many years on this earth. With his head shaved close, his receding, graying hairline was barely apparent. He motioned for me to sit on the couch and asked about my family.

As I signed the register, I remembered I had a gift for him. I slid a calendar that featured photos of Nyaka School from my backpack.

"This is to thank you for your support," I said.

"It is I who should be thanking you," he said, flipping through the calendar. "It amazes me what can be done with a little effort." He set the calendar on the coffee table and looked up. "The building will be finished this year?"

"Yes," I said. "We have only to cement some of the floors and add finishing touches. Doors, window shutters, awnings, and plaster."

Mondo nodded. "If our government was not so focused on bribes and favors, just think what we might accomplish in education."

"It seems all governments breed corruption," I said. "I think the best one can do is to keep it under control."

Mondo nodded heartily. "And to weed out corruption, one requires an educated population."

It seemed a vicious circle. Poor, uneducated masses voted for unscrupulous politicians willing to pay for votes. They, in turn, fostered their own interests over those of the people. Still, it seemed Museveni was trying to break the cycle. The Ugandan government had recently launched a major initiative to improve education across the country.

"We are doing our best," I said. "We now have 118 students in primary grades one through four. In January 2006, we will open our primary-five classroom and welcome thirty more students."

The Ugandan educational system includes seven years of primary, four years of secondary, and two years of high school. That is followed by two to five years of higher education in technical institutes, teacher-training institutions, colleges of commerce, or university education. In the past, university education was free. However, government funding had now been diverted to fully support primary education under the Universal Primary Education Program, with the worthy goal of ensuring minimum literacy skills for the entire population. Despite this, literacy remained at a mere 42 percent.

"Our kids are doing so well in their proficiency tests," I said, "that Nyaka is becoming known as one of the best schools in the district."

"As I expected," Mondo said.

"Our first class will graduate in December 2008," I reminded him. "We will invite you to the ceremony."

"And I will certainly be there."

"Thank you." *If we can keep the school running,* the back of my mind reminded the rest of me.

Mondo glanced at his watch.

"I have one other thing I would like to tell you," I said. "We have had some trouble with the local police in Kanungu District."

"The police?"

"Rwaboona Milton, one of our volunteers and a Makerere student, was beaten by police when he traveled out to the school a few months ago."

Mondo hung his head. Undoubtedly, over the years he had had firsthand knowledge of more beatings and killings than I could imagine. Even to this day, there were the rebels to the north, the

Lord's Resistance Army, coming across the Sudanese border, robbing and killing and raping and kidnapping, but in southern Uganda life was supposed to be more stable. Police beatings were supposed to be events of the past.

"Milton was taking twelve boxes of shoes from Kampala to Nyaka," I explained. "The bus people loaded them in Kampala, then unloaded and counted them in Kambuga. Milton hired a car to take the boxes to Nyaka. Sometime after he reached Nyaka, the bus people showed up. They claimed there was a box of phone calling cards worth six million shillings missing from the bus and accused him of taking it. They spoke with the driver and inspected each box Milton had, but did not find the phone cards.

"Milton thought the problem was over until he returned to Kambuga on a *boda boda* and was confronted by the bus people and a local police officer. They started beating him and insisted he knew where the box was. Of course, he had no idea. So the beating continued until his head was bleeding and his eye swollen shut."

"This is not acceptable," Mondo muttered.

"They were right in front of the hospital. But instead of taking him there, they put him in a cell and held him overnight. Not until the next morning was he able to contact my sister. She spoke with another local council official who got him out on bond."

Mondo frowned. "What is happening now?"

"Other authorities were told and the police dropped the case, but Milton is blind in the one eye. We were told the culprits escaped. There has been no justice."

"Misunderstandings happen sometimes," Mondo said levelly, "but there is no excuse for this treatment. Rest assured I will see what I can do, but I cannot guarantee anything. It is not always easy being a politician."

He did not have to say more. I did not know how Mondo tolerated the day-to-day drudgery of lawmakers. Everyone seemed to want something for themselves, but was unwilling to give. Professor Mondo did not belong with that crowd and yet he had outlasted all but a very few.

Mondo stood. "I wish we had more time," he said. "But someone has to run the country."

"I appreciate any time you can give me," I said, shaking his hand.

I grabbed my bags and left the office, nodding to the poor soul who must now wait longer since Mondo was due at his cabinet meeting shortly. *We all have our frustrations,* I thought, taking no comfort from it. But then I remembered that frustration can be a motivator for inaction or action, a great despairer or a great inspirer. It is how we choose to react that is important.

By the time I reached the elevator the bags in my hands felt lighter and my quick smile to the guard was genuine.

CHAPTER 18

A SONG OF HOPE AND DESPAIR

Three days after my visit with Professor Mondo, I rented a Land Cruiser and made the grueling drive to Nyakagyezi with Samuel Mugisha and Frank's son, my nephew Stephen. Sam was one of the orphaned boys Frank and I had helped in the village. He now lived in Kampala, where he and his wife owned and operated a travel company catering to international tourists. He remained an avid supporter of the school. Stephen had graduated from high school. Along with his interests in computers and technology, he was our school photographer. Whenever he visited Nyaka, I could rest assured that everything would be recorded on film.

When we arrived in the village that night, Faida greeted us at the front door.

"Where is Maama?" I asked.

"She is resting," Faida said. "The pain in her back has been bad today."

Since Faida had divorced, she was spending more time at my parents' home helping Maama.

"I am glad you are here to take care of her, sister."

Before I slept that night I prayed for Maama. She had suffered enough in her life. I wished I could remove her pain, but that was her burden.

The next morning, I rose early to inspect the work that had been accomplished in my absence.

The new gravity-fed water system had been installed. One of only ten taps in the village, a square cement basin supporting it and a drainage sluice, was located in my parents' backyard. Instead of water carted from distant streams, people had convenient water stations and relatively clean water.

Now that the main school building had been erected, the foundation was being dug for a guesthouse. The school's board of directors had recommended we build a guesthouse to make living at the school more comfortable for visitors and as a potential source of income. Many guests had lived at my parents' home, but housing our interns, who stayed for months at a time, was becoming disruptive.

When I arrived at the school that afternoon, the children were concluding their meal and washing dishes at the school's water tap. A welcoming celebration planned for that day was supposed to be a surprise. With students gathering at the school on a Saturday and the aroma of cooking goat meat wafting across the field, it was difficult to pretend I did not know. I would let the children think I was surprised. My happiness would not come from their gifts of food and song, but from seeing the joy in their eyes.

"Time to get ready," Lydia reminded the children.

They scattered quickly and she ushered us across the yard to one of the classrooms. Along the far wall, a table covered with a white cloth had been set with a banquet of traditional foods. The room soon filled with people, including teachers, supporters, and the school's management committee. Christine led the group in prayer and we lined up for the buffet.

I found myself behind Habib Museka, a thin, older man and an indispensable part of our leadership group. He had chaired the local management committee since Nyaka was founded.

Nyaka is unique in that it is an interdenominational school. The committee reflects that uniqueness with Mr. Habib Museka, a Muslim; Mrs. Leonarda Ndazororera, a Catholic; Headmistress Freda Byaburakidya, an Anglican; my sister Christine, a Seventh-day Adventist; and others from a variety of faiths. In an area where people segregate themselves along religious lines, I wanted Nyaka to be available to all members of the community, no matter their faith. Thus, Nyaka not only helped orphans but acted as a bridge and unifying force between community beliefs.

By the time we finished our meal, students had moved benches from classrooms to the shade under the largest tree in the school yard. Many were already seated and waiting. Guardians arrived in clumps, some sitting behind students, others on the grass or blankets. Maama and Faida set out a blanket at the edge of the group where Maama could recline. Taata sat on a bench with the children.

The festivities started with introductions. Freda introduced Christine as one of our school board members.

I was introduced next and kept my speech very short. Like everyone else, I was more eager to see the children perform than to hear me talk. I went back to my seat amid a polite round of applause.

Without further ado, the Anti-AIDS Choir marched from a classroom in traditional costumes. Irene, one of the brightest students, kept time with a drum while the others sang and walked in fluid strides. The girls wore brown skirts and red and brown striped shirts while the boys wore purple, pink, and blue striped shirts over their shorts.

As one of the shortest boys, Emmanuel stood out, especially with his flashing grin. He was a member of the primary-three class, but had a better command of English than many older students. After his parents died, his family had been unable to care for him and he was taken in by good friends of his uncle. As he often said, they treated him "very nice" and encouraged him to study. With such support and the love of his fellow students and teachers, it was no wonder he had scored over 90 percent on the government standardized tests.

"Where is Scovia?" I asked Freda, who had sat beside me on a bench. Scovia had been born with HIV, but without available testing no one knew. She had joined Nyaka as a frail nine-year-old girl, which is older than most HIV-positive children live to be. At first her health improved, thanks to the food, love, and care she received from the school, and she had even started to gain weight. It was not until recently, when she was overrun with infections and malaria, lost weight, and developed spots of Kaposi's sarcoma, that we knew she had HIV. With no antiretroviral medications available in Kanungu District, there was no treatment for her. Even so, she had attended school as often as possible and took great pleasure from participating in choir events.

Freda glanced away, then back. "We have been sending her food every day for weeks, but she is eating very little now."

Slim. My heart ached and I remembered Frank's bony hand in mine. Scovia had been so full of life the last time I saw her. I dared not imagine her appearance now.

God bless her, I thought. When her parents died of AIDS, Scovia and her brother had been taken in by a family with three children close to their ages, and they had quickly formed a close-knit family. Scovia's inevitable death would be a loss to everyone: her brother, her foster family, and the school.

"Maybe it is only malaria again," I said. It was obvious neither of us believed that. Freda was no stranger to the tragedy of HIV/AIDS, having lost children and a grandson to the disease. But such affirmations help us cope. I would visit Scovia as soon as my schedule permitted. With God's help, maybe she would rebound yet again.

Children's voices rang through the school yard, as clear and sweet as those of God's own angels. They sang the Nyaka School anthem, then a welcoming song and a Bible song about being resilient like Ruth in the Bible. Stephen skirted the crowd's edge, taking pictures with both still and video cameras. The audience listened raptly as the group began a series of short, traditional verses.

So many traditions. Some were good, such as the African proverb that says a child belongs to a community. Others were damaging, as in the tradition of ostracizing AIDS orphans, who were assumed to have the disease that killed their parents and therefore were not worth nurturing. Not every tradition is born of wisdom.

The first choir finished to a burst of applause, and the second choir took their place. Some of the girls tied scarves around their waists and eight dancers paired off in two squares of four, two girls and two boys. The boys jumped and stamped their feet; the girls undulated and swung arms high over their heads in a celebration of happiness and a good harvest. It was an appropriate dance, I thought, representing a harvest of good fortune from the poisoned soil of misfortune.

After this energetic dancing, the festivities became more serious. Students donned costumes and performed a play demonstrating the destructiveness of HIV/AIDS to families and communities. In a society where discussion of sexual behavior and its consequences is often taboo, this generation of children had to tackle the problem head-on. The only way to do that was with information and education. Even with education some students lost their way.

At age fourteen, Pleasant was lured to the nearby city of Rukungiri with rumors of employment.

"You will work in a canteen selling food and drinks," she had been told. It seemed an easy way to earn money to support her grandmother and brothers. When she arrived, an older woman fussed over her, having her hair styled and her nails painted. It was exciting to see the bustling city and be treated as someone special. She was happy.

Happiness was soon replaced by fear. Held in a house with other girls, she discovered they washed clothing during the day, but their real occupation took place at night. Her first evening there, the girls were transported to a small room in a motel where they met three men stinking of alcohol. When the men discovered Pleasant was new, they dragged her into the next room, plied her with gin, and raped her multiple times.

Pleasant threw herself into the older woman's arms, crying until she had shed every tear. "There, there," the woman said. "You will get used to it."

Pleasant continued to be prostituted. Her days were filled with washing clothing and her nights with satisfying drunken men. The girls worked together, ate together, and slept together, and although she was not strictly a prisoner, she was never alone. Escape seemed impossible.

It took the help of an undercover policeman to find Pleasant and bring her back to the village. Her grandmother fainted when she learned of Pleasant's ordeal. All along, she had believed Pleasant was working in a canteen, sending notes home saying: *Mukaaka, I am doing okay. Here is the money to help you out.* Pleasant was angry and embarrassed at first, but once she understood there were people who loved and supported her, and that she did not need to sacrifice herself for her family, she returned to school.

Thunder rumbled, drawing our eyes upward to the darkening sky. The students had not finished their play, but it appeared the weather would end these festivities early. Rain began to fall with a heavy patter and students rushed to get their props and the benches inside.

Even while the rain came down, children's voices filled the classroom with a song about the second coming of Jesus in Rukiga.

"Jesus has gone to prepare a place for us.

He promised he will come back and take us."

I thought again of Pleasant and Scovia. Yes, I fully believed Jesus would return to Uganda and everywhere else on this earth, but who would watch over and protect these orphans until then? Tears welled in my eyes. If I failed, if *we* failed, in this mission, it would be these children who suffered. I could not let that happen.

CHAPTER 19

ONE NEVER KNOWS

That evening I had interviews scheduled with two girls Beronda and I had been supporting in public school. Shortly after dinner, Maama escorted the first into the sitting room.

At fourteen, Brijati was a graceful young woman with bright, inquisitive eyes. She wore the light blue uniform of the government primary school but had no shoes. A twenty-pound jackfruit was cradled against her hip.

"I brought you one of the fruits from our garden," she said. The rough-surfaced, green fruit is solid inside except for hollows that contain seeds surrounded by a thick membrane as sweet as honey. Brijati's guardians were one of the first families to be assisted by the free-vegetable-and-fruit-seed program sponsored by Seed and Light International.

I welcomed her to sit on the sofa and joined her.

"How is school?" I asked.

"Good," she said, gazing at the floor.

"How did you do last term?"

"Tenth out of fifty-four. But that is good considering I have no textbooks."

"What about the textbooks I gave you last time I visited?"

"Our teacher borrowed and never returned them. I was the only one with a new version."

I should not have been surprised, but I was.

"I will be visiting the school later this week," I said. "I will ask the head teacher about your books. But I have other news for you."

Brijati glanced up, meeting my eyes for the first time.

"I plan to send you to Ishaka Secondary School next year. There will be no chores, so you will have time to read and study at night. There is even a small library at the school."

"Ishaka?" she repeated, as if lost in a dream.

"But you must raise your test scores or they will not admit you."

"I will work hard," she said. The smile that parted her full lips beamed joy. "I promise! My scores will be better."

I squeezed her shoulder and stood. Brijati was a bright girl and I knew she would go far with the right support.

"I expect to see higher scores on your December tests," I said.

"Yes, Director. You will." She curtsied and danced out of the room.

I snacked on a few tiny *kabalagala* bananas while I waited for Sharon to arrive. This would be my most difficult interview without a doubt. Sharon's father had been a polygamist who had died leaving so many children that her mother could not keep track of them all. Sharon had run away from school several times, and preferred boys to studying. Disaster loomed in her future, but I could only offer help, not force her to take it.

After a quiet knock, Sharon entered the room with arms crossed over her developing chest and an orange skirt hemmed too far above her knees. Her jaw was set with stubborn determination and her dark eyes focused on the wall.

"Welcome," I said.

My greeting was met with cold silence.

"Sit down," I said.

I sat beside her. "How is school?"

"I do not like it much," she said, crossing her legs and leaning away from me. "I am trying my best."

"Your sponsors wish to pay for you to go to boarding school," I informed her. She had made friends with one of the interns who had taught at Nyaka the previous year. The intern and her mother agreed to assist Sharon with her education, even at the university level.

"Are you interested?"

She shrugged. "Maybe."

"Maybe? They offer an education that most girls will never receive, and you say maybe?"

She looked away.

Enda ezaara mwiiru na muhima, I thought. A womb gives birth to different babies. Many girls would do anything for the opportunity to attend boarding school, and Sharon acted as if I had offered her a pair of worn-out shoes.

"Either you want to go or you do not."

"I do not," she said, looking bored.

My heart sank. Even with all the successes, there were bound to be failures.

"I cannot force you," I said, standing. "But I want you to think about this."

Sharon stood, smoothed her skirt, and strolled to the door. Without another word, she disappeared into the darkness.

I prayed for God to protect her and hoped things would turn out for the best. One never knows about these things. I had learned that lesson firsthand. It was 1982 and I was ten.

The rolling hills of eastern Kanungu District give birth to many springs and streams that flow into the Ekyambu. During the rainy seasons in March through May and October through December, the streams become brown with soil and overflow their banks, transforming the Ekyambu into a dangerous torrent prowling the *enengo,* waiting patiently for that one misstep or wrong turn that will allow it to claim a life.

Despite the danger, people must fetch cooking and drinking water. Cows must drink and children, with their reckless energy, must swim. Everyone takes chances with the water.

One sunny morning in March, four of us, Herbert, Stephen, Ben, and I, decided to sneak down to the river for a swim. It was Herbert's idea. With no permanent bridge at the time, his brothers made money by helping people cross the water, and Herbert spent a good deal of his time swimming.

"I know an island we can swim to," Herbert said as we left a banana plantation and slid down a muddy path toward the *enengo.*

"Where?" I had learned the river's shallow safe places and its deep and dangerous spots. I did not remember an island.

"You will see," he said.

"There is no island."

"There is too," he said.

"We should stay in the shallows," Ben said. Ben hunted on Sundays, our usual swimming day, but he was free to swim that morning.

"Why?" Herbert stopped and turned to face Ben. "Are you afraid?"

Ben put his hands on his hips and stared him in the eye. "I have crossed the river plenty of times."

"Then it is set," Herbert said. "We will swim to the island."

When we reached the muddy bank, the midday sun was hot. Herbert pointed out a narrow wedge of sand and grass in the river's center. It did not look like an island to me, but I was too interested in swimming to argue. We removed our shorts and shirts and hid them in a nearby hollow. That way our parents would never know we had been swimming. Tingling with the thrill of the forbidden, we splashed into a quiet section. A white crane was flushed from the opposite bank and coasted over Ben's head.

"This is too deep." Stephen frowned. The water was up to his armpits only a few feet from the bank.

I laughed. The river smelled sour and looked faster than usual between us and the island, but I remained confident I could swim the distance.

"Just follow me," Herbert said. "If you have difficulty, yell. I will come back and rescue you."

"Ha!" Ben shouted. "We will rescue *you*."

I laughed, but Stephen did not laugh with me. The frown did not leave his face as he grudgingly swam with the rest of us. Worried about Stephen, I focused on him while we crossed. The water grew steadily deeper until my feet could not touch bottom; the current pulled hard. I kicked with my legs and paddled with my arms to stay abreast of the island.

"Stay with us," I called to Stephen. "We will soon be out of the current."

Stephen struggled a bit, but kept his head above water and even managed a nervous smile.

"Almost there," Herbert yelled. Our goal was only a few yards away, but the water remained swift.

"This was a stupid idea," Stephen said, spitting water.

I kicked hard. "If Herbert can do it, so can we."

"Over here!" Herbert called, standing nearer the island in waist-deep water.

I stopped kicking and let my legs drop, but could not feel bottom.

"Come on," Herbert said.

I resumed swimming.

"We will never get there," Stephen said. The current pushed us past Herbert.

"Yes, we will." I made a final thrashing effort. Finally, my foot found mucky silt, and relief flooded me with warmth.

"We made it," Stephen said.

"Waaah!" Ben screamed behind us.

I turned and saw the top of his head slipping beneath the water. "Ben!"

Herbert splashed into the current, slashing wildly.

"Waaah!" Ben surfaced and sank a second time.

"Hurry!"

Herbert flew across the water, hands and arms pounding.

"He is drowning," Stephen screamed.

Well below the island now, Ben surfaced a third time and went under, but this time he did not call out. His eyes were closed and his mouth gaped. Herbert dove below the turbulent surface. I held my breath, praying they would both survive.

"*Nkakugambira*." I heard the word as plainly as if Taata stood next to me. How many times had he ordered me not to swim during the wet season? How many times had he warned me of just this sort of incident? More times than I could count.

Herbert burst, gasping, to the surface, which splashed and churned behind him as he kicked hard to reach the island.

"Where is Ben?" Stephen asked.

"I do not—" I saw something dragging in Herbert's wake. It was Ben.

I splashed through the water to meet them.

"I have him!" Herbert half swam, half crawled into the shallows. I grabbed Ben's limp body and hauled it ashore.

"He is dead!" Stephen cried.

"He is not," Herbert said. He rolled Ben onto his back and pushed against his stomach. Water flowed from Ben's mouth but he did not respond.

"We are in big trouble." Stephen paced back and forth.

"Shut up!" Herbert's eyes were wide.

I knelt beside Ben. Water glistened on his face and his lips were parted as if he were about to say something. I lifted an eyelid. The white of his eye was bloodshot.

"Wake up, Ben," I said.

"Put him back in the water," Stephen said, voice screeching. "The cold will wake him."

"That is craziness," Herbert said. "What if the water sweeps him off?"

I lowered my ear to Ben's chest, but could not hear breathing.

"We must warm him." Herbert slid back into the water. "I will get our clothes. You stay here."

"We need help," Stephen said.

I patted Ben's cheek. "Come on, Ben. Wake up."

"That is not going to work. He needs a doctor!"

"How are we going to get him to a doctor, Stephen? Swim him across the river and carry him up the *enengo*?"

Thunder rumbled in the distance, an almost everyday occurrence during the rainy season. I checked Ben's eyes again. There was no sign of life.

"God help us," I prayed.

"He is dead!" Stephen cried. "It is our fault. We should not have come out here. The water was too deep. I *told* you it was too deep."

"He said he could swim." I pressed Ben's chest as Herbert had done, but Ben did not respond.

Herbert waded in from the river, clothes in hand. He tossed us our sopping garments and tugged his own on.

Herbert and I struggled to pull soggy shorts up Ben's cold legs.

"How is that going to help?" Stephen asked.

"Shut up!" Herbert said. He sat Ben up so we could draw the shirt over his head.

Thunder rumbled nearer. Clouds darkened the strip of sky above us.

"He cannot be dead," Herbert whispered. Tears filled his eyes.

I went to my knees, praying with all my might. "Please, God. Please. Please. Please. Please. Please." *I will obey Taata with no question. I will do all my chores. I will help Maama without being asked. I will not tease my sisters.*

Lightning streaked overhead. Rain fell in large drops, splashing our heads, the sand, and Ben's face.

Ben gasped and sputtered. He rolled to his side and vomited.

"Ben!" Herbert yelled.

Ben sat up and coughed violently.

Stephen leaped into the air. "Thank God! He is alive."

"What happened?" Ben croaked.

"You almost drowned," Herbert snapped. "You said you could swim."

Ben's teeth chattered. "I said I have crossed the river."

It was not until our walk back up the *enengo* that we discovered Ben's lie. He had crossed the river before, but only on someone's shoulders.

If a boy could be revived from nearly drowning, Sharon could be saved as well. I would not give up on her just yet.

The Nyaka AIDS Orphans School, one year after its official launch. We had three classes, three teachers, and eighty-six students.

When I am at the school, I enjoy meeting with students and staff.

Staking a flagpole with my friend Sajjabi Mugerwa. Nyaka was built brick by brick, stone by stone.

Sempa Baker, my friend since childhood and now our national coordinator.

Freda, Nyaka's first headmistress, and her husband, both early supporters of and donators to the school, with their grandchildren.

Husband-and-wife teachers Lydia and Agaba with their three children.

Bruno, one of our star students, who lives all alone and walks several miles to school each day.

The Nyaka staff. From left to right, Lydia, Caroline, Alice, Emmanuel, Annet, Nicholas, Joram, Aggrey, Stephen, and Monica.

A portrait of my maternal grandparents (with my parents, standing in back), taken in 1978 during Idi Amin's regime.

My family having lunch after church in happier days, when I was a student. From left to right, Christine and her youngest son; my mother; my sister the late Mbabazi; me; and Faida.

At graduation from Makerere University with my brother, Frank.

My sister Mbabazi's burial.

My parents in front of their home.

Me; my wife, Beronda; and our son, Nicolas.

The primary-one classroom.

Students, on a break, playing drums in the schoolyard.

These are some of the heroic grandmothers whose children have died and who are caring for their grandchildren. We have created special programs to support them, in gratitude for everything they do for Nyaka.

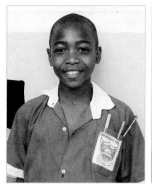

Arihihi Ronald   Atusiimire Precious   Komuhangi Irene

Children line up to test our clean water. Nyaka's clean water system is the first and the only one in this village. Our gravity water system serves more than 25,000 people.

Professor Mondo, a role model and hero for me and many others in southwestern Uganda, congratulating students on their graduation day.

OPENED BY
HON. MINISTER
PROF. MONDO KAGONYERA
ON
2ND JAN 2003
"FOR OUR CHILDRENS SAKE"

The foundation stone that was laid on the day Nyaka was officially opened. I remember that day so clearly.

CHAPTER 20

COWS IN AMERICA

The next morning I awoke to children's voices echoing up the hillside. Startled, for I had overslept, I dressed and hurried to the shortcut through the well-kept banana plantation. Dead fronds had been trimmed, chopped, and scattered, making a comfortable bed for the farm dog. While it dozed in the shade, chickens wandered among the fronds scratching for grubs.

Envious of the dog's idle approach to life, I wished I could have slept just a little longer, but my day was already filled with appointments. Such was the life of a "director."

I slipped through a narrow gate in the wire fence and entered the school grounds behind the building. Following a worn path, I came to the side yard where the cook filled jerry cans with water from the tap. The kitchen stood behind her, a temporary structure of poles and roughly hewn wood slats.

"*Agandi,*" I said.

"*Nigye,* Director." Rose was a robust woman with muscular arms who could lift the heavy cans without a moment's hesitation. Someday we hoped to build her a real kitchen with brick walls, a cement floor, and a hearth. Although Rose never complained, I knew she would appreciate getting out of the dust and heat of the current structure.

As I rounded the side of the school, the singing stopped and students poured from the primary-four classroom, a wave of purple dashing to their regular classrooms to begin their lessons. Lagging behind, ten-year-old Allan crawled, dragging his paralyzed legs. Without pausing, he crossed the dirt yard and scaled three steps leading to the primary-one classroom.

He had been physically handicapped since birth, but Nyaka School welcomed him as it did all orphans. The Indiana Friends of Nyaka had purchased a wheelchair that his classmates now used to bring him to school, but with no ramps, Allan had to crawl between classes. The sight brought tears to my eyes, but I only had to remind myself of where Allan would be without our school. He was happy enough here, certainly happier than he would have been begging in the village.

I followed Allan inside and strolled to the front of the classroom where Freda stood, waiting for the students to settle. Giggling started as soon as they saw me.

It was good to see the room furnished with desks and seats for everyone. Each student had his or her own workbook and pencil, and the walls were covered with cheery, colorful posters about nutrition and math, and drawings made by students. Most students had uniforms, but several wore overlarge sweaters to keep off the morning chill. One boy wore a blue Penn State sweatshirt, and another, a black AC/DC T-shirt over his uniform. The shirts had obviously come from bundles of charity clothing shipped from the United States to many countries in Africa. It was not unusual to see people wearing shirts with the names of American universities, American cartoons, or slogans for American products. I have seen Michigan State, Duke, UCLA, Harvard, and Stanford gear all worn by children who might never know where these universities are located.

"How do we greet our guest?" Freda said.

"Good morning, Director," they said in English. "How are you?" English is the state language in Uganda, and the younger children learn their lessons in both Rukiga and English.

"I am fine," I answered. "How are you?"

"Fine," they said, breaking into giggles.

Freda sternly waved a hand to quiet the clamor. These visits were expected of me, and I certainly did not object to interacting with the children and providing an example of someone who had used his education to find a better life. I did regret that my presence inevitably proved disruptive to lesson plans, especially with the younger children.

"Does anyone have a question for the director?" Freda asked.

Hands shot up. I selected one at random.

"Yes, Nicholas?"

He slid from his seat and stood, barely taller than the desk.

"Do they have *ente* in the United States, Director?"

A girl tittered, which threw the others into another giggling fit. Freda and I exchanged glances and waited for it to subside.

"That is an excellent question," I said. "Here in Uganda, we primarily have long-horned brown Ankole cows."

Nicholas nodded intently.

"In the United States," I said, "there are long-horned cows as well as short-horned cows and even cows with no horns at all."

"How can that be?" another boy asked.

"There are many different types of cows in the world," I said.

"Why?" Nicholas said.

"Do they provide milk?" another student asked.

"Yes, milk and meat," I said.

"Do they have hooves?"

"How many cows do you own?"

A vehicle crunched to a stop outside, saving me from the deluge. I lifted my hand.

"I am sorry, but I have an appointment this morning and cannot monitor the class."

Frowns replaced smiles on many faces.

"But I will send your teachers further information about the cows of the United States when I return to Michigan. I do not know all the breeds in my head, but this is an important topic and I wish you to have as much information as possible." Mainly I was thrilled to see their thirst for knowledge. I would send photos and books or printouts to the school via Sempa or Stephen. Perhaps I could introduce my own Nicolas to America's cows at the same time. Young brains largely share the same fascinations regardless of locale, I have found.

Sam Mugisha's Cruiser idled just outside the doorway. Alongside Sam sat Dennis Mwebaze, the Kanungu District water engineer.

"I am thinking of starting a Nyaka water tour," Sam said when I climbed into the backseat. "It seems we have many who are interested in seeing this project."

He turned the Cruiser around and I noticed a second SUV waiting beyond the hedge. As we passed the vehicle, I recognized two of the men inside as workers who had helped Dennis with the water project, but the third I did not know.

"We can use tour fees," Sam said, "to pay for our next tap system."

Dennis laughed.

"We might have to do that," I said. "I have been so busy raising funds for the school I have not had time to deal with a second tap system."

We bounced along the dirt road, gradually working upslope from the Nyakagyezi area.

"We should obtain government funding," Dennis said. "Every village in Kanungu District could use a system like ours."

We turned onto a muddy path between a pasture and a banana plantation.

"I do not think we want to wait for the government," I said. Kanungu District was last on the list when it came to upgrading living standards. There were no paved roads or electricity. How could we expect clean water?

"The local council has been fighting hard for improvements," Dennis said.

"I hope they win their fight," I said. "But I do not intend to sit idly by."

People from the United States had already funded two water projects, the ten-thousand-liter rainwater tank and now the gravity-fed system that served the entire community.

Sam parked at the side of the path.

"We are here," he said.

When I greeted the men in the other vehicle, I learned that the visitor, Mr. Namara, was interested in building a similar system in another part of the country. Dennis spoke to him as we walked a narrow trail, passing gardens of cassava, potatoes, and yams, to a mud daub hut nestled in the shade of a eucalyptus tree. Amid a disorganized collection of firewood, cooking pots, and old mats, a dog lay under a wooden bench near the door, one eye watching a rooster strut across the dirt yard. A white goat bleated, pulling against its rope.

"*Agandi.*" Rujokye left his shack, donning a blue baseball cap. A middle-aged man in his forties, he was tall and slender. Although his forehead had wrinkled from years of hard labor, he was a happy man and proud to be part of the village's water project. He had sold us the land around the springhead at a discounted price, but still managed a small profit for himself. So everyone was happy.

"*Agandi*," I said, shaking his hand.

"*Nigye,*" Dennis said. "We are here to inspect the water system."

"Your miracle tanks are still there," Rujokye kidded, taking up a walking stick propped against the side of the shack.

"Nyakagyezi is no different from hundreds of thousands of villages," Dennis told Mr. Namara while we followed a muddy trail. "The streams used for water are the same streams people bathe in and cows drink from. People who can afford iron roofs collect relatively clean rainwater, but the majority of people in Nyakagyezi do not have that luxury. In the rainy seasons human and animal wastes contaminate the streams. This leads to diseases such as dysentery, cholera, and foot-and-mouth. Babies die from diarrhea; children suffer coughs, swollen feet, and colds made worse by drinking polluted water."

The trail ended in a grove of saplings. At a clearing within the grove, the cement lids of massive twenty-five-thousand-liter tanks rose above a thorny hedge.

"We have two reservoir tanks," Dennis told Mr. Namara as we approached an opening in the hedge. Beyond the gap, cement steps led downward. Three girls in threadbare skirts and grimy shirts squatted on the cement pedestal bearing the tanks. They chatted while waiting for their jerry cans to fill up at taps fitted to metal pipes exiting one tank.

The girls glanced up. Sam greeted them and they smiled before returning to their conversation. *These girls should be in school,* I thought.

Dennis pointed to the tank on the left. "We excavated the area to provide a clean connection to the source. Spring water comes into the first tank unfiltered. From there, it flows into the second tank which contains layers of gravel, fine stones, and sand. This system does not remove all impurities, but filters out much debris. From the filter tank, water flows into the pipe system."

"There is no pump?" Mr. Namara asked.

"No," Dennis said. "The water flows by gravity only. The taps in Nyakagyezi are downhill from the source. No energy is required."

"And all the pipes are underground?"

"Yes. We have installed two and a half miles of pipe. Their routes are marked so that farmers do not cut them accidentally."

"How many families now have safe drinking water?" Mr. Namara asked.

"About eighty," Dennis said.

"Even though the water has been filtered," I said, "we still have problems with sickness." I pointed out the girls at the taps below. "The water is clean, but the containers are not. We must educate families to avoid using the same containers for contaminated and clean water."

After discussing a few more details of the system, Dennis suggested we continue to the next tap location a mile down the road in Zorooma. This tap served several families as well as Zorooma School, one of the primary schools I attended as a boy.

From there, it was a twenty-minute drive to the third tap in Rutooma, a small village with a clothing shop, a grocery selling fresh produce, and three pubs. Sam navigated the main road until we reached the tap, a cement slab with a faucet next to one of the pubs. Several women waited there, jerry cans at their sides. Two women carried babies, and toddlers played in the dirt.

"I will show Mr. Namara how safe our water is," I said. The day had grown hot and I was thirsty. I climbed from the Cruiser to find a crowd gathering. Attracted by our vehicles, men had wandered out of the pubs and shops.

I waited for a younger woman to fill her can and cupped my hands to drink straight from the tap. The cold water had a metallic taste but could not have been more refreshing.

"It should be boiled as a precaution," Dennis added. "But the water is of good quality."

"Aha!" A heavy man in an orange shirt marched toward us from a second pub. I did not recognize him, but Dennis smiled.

"*Agandi!*" the pub man said, waving. The crowd parted, letting him through. "I am so happy to see you. You have saved me from the wrath of the chief."

He shook everyone's hand vigorously.

"How have we done that?" Dennis asked.

"This clean water has been sent from heaven!" The pub man was so animated, waving his arms as he spoke, that I wanted to laugh. But I knew this was serious business.

"It has saved my pub and my life."

"And mine," another man called from the crowd. His companions laughed.

"People were sick from drinking my beer," the pub man said. "The chief threatened to toss it all out and close my business. But this is my livelihood. Without my pub I have nothing. With this new water I make great beer. My customers even have seconds!"

"We are glad to hear that," Dennis said.

"Please, come inside for a beer," the pub man said. "To celebrate this wonderful water."

"We cannot stay," Dennis said. "We have six more taps to inspect."

"And you should build six more!" the pub man shouted.

We excused ourselves and pressed through the crowd to the vehicles.

"Everyone is excited about this water," Mr. Namara said.

"Yes, they are," I said.

I thought of the Bible story where Jesus told the woman at the well, "I will give you the water of life." We had given the Nyakagyezi people "the water of life" and they had responded wholeheartedly, volunteering their labor, allowing pipes to pass through their land, and advising the engineers on where to position the taps. They had even formed the Nyaka Water Committee to sustain the project for many generations by collecting small fees from households to maintain, clean, and repair the system when necessary. The committee planted landmarks where the pipes passed through people's farms and educated the public on how to use the taps. They had even started levying fines on those who left taps running.

"Can we add more taps to the system?" I asked Dennis.

"Two more without losing pressure," he said.

"And if we want more than two?"

"We will need another water source." We reached the Cruiser. "I have found another source, but it will require two more tanks and miles of pipe."

"And that means more money," I said under my breath. The first water system had cost twelve thousand dollars.

"Can you ask Farmington Catholic Church?" Dennis asked.

I shook my head. "Even for Americans, this is an expensive project. I am afraid it is going to take a major fund-raising effort." Maybe Rotary International's matching grants would help, but that was far from certain and would still require finding a large amount first from elsewhere. Sometimes the thought of helping the children and the community was so overwhelming, I felt as if I were drowning. "I will see what I can do."

"Of course you will," Sam said brightly. "You are the director!"

When we returned to the school, Freda was standing in the yard, mouth set in a deep frown.

"Excuse me, Twesigye," she said. "I have news from the school nurse about Scovia. She is in the hospital."

My heart sank. "How did she get there?"

"Her *mukaaka* arranged it yesterday."

"Her grandmother has no money to hire bearers or a *boda boda*. Why was I not told? I could have arranged for the Cruiser to take her."

"I think they did not want to disturb you," Freda said.

Disturb me? Each and every day I was disturbed by people seeking handouts or wishing to tell me something that could not wait. Nothing, it seemed, could ever wait until the next day. And yet, when something important happened in the community, when I might have made a *real* difference, no one informed me? My blood warmed; I struggled to hold my tongue. This was not Freda's fault. It was no one's fault.

"I will visit her before I leave," I said.

Freda nodded, tears showing in her tired eyes. "Even as weak as she has been, she came to the school many times to be with her friends. We will miss her. Oh, Twesigye, why does God . . . ." Her voice choked and I pulled her close.

"We must content ourselves with knowing she will go to God. Through Him she will have everlasting life."

Her head nodded against my shoulder, but sobs shook her body.

"We cannot save every child," I whispered. *We must focus on the ones we can.* My throat clenched and I could not get the words out of my mouth.

I wished that I might comfort Freda as she had so often comforted me in childhood. I wished I could let go of my emotions and cry with her. But that was not wise. Were I to start crying now, I might never stop.

Life must continue, even as death pulls us down.

CHAPTER 21

IF YOU DO NOT REACH, YOU CANNOT GRASP

The next morning while I was taking a sponge bath with hot water that Faida had kindly heated over the fire, I thought again of Scovia, and Sempa's words came home to roost in my head. "Either we must build a health center or find a way to get people to the hospital."

Of course! I thought, pounding the soap down. *A van. We need a van.* We could also use it to transport the choirs. Why had I not thought of such an obvious solution?

The initial thrill died and I came back to reality. We were not even assured of continuing the school into next year, had barely started on the guest house, and here I was planning on a van.

I dressed comfortably and told Faida and Maama good-bye.

This morning was set aside for visiting local schools. Once students graduated from Nyaka, many would be ready to move on to secondary school. Our hope was to set up an endowment fund to make this possible. An endowment would be more difficult because people like to see their donations go to immediate use, but it was a necessary part of our vision. Primary school was only the first step in breaking the cycle of poverty and illiteracy.

I went outside and climbed into Sam's Cruiser, which I had borrowed for the day. Soon, Stephen arrived, video recorder in one hand and camera bag in the other.

"I brought three cassettes," he said.

"Good," I said.

He came around and climbed into the passenger seat. The door closed with a dull clunk.

"I promised Maama I would be back for lunch," I said, backing through a deep rut onto the roadway.

"You'd better drive fast," Stephen joked. Kambuga Secondary School was only a few miles away, but the roads were in desperate need of repair. Roads leading to Kinkizi School were better maintained, but that school was many miles to the west, near Kanungu Town.

"Sam loaned us this Cruiser," I said. "I do not want to return it with a broken axle."

Stephen raised the video camera to his eye. "I will record the trip. You can show Mukaaka the bad roads and why we are late."

I laughed. "We will be back for lunch. She is serving my favorites, *embuzi* and *akaro*. Besides, I came all this way to visit and have barely spoken with Maama."

We drove along the rutted road, splashing through streams that had carved their way into the *enengo,* climbing hills planted with banana trees and gardens. The engine groaned as I turned onto the steep drive leading to Kambuga School's green iron gate. I stopped at the guard shack, a brick kiosk standing outside the gate. To my surprise, an old classmate appeared.

"Twesigye Jackson!" Baguma reached through my open window and shook my hand. Except for his thinning hair, he was just as I remembered him, a quiet man with a wide nose and thin smile.

"It is good to see you again," I said.

"What brings you here?"

"We have come to visit the headmaster."

"Ah," Baguma said. "That must be why he is in a good mood today."

He opened the gate and I gave the Cruiser some gas to get it up the rest of the hill.

The school consisted of three one-story brick buildings around a central yard shaded by mature trees. The two older buildings had been built in the 1970s when Kambuga was a primary school. A recent coat of whitewash and blue-painted shutters brightened them somewhat, but their corrugated iron roofs were a patchwork of rusted and shiny sections. The newer building had a better roof, but its brick had not been plastered and the windows had no shutters.

Stephen and I climbed down from the Cruiser. He immediately began filming the area, panning over to the stocky headmaster now striding toward us.

"Welcome," the man said with a generous smile. "Welcome to Kambuga."

"Thank you," I said, accepting his handshake. "I was once a student here."

"It is a small world. I am pleased to see one of our own doing so well."

"This is my nephew Stephen." Stephen smiled and shook the headmaster's hand.

"And will you follow your uncle to the United States?"

"No," he said. "I am starting a Web business in Kampala."

"Most impressive," the headmaster said with a knowing nod. The Internet was like a rumor in rural Uganda. Everyone pretended to know all about it, but few actually had any idea.

He invited us into his office, a plain room adorned with a wildlife poster and a blackboard with posted schedules. The headmaster's desk was small, but relatively uncluttered.

"Please be seated," he said, offering a guestbook for us to sign. "You are both most welcome at Kambuga Secondary School."

"It is generous of you to schedule time for my presentation," I said.

He nodded. "Our anti-AIDS club has planned an assembly for your visit."

A secretary entered bearing a tray of bottled soda with straws.

Stephen and I thanked her and sipped our sodas. I told the headmaster I was considering the school as a future destination for our students.

He frowned slightly. "I would be happy to have more orphans in the school, but there is no way to fund them through the district."

"I plan to arrange for that," I said.

The headmaster steepled his fingers, appraising me intently.

An older man wearing thick-rimmed glasses peered inside. I recognized my old agriculture teacher and headmaster.

"Mr. Byanyima!"

He nodded gravely. Despite the addition of a few wrinkles, his rigid stance proclaimed him the same stern man. He had disciplined us without apology, insisting we would thank him someday. Sempa and I had attended his classes together, and even though we had not appreciated his strictness, we had certainly reaped the benefits of his structured teaching.

"Welcome, Twesigye," he said, shaking my hand.

"Come," the headmaster said. "The students are gathering for the assembly."

We strolled between buildings to find five hundred or so children sitting in the courtyard shaded by trees. Mr. Byanyima showed us to our seats near other teachers and staff.

The headmaster, summoning a booming voice I had no idea he possessed, quieted the crowd and said, "Let us welcome our guests."

Almost as one, the student body stood. I stood with them.

"Oh, Kambuga Secondary School," the children sang, "how proud I am that you are mine. I will sing your name wherever I go, because you are my lovely school."

I found I could still remember the words and joined in. Many students noticed my singing and acknowledged the gesture with smiles and applause.

Afterward, the students resumed sitting and the headmaster made a short speech about the value of a good education and the importance of studying hard.

When Mr. Byanyima stepped forward, a cheer rose almost as loud as one might hear at a soccer match. I remembered my days at the school, when Mr. Byanyima had been younger and less popular. But even then he had been more than a teacher to us, taking a personal interest in each student in his class.

"Quiet," he said. "Today I would like to present one of my star pupils." He nodded toward me. "Mr. Twesigye."

Students applauded.

I had not expected this.

Stephen's knee bumped my leg. "Star pupil? This does not sound like the stories I heard."

I wriggled uncomfortably.

A boy rose from the crowd and unfolded a note from his pocket.

"Thank you for coming to our school," he said. "You are very welcome." He then proceeded to read a list of items the school was in need of, ending with "and we are in need of a new truck to transport students. Thank you." With a smile and a nod of his head, he sat again.

I sighed.

Next, the school's anti-AIDS club performed traditional dances and songs. They wore green-and-white costumes and kept time with an old drum that was losing its head.

Finally, I was introduced. By now, the younger students were getting restless.

In my clearest speaking voice I explained that the reason for my visit was to support their anti-AIDS club. While I told them about Nyaka's Anti-AIDS Choir and our goal to educate all students about HIV and AIDS in Kanungu District, Stephen passed out brochures that presented frank, accurate information about HIV transmission.

"Preventing HIV/AIDS is simple to remember," I said. "ABCD: Abstinence, Be faithful, use Condoms, or Death."

The ABCD program had been incredibly successful at lowering infection rates from around 30 percent to 6.1 percent by the late 1990s. Unfortunately, when President Bush started offering faith-based, abstinence-only aid, President Museveni, in an effort to maintain political support, backed the program. Since then, condoms had been less available, and infection rates were on the rise.

"There is no cure for *slim*," I said, holding a pamphlet high above my head. "These contain information you must know. It is information that can save your life!"

Boys opened the brochures and glanced inside with nervous laughter. Embarrassed girls covered their faces.

Stephen took a few still photos of the crowd. The headmaster and Mr. Byanyima watched me, obviously waiting for something further. And I knew what, of course. That blatant request for school supplies had irritated me. I was here to speak about the anti-AIDS effort, not school funding. But I could not really hold it against them. Were I in their position I might have done the same thing.

"Before I go," I said, "I will tell you. I do not have money to buy you a new truck, but I will replace the choir's drum."

It was all the headmaster could do to smile, but the students loved my offer, cheering even more loudly than they had for Mr. Byanyima. Perhaps I was becoming a politician after all. Lord, help me.

From Kambuga, we traveled until we climbed the hill to Kanungu, a large town with wide dirt streets, many shops and hotels, and the district headquarters buildings. We followed the main street through town, passed a technical school run by the Anglican Dioceses, and turned onto a narrow, washed-out road.

The road ended in a circular parking area adjacent to a school yard, a square bordered on three sides by classroom buildings. These buildings were not quite as rundown as those of Kambuga School. The outer walls were plastered and painted red-orange and white, but the iron roofs had started to rust and the blue trim was faded and peeling.

"This is the place," I said, turning off the engine.

When I stepped down from the Cruiser, I noticed the same open-back delivery truck that had been there sixteen years before. The vehicle was rusty, but blue letters on the side remained readable: KINKIZI sss. That brought back memories of long, bumpy trips to far-off parts of the country including Mbarara, Kampala, and Jinja. We took that truck everywhere, visiting national parks, participating in school debates and conferences, and even traveling to school dances, since, at the time, Kinkizi was a boys-only school. While the truck bounced along rutted roads, we would cling to metal rungs in the back. Avoiding low-hanging tree branches became a game to pass long hours of travel. I smiled, recalling the time one boy did not duck fast enough and a tree branch ripped away his shirt.

We walked to the headmaster's office, a small room located at the end of the nearest building. When I peered inside, an older man with graying hair and a tight smile stood.

"Welcome," he said. "May I help you?"

"Yes," I said, entering the cluttered office. "I am Twesigye Jackson, director of Nyaka School. I was once a student here and recall it fondly."

His smile grew warmer. "We have something in common," he said. "I was also a student of Kinkizi who returned to serve the community."

He handed me his guestbook and asked us to sit on hard-backed wooden chairs.

"We have heard of your efforts to help the orphans in Kambuga," he said. "It is an honor to meet you."

"The honor is mine. Kinkizi is a fine school. And that is why we have come to visit. In two years, Nyaka will graduate its first class and some of the students may attend Kinkizi." I passed the guestbook to Stephen. "While I am visiting the area, I wanted to see your facilities."

"Where are you living now?" he asked.

"The United States. In Michigan."

"The United States? You are very far from home! No one has done a thing for Kanungu District in a decade. It is wonderful, your good work. We thank you and God bless you."

I had not come to hear compliments. I changed the subject.

"How many students do you have?"

"We have three hundred fifty, but expect more each year, especially with schools like Nyaka producing high-quality students. Nyaka has had an impact on the community and district, you know."

I checked my watch. "Could I impose upon you to give us a tour?"

"Certainly," he said, standing. "Let me show you the school grounds."

Next to his office was a staff room and beyond that a classroom with unfinished walls, a dirt floor, and a blackboard where three students worked on an advanced mathematics problem. I saw no teacher and only a single book between them.

"This is a new room," the headmaster said. "We use it for study at this time."

We looked in on a physics class in an adjacent building. A dozen boys stood around a table with one experimental apparatus and a meter stick. A teacher wrote an equation on the blackboard.

"Welcome," the teacher said.

The headmaster introduced us. Stephen took a few still pictures.

"I have heard good things about Nyaka School," the teacher said. "As you can see, we are short of lab supplies, but we make do." He gave us a tour of his storage room where he had accumulated a random assortment of glassware, measuring scales, and other equipment. "Sciences are difficult to teach with so few supplies. It should be no surprise we have a lack of doctors and other health professionals in this area."

I nodded. "It was the same when I attended school."

Excusing ourselves, we walked behind the building and downhill to two additional buildings with fading paint and corroding roofs. Here students sat at long tables reading.

"Studying for proficiency exams," the headmaster said, entering a room.

I followed, but Stephen remained outside. Three girls at the front table glanced up before returning to their reading.

"I would like your attention," the headmaster said. "I want to introduce a former student who now lives in the United States."

Eighty eyes latched onto me.

"When Mr. Twesigye attended this school, there were few books and no equipment. But he worked hard with what he had. He did well on his exams and was accepted to Makerere University. Now he is an accomplished man. Although he lives in the United States, he has built a school for AIDS orphans right here in Kanungu District."

Several students applauded.

I nodded. To be successful in life, these students would not only have to work hard but also possess the courage and self-confidence to push forward. Strong role models were useful.

"I wish you success with your exams," I said.

After a silent pause, the headmaster spoke. "Back to work!"

We exited the classroom and walked behind the building and up a slope to another structure. The main walls were up, but it lacked a roof and cement floor.

"This is the new girl's dormitory," the headmaster said. "It was being funded by an international group, but they ran out of money."

"Funding is often temporary," I said. I glanced inside. It was large enough to sleep at least fifty girls.

"I do not know how they can promise a building and not complete it," he said.

"Costs were probably more than anticipated," I said. *Too many people getting kickbacks along the way,* I thought. That was one thing I had avoided with Nyaka.

The headmaster shook his head. "So we must wait with a half-finished building and the students suffer. It is difficult to watch their suffering." He looked me squarely in the eye. "I realize you are a busy man with many responsibilities, but could you help us?"

I looked away. Like the headmaster at Kambuga School, this one expected me to have money at my disposal.

"I would be grateful for any help you can find," he said. "I will write letters, fill out applications, speak to officials, whatever is required."

I nodded, but inside, my heart ached. This was a man who loved his community and wanted to help. If I had had money to finish his dormitory, I would have given it to him right then. I would have counted the bills directly into his palm. As it was I barely had enough cash left to return to Kampala in a few days.

We reached the Cruiser. Stephen climbed inside and I opened the driver's door. I shook the headmaster's hand.

"I will do what I can."

CHAPTER 22

NOTHING WORTHWHILE IS EASY

My early-morning run is a time when I am free to think about the day's events and plan for upcoming business. On this morning, light filtered through mist blanketing the road. Beyond hedges hugging the roadside, *ente* were brown ghosts, banana tree fronds fluttered like winged angels, and houses crouched in shadow. In the distance a baby cried. I increased both stride and pace. My lungs strained to keep up as I ascended a moderate incline. *Life is a struggle,* I thought, *but if one trains for struggle it becomes less difficult over time.*

My muscles warmed. Sweat gathered on my skin. I reached a steady rhythm and my breathing eased.

Recently, as part of our HIV/AIDS education program, Nyaka School had sponsored an essay competition for primary-seven students from surrounding area schools. The subject was: *What has been the impact of HIV/AIDS in your community?* I had spent the previous evening reading through top entries. From those, I would be making awards. Most students had done a good job, but the assignment was more than a writing contest. It was a platform to bring our AIDS problem out into the open and begin to dispel the stigma surrounding the virus and its transmission.

Ente bellowed. I heard a boy call out to the animals.

In rural communities like Nyakagyezi, where most of the population is illiterate, myths about AIDS abound. Some believe it is caused by witchcraft and can be transmitted by touch. That is why so many with the virus are shunned and ostracized when *slim* begins to cause illnesses. Others believe condoms have been infected with the virus by foreign governments in order to destroy the African people, or that the virus can infect only a certain class of people. Rumors abound that there is a magic pill or cure, and people routinely buy fake remedies that range from vitamin supplements to weight-gain products to outright poisons. The most destructive myth of all, however, is the persistent belief that AIDS can be cured by having sex with a virgin. Not only does this lead to the rape of many young girls, it spreads the disease more thoroughly than any evil foreign design.

Part of AIDS prevention is identifying who has the disease. I had spoken with a local doctor about having the Nyaka students tested. It was not a simple process; I first had to obtain consent from the children's guardians, supplies then had to be ordered and the testing scheduled. Measures also had to be taken to protect the children's privacy.

A boy from Nyakagyezi Primary School wrote: *It has led to poverty, whereby the youth who would lead and develop the country are being killed by this disease.*

At this point we could treat only students who showed signs of *slim*. And that was not good enough. HIV/AIDS is a death sentence for the poor. Even those who sell their land and possessions to purchase medicines eventually die when their money runs out.

At the top of the hill, I left the road and jogged across the wet grass of the Nyakagyezi School grounds. Beyond the school, the brick Nyakagyezi Anglican Church stood quiet and dark, arched window openings devoid of glass. I loped past the wooden doors, wondering how many AIDS victims had been carried through that entry in the past ten years.

From the churchyard, I took a narrow path that wound between fields and family graveyards filled with wooden planks and crosses. Some markers were hand carved; others with painted names had faded over the years. With no family left to tend to them, many of the graves would soon be overgrown by wild grass and vanish from sight. Entire families had been lost to *slim*. Now they would be lost to history.

My legs began to ache as I jogged by a millet field. The grassy plants were tall and the seeds about ready to be harvested. A *waringa* stood guard, its banana-frond arms waving gently in the breeze. Just a few days before, Arineitwe, an orphan at the school, was telling me about his *waringa* business.

"Mine are the best in the village," he had said. "Everyone says so."

At the age of eleven, he was already an entrepreneur, making money to buy soap for his family. I had to shake his hand. He was trying to make something of his life.

When I finished my run and returned to my parents' house there was a message waiting on my cell phone to call Christine. I washed up and changed, then dialed her number. It took two tries to get through even though she lived only two hours away.

When she picked up I said, "Hello, Christine. How is your family?"

"Twesigye!" The anxiousness in her voice raised goose bumps on my skin.

"What is wrong, Christine?" *Slim,* my thoughts whispered. So often that is the cause of tragedy in Uganda. But Christine had looked healthy, even radiant, earlier in the week and I knew of no health problems in her family.

"They're going to shut the school down, Twesigye! They say we have not filed inspection reports and they're going to shut us down."

"Slow down," I said, adopting my director's voice. "Start at the beginning."

"How can you always be so calm?" Christine asked.

"I am the director," I said, hoping to change her mood. In truth it was an important matter for me. I had learned over the years that in order to be taken seriously one must avoid emotional thinking. Emotional thinking engages passions, it is true, but clearheaded, rational thought solves problems. Consequently I am a guarded person in public and seldom allow my emotions to show. My belief is that any problem can be solved with patience and clear thinking.

"Start at the beginning," I said.

"They sent a document—"

"Who?"

I heard Christine breathing. When she spoke again, her voice was normal and she was back to her effective self. She proceeded to tell me that the Nyaka Board had received an official letter from the district departments of Health and Education threatening to close Nyaka School because inspectors had not filed necessary reports. This was the first I had heard of these reports, though we had taken great pains to make sure our various permits were arranged in advance of breaking ground for the school and we had made certain to provide Nyaka with the same facilities as any other school in the region. We had toilets for girls and boys. We had a separate area for food preparation and we made sure our teachers were qualified.

"So, it is mainly a matter of getting inspectors to the school?" I said when Christine had finished. It seemed to me that if the necessary reports had not been filed, we should have the inspectors file them. If they found minor infractions we could fix them and move on.

"They will not come," Christine said.

"What?"

"We tried to get them out last year, but they refused."

"What was their reason?"

"It is too far from their normal route. They had no money for the extra petrol."

"They want a bribe," I said.

"But we do not pay—"

"Nor will we start now," I said. I had been adamant about refusing to pay corrupt officials. Once you pay one, you find a line of them on your doorstep. And I could not ask donors to give money toward a cause that supported corruption. One of the school's greatest strengths was that I could honestly tell donors that every dollar went to the school, students, and their support structure.

"They will close Nyaka," Christine said quietly. "All the progress we have made will be lost. Those kids will be thrown out to fend for themselves and we both know what happens to them then."

"No," I said. "They will not shut us down and we will not pay these bribes."

"How can you be sure of that?"

"I will talk to Josephine Kasya and Peter when I go to Kanungu. They will help." Joesphine was the district chairperson, which is similar to a governor in the United States. Peter Mugisha was the district house speaker and owner of the Kanungu Inn.

"I hope you are right about this," Christine said. "So much is at risk."

"I am right," I said. "You will see."

Christine sighed heavily. "Why must every step be so difficult, Twesi? Surely God sees the value in what we do."

"Nothing worthwhile is easy," I said.

"I suppose so," she said.

We talked about her family for a few minutes, and then said our good-byes.

I could not help feeling a wave of sadness. What if I was *not* right about this? What if the district had been looking for an excuse to shut us down from the beginning and I had simply been too naïve to see it? What if these inspectors would not relent and we were forced to pay bribes? Once the donors found out, not to mention the Stephen Lewis Foundation, it would be the end of Nyaka School as surely as if the Health Department shut us down. Everything depended on this, on me.

CHAPTER 23

SCOVIA

Cell phone reception in western Uganda is sporadic at best, so I was happy when I found a good spot out in the front yard to talk to Beronda. She and Nicolas had been surviving well without me, but Nicolas was certain I was coming home immediately. Each morning he could not understand why they were not going to the airport to pick me up.

"I miss you both," I said. "But I will be home soon." My two weeks in Uganda were quickly coming to a close.

"Have we received word from the Stephen Lewis Foundation?"

"Nothing yet," Beronda said.

"No news is good news, they say. I know God will help us." I chose not to mention the latest problem concerning the inspection. No use both of us worrying. "We will find a way."

Most of our teachers would keep working even if their wages were cut back. Some would work for nothing, such was their dedication. But they were professionals deserving of an income.

We talked for a little longer before the signal began breaking up. I told Beronda to give my love to Nicolas and ended our conversation.

Now for the more difficult part of my day. I had canceled an appointment with the teachers in order to visit Scovia. Skipping breakfast, I changed from shorts into longer pants. On my way out of the house I grabbed one of the loaves of *mugaati* bread I had brought from Kampala. The bread would be a treat for Scovia. I hoped that she would eat some and restore her strength.

As I drove the grassy path to Kambuga, optimism deserted me. What if she were beyond eating? I had seen the same with my brother in his final days.

I pulled up to the entrance gate to Kambuga Hospital and was greeted by the *asikali,* a lanky guard in a green uniform. When I told him I was there to visit a sick student, he waved me through.

Kambuga Hospital occupied more than twenty acres on a wooded hillside. Four wards, designated for men, women, children, and maternity, held about twenty-four beds each. All were constantly busy, but the mortuary house, a separate building near the maternity ward, saw more traffic than any. The district the hospital served had not seen so much death since the Amin regime, when district administrators commandeered part of my grandparents' land to bury unclaimed bodies.

The hospital would have been even busier, but for the fees. When I was taken there as a boy, treatment was free, but now a co-payment of eighty cents per visit was required. In this district, that was more than many could afford. Scovia's *mukaaka* had probably sold a precious chicken or goat to pay for her granddaughter's transport and stay in the hospital.

I followed the road to the left, feeling more and more anxious. Mere proximity to the hospital brought back memories of throbbing pain, the groans of the men in the ward, and the stiff bed I laid on for months. I eased the Cruiser past the X-ray building and came to a stop at the outpatient ward. Taking a deep breath, I forced myself to get out. My legs shook so badly I could barely walk.

"God give me strength," I whispered.

When I entered the outpatient building and smelled urine and blood, my old wound throbbed. The walls may have been newly painted, but it was the same as I remembered. Old and sick people waited on cement benches near the door, nurses and other medical personnel scurried through the admissions area, patients groaned in adjacent treatment rooms. I was once again Twesi, a little boy terrified of dying.

"Twesigye!" A light-skinned man strode toward me, white coat flaring. The surgical uniform beneath was bloodstained.

"*Agandi,*" I said, putting my fear behind me. Dr. Mubangizi was the medical superintendent. We had met the previous year at the school when Nyaka donated medical equipment to the hospital. He had been overjoyed, since the facility lacked funds for expensive supplies. The hospital did not even have electricity; the surgical suites relied on gas-powered generators. Everyone knew of someone who had died at the hospital during an electrical outage in the middle of surgery or for want of equipment and supplies.

"*Nigye.*" The doctor shook my hand. "What brings you here?" I am sure he was hoping I had arranged additional aid for him. Unfortunately, I was not there with good news.

"I am here to see a patient," I said. "A Nyaka student. The little girl battling AIDS."

"Yes, of course," he said. "I seem to remember her from last year as well."

"She was here with two other students last year. They all had malaria." I remembered visiting the children's ward, the potent smells of unwashed bedding and overloaded toilets. The ward had been jammed with children, many suffering from tuberculosis or malaria. Mothers and fathers sat by them with masklike expressions, resigned to impending deaths. I had found our student Desmond next to a dead child who had not yet been removed because the morgue was full. That experience had only added to my discomfort around hospitals.

"She is a fine, spirited child." Dr. Mubangizi clasped my hand between his. "I am very sorry, Twesigye. She is in the women's ward."

"Thank you, Doctor. It was good to see you again, even in these unfortunate circumstances."

"You are always welcome here, Twesigye, as are your students." He meant the words to be kind, but this was the last place I wanted my students to be.

While Dr. Mubangizi rushed off to his duties, I strode resolutely toward the women's ward, where two old women in worn clothing and a man who looked ill enough to be a patient loitered outside the double-door entrance. I pulled open a door and entered a foyer with chairs and a single wooden table. An old man in green pants slept across three of the chairs. Next to him, a woman sat quietly, staring into space.

Crossing the foyer, I came to the central hall, which was lined with open doors to private rooms that now held four or more patients each. Beyond the private rooms, the hall opened into the ward area.

The ward was filled wall-to-wall with patients. Some women were in beds; others slept on mats on the floor. It was a dismal sight, but unlike the other wards, the women's ward was at least clean. This was mainly because women patients and their relatives took on the responsibility of changing sheets, emptying bedpans, and washing the sickest among them.

God bless these women, I thought, remembering the women in my life who had helped me over the years: my grandmothers, Maama, my sisters, Freda, and, of course, Beronda.

"May I help you?" a young nurse in a blue uniform asked.

"I am looking for one of my students," I said.

"What is her name?"

"It is Sco—" I spied Scovia's *mukaaka* sitting on the floor. "Never mind. I see her."

The nurse tilted her head down and hurried away.

Scovia lay on a mat, covered to her chin with a yellow blanket. Her *mukaaka* sat on a matching blanket, where she had created a home away from home, with fresh fruit, a thermos that probably held milk, and a wash pan and towels.

"Uncle," Scovia whispered when I knelt beside her.

I could hardly hold back my tears. Scovia had always been a thin girl, but now she was like a shell of brown paper, lips pulling back from her white teeth.

"I am here," I said. I took her hand.

As my *mukaaka* had done for me, I said a prayer from the Book of Psalms. " 'Bless the Lord, O my soul; and all that is within me, bless his holy name. Bless the Lord, O my soul, and forget not all his benefits: who forgiveth all thine iniquities; who healeth all thy disease; who redeemeth thy life from destruction; who crowneth thee with loving kindness and tender mercies.' "

"Thank you for coming," her *mukaaka* said.

"I should have come earlier," I said. Every child at Nyaka was my child. "She is my adopted niece."

I turned my attention to Scovia.

"I have brought you something." I unwrapped the bread and offered her a piece.

Scovia managed a weak smile.

"She cannot eat much," her *mukaaka* said. "I will soak it in milk that she might swallow a little piece."

Her *mukaaka*'s hand trembled when she took the bread. She dunked it in a cup near Scovia's mat and leaned over the girl. Scovia took the bread between her cracked lips. Milk trickled down one side of her face, but she swallowed a bit of the bread. Her eyes closed.

Her *mukaaka* wiped the milk away and smoothed the white collar around her neck.

"She's wearing her uniform," I said.

"She wants to be ready for the resurrection." Her *mukaaka* pulled back the blanket. "She wishes to be buried in her uniform so she will not worry about dressing up when Jesus calls."

I stared at the Nyaka emblem over Scovia's heart. The patch had faded over many washings, but the words, *For Our Children's Sake,* were visible. I could not believe this was the same Nyaka student with the shy smile whom we had admitted three years before. She liked to read and tell stories, especially when she thought no adults were watching. Whenever I spoke to the children and asked for questions, she was always the one to speak up. I remembered the time she asked what district America was in. Her teacher had laughed, but I answered the question seriously. Later, I told the teachers that the students must learn more geography. The next day I went out and bought a world map for the school and showed Scovia the Atlantic Ocean, Africa, and North America.

"That is a very big lake," she said.

"That is an ocean," I said.

An ocean she will never see, I thought. Closing my burning eyes, I prayed to God. *Do not let her suffer.* I was still on my knees when a nurse announced that visiting time was over.

"Thank you for coming, Director," her *mukaaka* said.

I squeezed her hand. "God bless you," I said. "Be strong."

Tears flowed down her cheeks. She shook her head.

"I will be back to visit later," I said, knowing it would not be long until Scovia became another statistic to be posted on the Internet, another nameless death in Africa. But she was not nameless to me. She was a child with hopes and dreams just like my son.

CHAPTER 24

WHO IS MY NEIGHBOR?

In the 1970s, intent on allowing the practice of only certain religions—Islam, Catholicism, Anglicanism, and Greek Orthodoxy—in Uganda, Idi Amin's militia was on the hunt for members of other faiths. Announcements were made from the local radio station that Friday would be a day of rest and Saturday would be a school and work day. That would prevent people of unsanctioned churches from attending Seventh-day Adventist services on Saturdays.

This might have discouraged some, but not my *shwenkuru,* Stephano Rukwira, God bless his soul. As in the story of Daniel, when Nebuchadnezzar built a great idol of gold and commanded everyone to fall down before it or be cast into a fiery furnace, Stephano was like Shadrach, Meshach, and Abednego. He refused to worship another god, willing to give up his life for his beliefs.

Stephano had originally been a polygamist with five wives. My maternal grandmother was his first wife. After bleeding problems following the birth of her last child, she was taken to the Ishaka Adventist Hospital in Bushenyi District where she spent several months recuperating. Stephano had been so impressed and humbled by the Adventists' hospitality and spiritual healing methods that he accepted Christ as his personal savior.

Being a wealthy man with a fishing business and acres of banana plantations, he gave up four of his five wives, but continued to financially support them and their children. He donated land for a church, constructed the building, and paid for the furnishings himself. He also paid his servants' wages for Saturday so that they would not have to work on the Seventh-day Adventist Sabbath, and fed everyone who attended church. There were always people at his home: sick, poor, and orphaned. It became a refuge and a stopover on their way to the hospital.

Yes, Stephano was a true man of God.

When Amin assumed power, the local militia closed the church, but could not stop Stephano. He possessed a twelve-room house with an iron roof, corrals out back for *ente* and *embuzi,* and a banana plantation off to the side. In the house's central room was a long table surrounded by chairs. On Saturdays, his family, neighbors, and servants secretly congregated around the table and Shwenkuru slid his Bible from a drawer to worship.

Stephano and his congregation did not escape Amin's wrath, however. Someone must have heard them singing and news that he was holding Christian services spread to local officials. One night during prayers, there was a knock at the door. Everyone went to their knees and prayed that the intruder would leave, but, as they feared, it was the local militia. Soldiers kicked in the door and dragged Stephano off to the sub-county offices. Stephano was jailed for three days that time, refusing food until the local chief persuaded the militia to free him.

It was not the last time my *shwenkuru* was arrested for his faith. Each time they put him in jail, he would pray for their salvation. And in the end it was Stephano who triumphed. Amin was forced from power in 1979 when Ugandan exiles and Tanzanian army fighters routed him from the country.

———

Now a new Adventist church stood on the land my *shwenkuru* donated all those years ago, a square building crafted from local red brick, situated in a grassy field bounded by trees. The floor had been cemented, but as with most churches in the area, there was no door and no glass in the window openings.

The new church was larger than the old one, with a capacity of 120. The pastor's plastered house stood beside it. A thin man with a wife and three children, Pastor Ndimu Joseph had been appointed by the union in Mbarara to lead our parishioners. He was a kind man and an inspiring community leader.

I entered the building and walked up the aisle between rows of wooden benches, Scovia's illness fresh on my mind. Sitting in the front row, I looked at the simple altar and dais, and recalled the Saturday when I had given the sermon at Pastor Ndimu's invitation.

Worship began with Sabbath school and at least sixty worshippers in attendance, including many children and teens. As it progressed, I became more and more nervous about my impending speech, even though I had addressed countless church and civic groups about Nyaka School. This was the church of my childhood and my community. Often it is easier to speak in front of strangers than friends.

After Sabbath school, Pastor Ndimu came forward to pray and accept offerings. Heart thumping in my ears, fearing I would forget everything I was about to say, I reminded myself of Maama's words: "It is not what you believe that counts; it is what you believe enough to *do*." No matter how difficult it might be to speak in front of this group, nothing would be accomplished if I did not act upon my convictions.

"Please welcome our own honored son and brother who has

traveled far to speak with us today," Pastor Ndimu said. "Twesigye Jackson."

I stood and my fear suddenly melted.

"Who is my neighbor?" I asked.

I began with the parable of the Good Samaritan, a story from the Book of Luke about an average man who aids a stranger left beaten at the side of the road. Two thousand years ago, Jesus had used this story to challenge the religious establishment of his day. I wanted to impel others to consider their responsibility to the community through a fresh perspective.

"This is a simple and yet most profound parable," I said, glancing at some of the orphaned children in the room before me. "It can be applied to the HIV/AIDS pandemic that has claimed forty million lives, turned fifteen million wives into widows, and robbed fourteen million children of their parents. The parable challenges us today to ask, 'Who is my neighbor?' Is it only the person who lives in the house next to us? Is it only the people who attend our church? Is it only the people we know? What about the complete stranger who lives in the neighboring village? The stranger living in another country? The stranger living halfway around the world? Are they not our neighbors too?"

Many in the audience nodded. The parable was one of the most foundational and universal tenets of moral law, a lesson Jesus demonstrated through the actions of four characters: the victim, the priest, the Levite, and the Samaritan.

"At the beginning of the story there is a victim on the road, but who is the man? We know that he was beaten by robbers and was in dire need, but we do not know his ethnicity or nationality. We do not know if he was involved in some illicit activity that led to the attack or if he was just a careless traveler. He may even have been one of the robbers, beaten by his fellow thieves.

"The power behind the parable is not how the man came by his situation, but how he is helped by the Samaritan. It is not relevant whether the beaten man is at fault. We are bound by Scripture to respond to all those who are downtrodden, no questions asked.

"Should we distinguish between those who become victims because of sinful behavior and those who are innocent?" The HIV/ AIDS issue was complicated by the fact that many Christians considered the disease retribution from God for sinful behavior. "The Scripture makes it clear who has the right and responsibility to judge. It is God. Not us. Amen."

"Amen," the congregation responded.

"In the parable, it is the men of God, the priest and the Levite, who fail to help the beaten man. It is the Samaritan, a person despised by the religious community as heretical and unclean, who comes to his aid."

I found it sadly ironic that the HIV/AIDS crisis paralleled the Good Samaritan story. While many religious establishments turned a blind eye to the pandemic or condemned victims of the disease, the secular community reached out their hands. The United Nations, the Gates Foundation, TV personalities and actors such as Oprah Winfrey and Elizabeth Taylor, the homosexual community, and political liberals had all gotten involved. And who would have expected that a rock star would be leading the charge? Bono, the front man for the group U2, was doing more for the HIV/AIDS crisis than any single person in the world.

"Too often our beliefs do not translate into action," I said. "We are the ones who turn away from those in need."

When I lived in Manhattan in 1998, I worked for a renowned women's rights advocate who had recently won a United Nations award. She did not believe in God, but held many of the views of Peter Singer, a radical ethicist from Princeton University. Singer's views were morally shocking to many Christian audiences, yet his writings challenge us to think through the ethical implications of our behavior, particularly the connection between knowing and doing. Singer used an example of a drowning child to make a point about choice. How many of us would refuse to save a child if it meant sacrificing nothing? I think none of us. But at what point do we ignore the child, putting our own needs first? Apparently, millions have drawn that line.

"The Samaritan not only took pity on the man at the side of the road, he bandaged his wounds and poured oil and wine on them as a salve. He let the man ride his donkey to a nearby inn and left money for his care. He even promised to return and check on his condition. This was more than a minimal response. This was complete engagement." I paused. "Can we ask anything less of ourselves?"

"No," the crowd answered.

"As Christians, there are three things we can do," I said. "We can pray. We can give. We can act. Or we can do all three."

I wondered how this time of crisis would be chronicled. Every generation struggles with events and disasters that ultimately define it. Every generation has its own sins of commission and omission. One has only to look at a world history book. No one could predict the outcome of the HIV/AIDS crisis with certainty, how soon or whether a vaccine would be found or how many would die. But one thing was clear: what Jesus would have us do.

"I am certain of God's expectations for his people. I am certain that God sees the widows and orphans as our neighbors. It makes no difference if they live in Nyakagyezi or Kampala. It makes no difference if they are Protestant, Muslim, or Catholic. They are our neighbors, lying beaten and bleeding on the side of the road, helpless and hurting. Does God not call us to stop? Does God not ask us to show compassion, to comfort them, to bind their wounds, to care for them?"

The congregation echoed my "Amen."

That Saturday, the church buzzed with expectation. People had been inspired to pray and to give. But this morning I sat alone with God in the dim silence. I might have felt the pain of Scovia's sickness that much more intensely, but instead hope filled my heart. I thought of the words in Matthew 25: "Come you blessed of my Father, inherit the kingdom prepared for you from the foundation of the world, for I was hungry and you gave me food, I was thirsty and you gave me a drink, I was a stranger and you took me in, I was naked and you clothed me, I was in prison and you came to me."

"Assuredly, I say to you, inasmuch as you did it to the least of these, my brethren," I whispered, "you did it to me."

When Jesus ended his parable of the Good Samaritan, he asked the holy man which of the three men had been a neighbor to the fallen man. The holy man replied that it was the man who had mercy on him. Jesus responded with his most powerful message.

"Go and do likewise."

"I will," I whispered, thinking of Scovia.

That is a very big lake, Director.

It was indeed, but I could not let a mere ocean slow my efforts.

CHAPTER 25

BIG TRUCKS AND SODA POP

On Sunday morning, I arrived at the school on foot and found it alive with activity. Some students sat beneath the shade tree, finishing their morning snack, while others washed their plates at the tap. Agaba and Lydia strode through the crowd, prodding them to finish.

An open-backed Nissan cargo truck waited in the school yard beyond, surrounded by boys, some barely as tall as the tires.

"Director! Director!" Little Barigye ran from a group near the vehicle. His eyes were wide with excitement. "Are we going to ride in the truck?"

"Yes," I said, touching his soft, curly hair. I had originally planned to hire a pickup to transport the choir to the Independence Day celebration in Kanungu. Since the school opened its doors, our Anti-AIDS Choir had traveled throughout the district on weekends and public holidays. In 2005 alone, the choir had visited more than thirty schools and a dozen churches. The Independence Day event always drew a large crowd, and I saw it as an opportunity to spread our message.

BIG TRUCKS AND SODA POP   189

I am not certain who initiated the idea of the entire school attending, but it was Izidol who approached me with several boys from the primary-four class.

"Why is it that only the choir is going to the celebration?"

"It is a long trip," I said. "We cannot walk so far, so I have planned to transport the choir to represent Nyaka."

"We are *all* Nyaka students," Onesmus said, jaw set with determination.

"We want to go," the gangly group said in unison. "Please. Can we go?"

Later that day, several primary-four girls mustered the courage to speak with me privately. Irene, one of the class leaders, was their spokesperson.

"Can we all go to the celebration?" As a secondary-choir member she would attend either way. "We *all* wish to represent the school."

Akampurira peered over Irene's shoulder and smiled sweetly.

"We have never been to Kanungu Town."

"Please, Director," they said, grasping my hands and kneeling. "Please! Please!"

"Stand up," I said. "You do not kneel and beg."

"Yes, Director."

Most of our students who were not in the choir had never ridden in a motor vehicle or even traveled outside the village, but it would be a logistical problem to transport so many. We had no local buses and it would require many pickup trucks.

However, after another dozen students begged me to go, I spoke with the teachers and guardians, who decided it would be a great experience for the children. I negotiated with a local cargo-truck owner to transport them.

"It is a big truck!" Barigye said, drawing my thoughts back to the present. "It has six tires."

"Yes," I said. "It has extra tires in the back to carry heavy loads."

The truck dwarfed our Cruiser, its blue engine compartment tower-ing over the students. Normally used to transport stone and building materials, the open-top bed had enough room to hold one hundred standing children.

The truck's back gate screeched when the owner lowered it. Agaba ordered students to form groups according to class.

"If you want a ride, go get in line," I told Barigye.

Students climbed up and moved to the front of the bed, older stu-dents packing themselves into rows behind the cab. Teachers helped younger students onto the truck.

Agaba, his assistant, Matia, and a couple of men from the village climbed onto the sideboards, and the engine started. A boy ran from the school's entrance gate to the truck, shoes and socks in hand. I rec-ognized Nicholas, who had been consistently tardy the prior week. I initially assumed he had been delayed by chores, but later discovered he walked several miles to school each morning. Even when he left at daybreak, he barely made it before morning prayers and songs.

Milton had been harsh. "We all have our obstacles, Nicholas. You must leave earlier."

"He has miles to walk," I said to Milton one morning. "Should you be so demanding?" Nicholas was one of the smarter students in his class, and I knew if Nyaka could keep him in school he could accomplish great things.

"If I let one student arrive late," Milton had said, "they will all make excuses. Rules are meant to be followed."

While Nicholas scrambled into the truck, Sam, Stephen, and Auntie Joseline arrived in the Cruiser. I climbed into the front seat, taking one of the youngest orphans, four-year-old Suzan, onto my lap. The students in the truck broke out into a song: " 'This is Nyaka AIDS Orphans School, shining as stars; we are boys and girls des-tined for success. It is time to celebrate because we are destined for success.' "

Kanungu Town is about fifteen miles from the village, but with poor road conditions, the going was slow. In the forty-three years since Uganda had achieved its independence, one would have thought Kanungu District would at least pave a road from Rukungiri to the district headquarters. No, we were lucky to have dirt roads that did not completely wash out. Uganda's freedom from Britain had not meant freedom from poverty or politics.

The Cruiser slowed as we climbed a steep hill and followed a curve to the north. Sam gripped the wheel hard and leaned forward, watching for ruts and roots. Children still sang in the truck ahead.

How can they sing while the world falls to ruin? I thought, feeling irritable, but only for a second. These children were not to blame for the poverty they were born into or the virus that threatened the fabric of their existence. Yet much was expected of them as Uganda's hope for a brighter future. Sometimes I was as guilty as anyone of expecting more of them than was fair. It must be human nature to want to mold those around us. If only we would put that energy into remolding ourselves.

While Western leaders sat in air-conditioned offices ignoring the African AIDS epidemic, earmarking AIDS funds to comply with their political agendas, or setting up vacation conferences, small groups of supporters from around the world were making a difference at the community level here in Nyakagyezi and in other places. Every AIDS orphan who completes his or her primary education represents a vote for a better future. It will be these children's votes that eradicate corruption, improve the educational system, eliminate poverty, and stop HIV/AIDS's insidious destruction.

About an hour later, the truck crested a hill and its brake lights flashed. We had arrived at Kanungu Town to find its wide main street of red dirt and gravel congested with pedestrians.

"It looks like everyone in the district is here," Sam said. We inched along. Kanungu District's administrative offices, single-story brick buildings, sat off the road to the left. To the right and up a short slope was the soccer field. A blue tent and a white tent had been set up to shade guests and other public officials at the field's far side.

"Green," Suzan said, pointing to a group of students in green uniforms.

"Yes," I said. "Those students will be in the parade."

The truck's brakes screeched and it drifted right. Sam stopped behind it.

"We will get out here," Auntie said. Faida took Suzan and climbed down from our vehicle. Teachers helped students from the truck.

Sam parked the Cruiser beneath a shade tree near the soccer field. A crowd of at least one thousand had already assembled. Alongside the field, children from surrounding schools gathered in groups, wearing their schools' colors. The Bishop's Band, a menagerie of men and women playing used drums and brass instruments, marched around the field's perimeter. Military units, including the army and local militia, stood at attention in the hot sun.

After making sure the Nyaka students had been included on the day's program, Auntie Joseline clasped my hand and escorted me to the blue tent. The front row held military officers in pressed suits gilded with war medals, politicians and their wives, and priests and pastors in colorful robes.

"Here is the director of the Nyaka AIDS Orphans School," a woman announced over the public address system.

I donned my director's smile and hurried into the shade. Although there was a slight breeze, the day was already growing hot.

"Nyaka provides for orphans and has changed lives," the woman continued. "As you will see, because the kids are in the program later. Please welcome him. Director, please wave to our people."

I waved and moved farther back into the crowd.

More officials arrived, transported across the field in SUVs. Men climbed from the vehicles in black or navy blue suits and women arrived as explosions of color, in yellow, pink, or blue silky *busuuti* dresses. Announcements were made, soldiers marched in single file across the field, and the crowd around the field thickened. A few *muzungu* women came in a white truck affiliated with CHIF-COD, the Child to Family Community Development Organization founded by Hamlet Mbabazi. Hamlet was a member of Parliament and the guest of honor at this celebration. I had had the privilege of speaking with him several times and our organizations served the same goal of community improvement.

After a short announcement, a choir of older girls from the local school stood before the flagpole and sang a song of greeting in English.

"'Our dear visitors, we are very happy. Our dear visitors, to entertain you. You are welcome.'" As they sang, they made intricate hand motions and swayed, gray uniforms catching the slight breeze. "'This is the time to celebrate; this is the time for you and me. This is the time, time, time. This is the time to shine again.'"

Festivities began with military units in camouflage or khaki marching to the beat of the band's music. Student groups fell in behind the units in blue and green, pink and white, green and white, gray and white, and blue uniforms. They marched around the field's perimeter, soldiers high stepping and saluting the main tent, students striding proudly. Nyaka School was positioned toward the rear of the procession, displaying their Nyaka AIDS Orphans School sign: PROVIDING FREE EDUCATION TO HIV/AIDS ORPHANS. Indeed, Nyaka was the only one among fifty-eight schools in the district that provided totally free education.

When the Nyaka students crossed in front of the tent, everyone around me applauded. The children stepped up their pace, faces beaming so brightly that they challenged the sun. I smiled too. It was thrilling to see such acceptance. So many African countries struggled with the stigma of AIDS, abandoning orphans to fend for themselves.

Here in Kanungu District, the stigma was being overcome. People were no longer afraid to discuss AIDS openly. This was a main reason Uganda had made progress in reducing its infection rates. In order to defeat a serial killer, one must first admit it exists.

After marching twice around the field, the students took a break, and the choirs were called forward to perform. One group after another sang and danced. Speeches filled the gaps between performances.

By now the sun was high in the sky.

"I intend to reduce the illiteracy rate by encouraging functional adult literacy and supporting universal primary education," one politician said, ". . . provide improved hybrid seeds and animals; and safe drinking water . . ." another promised. "Silk production has been recently introduced. Mulberry trees, integral to any silk industry, have been found to grow well, but shortage of market has hampered expansion in production," said yet another.

A girl squeezed between chairs, offering bottled soda. I downed an orange Fanta in three gulps and wondered about the children. It was 1 P.M. and our choir had not yet sung.

They stood at the side of the field, ready to take their turn, but their uniforms were dark with sweat and I began to worry about the younger kids. From where I was seated, I could barely see the other Nyaka students. Afraid that the teachers were not watching them closely enough and that they were thirsty and hungry, I excused myself and bought water and sugarcanes to tide them over.

When I returned, the Nyaka choir was just beginning. I do not have an especially musical ear, but even to me it was clear their voices were strong that day. Like a chorus of angels in purple, they sang the Nyaka School anthem. In a way, I envied them. It was as if they were able to lose themselves in song. They were no longer double-orphans dealing with death and poverty, but parts in a glorious creation larger than themselves. This was their passion. Just as a farmer loves the texture and smell of rich loam, these children in our choirs loved melodies.

They sang three songs. When they finished and the crowd applauded heartily, my heart soared. I had been worried deep down that the quality of the audience's reaction would be muted by the stigma attached to HIV/AIDS. It was more encouraging than I can say to hear that was not the case. We were making progress.

I informed the other guests and teachers that we had to go early because of another scheduled event. Indeed, we did leave before the guest of honor spoke, but the surprise I had planned for the kids was well worth missing another speech.

Instead of returning to the truck, we walked a few blocks to the Kanungu Inn, owned by Peter Mugisha. At the rear, overlooking green hills, was a rustic open-air restaurant. Students whispered and giggled when we approached the back steps and teachers instructed them to wash at the tap near the entrance. While they took turns over a rusty rain barrel, soaping hands and turning the spigot to rinse, whispers grew into open talk.

"Everyone line up," Freda said sternly.

The teachers and I went ahead to a small inner lounge with cushioned bamboo chairs. Wood pole walls trimmed with bamboo held posters of some of Uganda's more popular lagers, Nile Special, Bell, and Club. A TV stood in one corner, powered by a small generator. Agaba remained behind, directing the children to a dining area beyond the lounge, where tables had been replaced with benches to seat our students.

Excitement bubbled through the group as they were seated, but when glass bottles of Coca Cola, Fanta, and other sodas were passed out, the excitement turned to amazement. Only students present at the Nyaka opening ceremony in 2003 had tasted soda before.

Chatter echoed. Boys belched and girls giggled. Soon, the staff brought plate after plate loaded with steaming *matooke,* rice, and greens. I sat back and sipped my orange drink. No meal could be as filling as the joy I saw on these children's faces.

Thank you, God, I prayed. *Thank you for giving me the opportunity to change these hundred lives for the better.*

Two dollars feeds a child for a week, I thought as I began my meal. *Fifteen pays for books for a trimester. We can do so much with so little.*

In seven years, Uganda would celebrate fifty years of independence. By then, God willing, Nyaka would have graduated five classes, and would serve more than 250 students annually. Many would remain in Nyakagyezi, but some would go on to high school and university, and perhaps into politics. One of these giggling children might even become the future president of Uganda. On this Independence Day, my hopes for the students were endless.

CHAPTER 26

IDEAS AND IDEALS

Kanungu District headquarters consisted of two one-story build-ings across the road from the Independence Day celebration field. I had visited Josephine Kasya, the district chairperson, several times in the process of registering the school. She was supportive of our efforts to help AIDS orphans and open to my advocacy for free compulsory education for all school-age children.

I parked the Cruiser near the complex and walked across red clay toward her office. As usual, the morning was sunny and hot and I kicked up dust with each step. I entered the building and made my way from the central atrium along a narrow hall to Josephine's office door.

Josephine's secretary, a thin woman with accusing eyes, looked me up and down from behind her desk, probably wondering why I was not wearing a suit and tie. The dress code, even in rural Uganda, is formal. Even street hawkers wear shirts and ties. Jeans are considered weekend wear. I did not usually bring a suit when I traveled, choos-ing to bring gifts rather than stuff my bags with extra clothing.

"I have an appointment," I said.

"Your name?"

"Twesigye Jackson. Nine o'clock."

The woman frowned skeptically and shuffled through her papers.

"Josephine is expecting me."

She searched through her stack twice before finding a small note. Without acknowledging me, she leaned forward and pressed an intercom button. "Twesigye Jackson is here to see you, madam."

"Send him in," Josephine's voice echoed from the box.

The woman ushered me inside without another word. She left the door ajar, implying I would be leaving soon.

"Close the door," Josephine instructed. The door closed slowly with a click.

From behind her mahogany desk, Josephine adjusted her suit collar and turned her attention to me. She smiled and extended a hand toward the overstuffed sofa on the opposite wall. "I welcome you, Twesigye. How has your visit been so far?"

"It is good to be home," I said. Through the windows behind her, I saw distant mountains, green with life. "But there are always problems to keep me busy."

Josephine nodded. "I have visited Nyaka several times. The last time I was at the school, one of your students had been killed by lightning. It was a sad day."

"Yes," I said. After dodging diseases and coping with the hardship of losing both parents, it had been doubly tragic that a natural accident took away the boy's life. Scovia flashed through my thoughts. Soon there would be another death.

"But we are growing by leaps and bounds," I said, "Despite our setbacks." I had talked briefly with Peter Mugisha about the problem with the inspectors after our gathering at his restaurant. Peter had agreed to do what he could to help, and emphasized that I needed to speak with

Josephine as soon as possible. Of course, the last thing I wanted to do was storm into her office demanding she force the inspectors to cooperate. Thus, I thought it best to approach the subject in its due time.

I outlined our accomplishments over the past year, informed her that the school building was almost complete, and that we would start our primary-five class in 2006. I updated her on our nutrition program that would soon be serving breakfast as well as lunch, the community gardens, and our plans to change our part-time nurse to full-time. I also described our water program, sponsor-family program, and teachers' workshop.

Josephine listened intently, taking notes and nodding.

"I apologize that the district cannot offer more help," she said. "But I assure you we share the same hardships. Kanungu District is like a poor stepchild asking for crumbs."

I saw an opportunity to raise my concern, but before I could get the words out, she continued.

"How do we provide for a generation that has no parents? How do we educate them? How do we lift them out of poverty?" She spread her hands atop the desk. "We have one of the largest populations of orphans in Uganda, the highest illiteracy rate, and the highest child mortality. The demographics do not look good. There are more people under the age of fifteen than over. Certainly, agriculture is not the answer."

I nodded. People in the Kanungu District depended on agriculture for subsistence, but land had grown scarce in the last century. Fathers passed land on to their sons by dividing up what they owned. With no birth control or family planning, and a soaring population before the AIDS crisis, each generation's share was smaller. Now, not only were plots of land too small to adequately support families, there were few working-age adults to till the soil.

"We need education and vocational training," I said.

"I agree." Josephine's brow furrowed. "But there are only two vocational schools in the district."

"We could help," I said. This was working out better than I had hoped. "We would like to start tailoring classes as soon as we can afford sewing machines."

Josephine's frown softened to a grin. "Tailoring classes. Good idea."

"We could also train boys in brick making."

"You continue to amaze me, Twesigye," she said, breaking into a full smile.

I shrugged. I amazed myself sometimes. Here I was, planning on starting new programs when I did not even have consistent income to maintain the school and might not even have a school to maintain shortly. "I am only trying to serve the community."

"The district can advertise your products," she said.

"That would be helpful." Now I was getting caught up in her enthusiasm. Once the tailoring class began, we could make school uniforms, but we would need to get the word out. This could be another stepping-stone toward making Nyaka self-supporting so that I would not have to be continually fund-raising and applying for grants.

"We could also offer health care to the community," I said, remembering Sempa's news of babies born at Nyaka. It was difficult to keep doctors in Uganda once they were trained. They became businessmen or members of Parliament, moved to the city where they could make a decent wage, or left Uganda altogether.

"Health care is always a problem," Josephine said, "but without better infrastructure and more advertising of what Kanungu District has to offer, it is difficult to attract educated people."

"We should offer an incentive," I said.

Josephine swiveled and retrieved a videotape from a shelf. "This is our new documentary video. We are on a campaign to show that the district is not the poor backward bush that people believe it is." She handed me the box. "Take it home with you. It has information about our education system, national parks, ethnic groups, health services, and agriculture. We hope to draw more tourists to see our mountain gorillas and pristine natural areas. Places people love to visit."

Of course we both knew that in order to attract more tourists we would need improved roads and electricity. Three times I had dropped American guests at Bwindi Impenetrable National Park to see its mountain gorillas. While foreign guests paid $350 for a chance to see gorillas in the wild, the poverty outside the park remained unmistakable. Locals made small amounts of cash selling crafts from huts outside the park's gates. In the evening, the children would sing and dance to collect money from tourists. Older children begged for dollars, calling out in English, a language they did not understand, "*Muzungu,* I want my money."

A knock on the door interrupted our discussion. The chief administrative officer, Elias Byamungu, hurried inside.

"*Agandi!*" he said.

I stood and shook his hand. "*Nigye.*"

"I did not wish to disturb you," he said. "But I wanted to take a moment to thank you for the wonderful water project you have developed in Nyakagyezi."

"I am not the one you should thank," I said.

"I am excited about this gravity-fed system," he said. "I am certain it can be implemented in other areas of the district."

"Without doubt," I said.

"You know, only forty-one percent of the people have access to safe drinking water in this district," he said. "In some areas that figure is as low as twelve percent."

I nodded.

"There is much to be done." Elias grew more animated, waving his hands. "We need cisterns and pipe and people and equipment. We must convince the government that clean water is essential for Kanungu District."

"I agree. Clean water will do more for the health of the people than anything else."

"We just need funding to pay—"

Josephine's intercom buzzed.

"Madam, your next appointment is here."

"Thank you," Josephine said. "Well, gentlemen, I hate to interrupt your conversation, but I have another appointment."

I was surprised to find my time with her was over. I had not mentioned the inspectors.

"Excuse me, Josephine, but I have one other matter I would like to bring up."

She glanced at the intercom. "Well, I do have other appointments today . . ."

"It is important."

She smiled. "Very well, Twesigye. Can you give us a few moments, Elias?"

"Surely," Elias said, stepping outside and closing the door quietly.

"I have a problem with the Health and Education inspectors," I said, watching her face for signals. Did she know about this?

Her expression remained blank and I relaxed. This was something the inspectors were up to on their own.

"They will not come to the school."

"Why not?"

"They say it is too far and they have no budget for travel."

"Is that so?" I saw storm clouds brewing behind her steady gaze.

"Because the inspectors will not come, we have no reports filed with the district and now we are told we will be shut down because of it."

"I will look into the matter, Twesigye. If the inspectors cannot find a budget for travel, perhaps we will fire a few inspectors to free up money for that budget."

"Thank you, Josephine." I presented her with a Nyaka calendar to keep the school in the forefront of her thoughts.

Josephine pressed the intercom button. "Hold my next appointment. I have another matter to deal with first."

"Yes, ma'am," the secretary's voice crackled.

I left her office feeling lighter than I had in days.

Outside, Elias was beaming.

"As I was saying," he said, squeezing my shoulder. "I am excited by your water project and would love to discuss strategies for implementing and funding it with you."

"I do not have extra money for that purpose at present," I said. "The school must be my priority."

"You have something better than money," Elias said with a wink. "You have a resourceful nature." He laughed and we carried on our discussion through the outer office and into the hall where Muhumuzu Fulgence, the head of the Health and Social Services Department, and Peter Mugisha nearly ran into us. Our conversation continued, with Peter describing what a godsend the tap installed near his house was for the area. I told him what Josephine had said about our inspectors and we shared a good laugh at their expense.

My thoughts buzzed when I left the district headquarters that day. I was energized to see evidence of Nyaka's positive impact on the entire district and pleased to have overcome an important obstacle.

Driving back to Nyakagyezi, I passed children with distended bellies carrying jerry cans. My thoughts returned to Scovia lying on her death mat at Kambuga Hospital, and my grand visions collapsed. No matter how quickly all this progress might come about it would not be soon enough for that dear child. I felt a sob bulging in my throat and choked it down.

"No," I whispered, clenching the wheel. I will *not* dwell on tragedy.

CHAPTER 27

IN THAT RICH DARKNESS

At five o'clock in the afternoon, I found myself outside the school watching the students who had stayed to clean classrooms. Where had the days gone? It seemed I had only just arrived, and tomorrow it was time to return to Kampala. This day, Bruno, Irene, Ivan, Natukunda, and a dozen other students loitered longer than usual because they had heard a visitor was due to arrive. They were naturally curious, and meeting anyone from outside the village was a treat for the children. This visit was also a treat for me.

We heard the car coming up the road before we saw it. Bruno stood on tiptoe and looked toward the road, as if that would help him see beyond the hedges and trees. Irene shouted, "They are coming!" Children ran from the classrooms giggling, some waving brooms in the air.

A dust-covered white Toyota Corona bumped through the school's gate, turned onto the grass, and drove straight for me, stopping only inches away. The engine rattled and the smell of diesel and oil penetrated the fresh air. A smiling driver peered mischievously from beneath his baseball cap. I recognized him as a classmate from one of my many schools. His name was Stephen like my nephew and he had that same prankster nature. Maybe it was the name. I shook my fist at him and laughed.

Emma Mugisha sat in the passenger seat looking neat and composed, hair pulled back from her round face. Nyaka AIDS Orphans School would never have been built if not for a core group of volunteers that included Sempa Baker, Sam Mugisha, my sister Christine, school-board chair Habib Museka, and two teachers, Freda Byaburakirya and Agaba Innocent. But when the school was merely a dream that Beronda and I shared, it was Emma's plans and protocols that had been invaluable.

Four years later, Emma was a treasurer at Barclays Bank, the largest bank in Uganda. Even though she had been actively involved with the school, this was her first visit. I had received a call from her the night before saying that she was visiting her in-laws in Bushenyi. With the recent headlines about the Global Fund being embezzled in Uganda, Emma had decided to take advantage of her proximity to the school to stop for a quick inspection. She could reassure Barclays on her return to Kampala.

As Emma climbed out of the car in her denim dress, the children rushed forward and surrounded her.

Natukunda was younger than Irene and Bruno, but took the initiative to speak. "Welcome, Miss Emma," she said, bending her knees slightly. "We welcome you to Nyaka." The tradition of kneeling as a greeting was a custom not practiced in this part of the country, but bending slightly at the knee remained a sign of respect. Natukunda was the most courteous child in her class. After her parents died, she had gone to live with her *mukaaka,* but her *mukaaka* had died soon thereafter and she now lived with an aunt and cousins.

Natukunda hugged Emma's waist. "I thank you," she said, "for the free-tuition education, books, and pens."

Emma glanced at me. "It is the director you should be thanking."

Irene gathered the children into a line. "Miss Emma will hug everyone," she said. They waited patiently, giggling and whispering. Even shy Bruno gave Emma a hug in the end.

I chuckled. Visitors were such a special treat. The students could name all the school's past visitors who had taught them, from Stephen Kerns, one of our first interns, to Sarah Vaadia, who had just been there that summer. She had remarked on the children's interest in education: "The kids work so hard on their chores at home but are always on time for school."

I helped the driver unload Emma's bags and paid him the fare while children gathered in two rows and sang the school's anthem and another song of greeting. By then, the teachers had joined us.

"This is the first time I have traveled the *enengo*," Emma said as we walked to the building. "It was a spectacular sight. I have seen nothing like it in my life. And then this magnificent greeting. Such wonderful, well-behaved children. And look at this fine building. I see my plans have grown into reality."

"It is time for all students to go home," I said loudly. Clouds had gathered in the sky, a sure sign of rain. "It will be dark soon and you have homework and chores waiting."

Most of the children returned their brooms and strolled toward the road, but Bruno, Irene, and Natukunda dawdled with a few of the youngest students.

"What is it?" I asked. I assumed they were hoping for a ride, but wanted them to be assertive. If they desired something, they should ask for it.

"The distance from my home to the school is very far," Natukunda said.

Irene stepped forward, looking at her feet. "Would you give us a ride home, Director?"

"I cannot hear you when you speak to your feet," I said.

Irene raised her chin. "Would you give us a ride home, Director?"

I smiled to myself. "I will take you as far as Muhokya. But you must wait."

When I entered the primary-one classroom, Freda was giving Emma a tour of its various school and office supplies, students' and teacher's desks, and wooden cabinets. She showed Emma textbooks and the students' work papers, printed alphabets, and colorful drawings.

"The class is well organized," Emma said to Freda. "You have done a wonderful job."

"Thank you," Freda said. "We all work very hard."

That reminded me to retrieve a stack of letters from Freda's desk that students had written to some of Nyaka's American sponsors. With no money for the cost of a one-dollar airmail stamp, neither the children nor the school could afford to send mail from Uganda, but they certainly enjoyed receiving mail. I would take the letters back to the United States and mail them myself.

"When the teachers' offices are completed, we will have more room in here," I told Emma. "We expect to have the rest of the classrooms finished in a few months and a guesthouse for interns and visitors by next summer."

"I have been signing checks for programs and teachers' salaries," Emma said. "But I had no idea how far you had come with the school."

Next, we toured Martha block, which housed primary-two and -three classrooms, and Bethel block, which was now complete enough to house primary four. I thought of the baby that had been born outside that classroom. Like that baby, Nyaka was a newborn. If we cared for it and nurtured it, it would grow strong.

By the time we finished, Emma looked tired. I carried her bags up through the banana plantation to my parents' house, where she received another warm welcome. I wanted to visit with her, but could not. Darkness was quickly descending and I had a promise to keep.

I made my way to the front of the house and started the Cruiser. Rain drizzled as I drove to the school yard where Irene and Bruno waited with the younger students beneath the tree.

I rolled down the window. "Get in."

"Thank you, Director," they said in unison. Irene and Bruno shared the front seat; the remaining half dozen crammed into the back. While we bumped over the uneven road to Kambuga, rain poured down.

"How are you doing with your studies?" I asked.

"I am doing well at school," Irene said. "I am head girl at Nyaka."

"And you are working hard?"

"Yes, Director," she said. "I would like to be a lawyer."

I nodded. Irene was one of the most intelligent girls in her class, and I hoped we would find the funding to send her on to secondary school.

"And you, Bruno," I said. "You are studying hard?"

"Yes, Director." Bruno had tenacity and drive. His school marks were not as high as Irene's, but I knew he would succeed.

When we reached Kambuga, I could barely see the road. The rain slowed by the time we came to Muhokya, a town consisting of a row of shops near the hospital. I had promised to take the students this far, but felt guilty leaving them off in the rain. If this had been my son and his friends in Michigan, each child would have been dropped at his or her doorstep. But these children had no expectation of such treatment. As soon as I stopped, they tumbled from the Cruiser, excited that they had gotten a chance to ride so far.

"Thank you, Director," Irene said. I saw that glimmer of hope that was in all Nyaka students' eyes.

There is no magic formula for success, I thought. There is only hard work, determination, and a passion for life. As long as our students possessed excitement for the future, the battle was won.

Roads are the darkest on rainy nights when not even a single star is visible. The Cruiser's lights reflected off thorny hedges, forming an eerie tunnel around me. Rain pattered like drumbeats and water splashed from deep puddles. In that rich darkness, I was once again that *embuzi* boy sneaking off to school, wading through dangerous water that could have swept him into the *enengo*. I was the injured boy who lay in the hospital for months recovering. I was the rebellious teen defying my father's wishes.

I was the entirety of myself.

CHAPTER 28

MORE THAN A COMPOSITION

Morning came too quickly after a final evening with family and friends. I packed the back of the Cruiser with my bags, then added Faida's and Emma's things, for they were going to attend the Nyaka fund-raising banquet being held in Kampala the next night. I wished I had one more week to spend with family, but soon it would be time to fly home to America.

Maama insisted photos be taken in front of the house, and I said good-bye to neighbors and friends, shaking more hands than I could count. Emma thanked Maama for her hospitality before climbing into the front passenger seat. Faida's young son, Sam, cried when he saw that his mother was going to leave in the vehicle without him.

We will all be crying shortly, I thought. It was probably the same for all families around the world. An awkward silence before leaving when one does not want to say good-bye, when the pain of family being pulled apart is too much to bear.

"*Mukama akurinde okuhisya obuturirebana,*" Maama said, breaking our silence. *May the Lord keep you safe until we meet again.* She had been telling me that since I first went away to boarding school. I gave her a long hug and wished I could bring her home with me to see that faraway place called America.

"Izidol and Fortunate are at Miss Lydia's house," Faida said from the back as I climbed in beside Emma.

Izidol and Fortunate had been chosen to represent the school at the Kampala banquet. It had been difficult to decide which two students should attend. They were all worthy, and if we had had the means, we would have taken them all. In order to select only two, our teachers had created a writing contest in both Rukiga and English. The boys and girls with the fewest errors were eligible. When I arrived, I added a second criterion meant to find the most generous students from the eligible ones. I asked for volunteers to help me collect letters written by students to Nyaka supporters. When Izidol and Fortunate jumped at the chance to help I knew they were the ones.

As I backed the Cruiser from the yard, Maama cried. Taata and the others waved.

I drove slowly, waving until the house was out of sight. We came to the school property, where children waited all along the fence line like purple flowers. When we passed, they waved, jumped up and down, blew kisses, and chased the vehicle to the edge of the grounds. I wanted to stop and hug them all, but we had a long trip ahead. With a break for lunch, we would not make Kampala until almost nightfall.

It was not far to Kayenje, a small town with narrow shops and a couple of taverns. There, I stopped in front of Miss Lydia's white-washed brick house. Before I could turn off the engine, she had left the house with her husband and oldest daughter, Izidol and Fortunate following on their heels. I added Lydia's overnight bag to the luggage in the back.

When I returned to my seat, I could not tell from their wide-eyed stares whether the children were excited or afraid. The farthest from home they had ever been was on the trip to Kanungu the week before. Now they would travel 250 miles, halfway across Uganda.

"This will be an exciting adventure for you," I said, starting the Cruiser.

Izidol nodded, but Fortunate seemed unsure.

From Kayenje, we descended into the *enengo* to the bridge. We crossed slowly, metal rattling beneath us. In the rearview mirror I saw that Fortunate had closed her eyes.

"Are you sick?" I asked, reaching for a plastic bag beside the front seat. Many children would get carsick when they traveled for the first time.

Fortunate shook her head. We reached ground on the other side and Fortunate opened her eyes slowly.

"I thought we would fall," she said. "Drown in the water. How can the bridge hold this huge car?"

I could not help but chuckle. "It is very strong metal," I said. "It will not only hold a car, but also trucks and buses."

Fortunate peered back at the bridge as we climbed the steep road. I stopped halfway up on a flat stretch that had been graded recently.

"Why are we stopping?" Izidol asked. "Is something wrong?"

"I want to show you the village," I said, climbing from the Cruiser.

Fortunate was hesitant to stand too near the edge of the road, which dropped precipitously toward a thatched house below. Izidol perched on a grassy mound, oblivious to height.

"There is Kambuga Hospital," I said, pointing. White buildings stood out against the green hillside across the gorge.

"Look!" Izidol said, pointing. "I see Nyaka!"

"Where?" Fortunate moved closer, but did not join him on the mound.

"There! Left of the hospital." The end of the building was just visible through the trees.

"Yes, I see it," Fortunate said. "It is not very large."

I smiled. Already their world was broadening. They saw the school as a small part of a greater whole. As we continued our journey and visited other new sites, they would begin to understand that their lives need not be restricted to one village or one district. The whole world stood before them.

After a few minutes I herded them back to the Cruiser, where Lydia and the other women waited patiently. I started the engine and resumed our climb out of the *enengo*. When we crested the lip, a series of red-roofed buildings came into view beyond a metal gate and security fence.

"What is that?" Izidol asked.

"Makobore High School." I slowed. "And Kinyasano Girls' High School."

"It has many buildings," Fortunate said.

"It is the same for all secondary schools," Emma said. "Some have more buildings than others."

"The older buildings are for the boys," I said, pointing to the left. "There are offices, classrooms for seniors, dormitories, a canteen, and a chapel. The church is Anglican. The girls' school is newer."

"Do they take orphans?" Izidol asked.

"Secondary and high schools will take students who have good grades," Lydia told them. "They will not care if you are orphans."

As long as we pay your tuition, I thought.

Izidol pressed his face to the window, watching the schools pass by. These large complexes were palaces compared with Nyaka School.

"I like this school. It is very nice."

"Yes, it is," I said. I sent a quick prayer to God. In order to send all the students on to secondary and high school, some sort of miracle would have to happen. Thirty students at a cost of $500 per year was $15,000. Then there would be graduates from the following year and the next. Even if only half or a third of graduating students went on, I had no idea where the money would come from. The best strategy would be to begin a permanent scholarship fund. I had drafted a policy for it, but had yet to contact anyone.

I must have faith. God had helped the Israelites escape from Egypt, how much strain could an endowment be? Still, I could not stop fretting. The endowment was in God's miraculous hands, but these children had been entrusted to my very human ones.

I followed the road through to Rukungiri to the tarmac road leading to Ntungamo. This road was paved, but meandered like a river, skirting rocks, farms, banana plantations, streams, and swamps. At the foot of a long downgrade just north of town, Immaculate Heart School for Girls was visible from the road, a collection of whitewashed buildings erected near the cathedral.

"This is another girls' school, Fortunate," I said.

"It is beautiful," she said.

"It is the best girls' schools in the district," I added. The school had been founded by Catholic sisters. "Students here have the highest passing grades at the secondary and high school levels."

"You will have to study hard to be accepted at that school," Lydia said.

"Two of my high school buddies teach animal and crop science there," I said.

We continued north and east, traveling through open farm country. I stopped when we reached Ntungamo, a crossroads town with fresh-vegetable stands, clothing shops, and a tavern. From Ntungamo, one could take Kabale Road south to Kabale District and Rwanda. Kabale District has been described as the Switzerland of Africa, with interlocking hills, cool morning temperatures, and beautiful scenery. Being positioned between two ridges, the morning fog could be so thick that children got lost. I would have loved to show Izidol and Fortunate that area, but we were going in the opposite direction.

"Time for a break," I said.

"The children are sleeping," Lydia said.

"Go ahead and wake them," I said.

I wanted them to witness Ntungamo's electricity, paved roads, and bustling traffic.

By the time the kids were fully awake, the Cruiser was surrounded by *batembeyi* selling *gonja, mukyomo,* roasted beef on a stick, *nyama ya mbuzi,* roasted goat, water, and soda.

"We are getting out for a break." I looked back at Izidol. "Do you need to use the latrine?"

Izidol glanced uneasily at the boys mobbing our vehicle. "Out there?"

"Come on." I motioned for him to exit through my door. He climbed between seats as Fortunate got out through the side door with the women.

"Are we in Kampala already?" Izidol held my hand. I guided him through the crowd and behind a clothing shop. Out back, past a pile of debris and trash, wooden latrines stood with gaping doors.

"We still have a long way to go until Kampala," I said. "Kampala is a much larger place."

"Larger?" His eyes grew wide.

"Much, much larger."

Returning from the latrine, we bought *gonja* to delay our hunger.

Now wide awake, the children were fascinated by the paved roads and fast-moving traffic on our way to Mbarara. They asked Faida and Lydia many questions.

The conversation eventually turned to their hopes for the future.

"I want to be a medical doctor," Izidol said.

"We are in need of more doctors," Emma said, encouragingly.

"I will build hospitals and train nurses so that everyone in the village can receive care." Izidol paused. In the mirror I saw he had bowed his head. "No one will have to die then. I will end AIDS with my hospitals."

Emma's gaping mouth revealed that she was as shocked as I. Sometimes adults think children do not understand the gravity of a situation, but Izidol was a smart boy. We needed more adults with his comprehension.

"Mbarara University offers science and technology," Emma said. "That is a school for you to attend when you are ready for medical training."

I wanted to hug her then and there. *When* you are ready, she had said. Several years before, I had instructed the teachers and volunteers to avoid using *if* when discussing the students' future as a way to encourage them. Our students should declare their success and speak it into action. I had mentioned this positive-speaking concept to Emma after her arrival, and she was already incorporating it into her conversation with the children.

"We will see the university when we reach Mbarara," I added.

"Where do I learn to be a teacher?" Fortunate asked.

"Teacher training schools," I said. Fortunate and I had discussed her interest in teaching before.

"I could live in Ntungamo," she said. "And teach at one of those schools we saw."

"Yes," I said. "But even if you live in a city, you can always return to the village to visit your family." I expected she would become as homesick for the village as I had.

In Mbarara, we passed iron gates leading to a compound of large buildings. A sign on the gate said MBARARA UNIVERSITY OF SCIENCE AND TECHNOLOGY above the blue and yellow school crest.

"That is the university, Izidol." Emma pointed at the campus buildings.

Lydia told the children about the history of Mbarara, how it was the capital of the Ankole Kingdom and that the long-horned Ankole cows came from that area. I drove slowly, giving them time to ask more questions about multistory buildings and electrical wires strung along the streets. They were soaking up everything; it was an education they could not receive from books, an education they sorely needed.

Rural children were at a disadvantage when it came to taking national exams. Some test questions assumed familiarity with city life. I remembered one question about people on the first floor of a building, which in Uganda was considered the first floor above the ground floor. For children who had experienced only one-story houses, it was an alien concept. They had little chance of answering such a question correctly.

The trip continued, with Lydia pointing out landmarks such as Mburo National Park and the president of Uganda's Rwakitura Ranch. That led to lessons on geography and history and how the president was from this region. When trucks carrying goods passed, Emma explained how important the highway was in trade with the neighboring countries of Kenya, Sudan, and Rwanda, since Uganda is landlocked.

A smile stretched my lips taut. Many children came to Nyaka with debilitating shyness, and I had wondered if they would ever be able to carve out a place for themselves in the world. When we first started the school, I told teachers that I wanted our students to gain the self-confidence necessary to compete. They must not fear being themselves or asking questions. As director, I had played with them, sung with them, but also corrected their mistakes. I showed them they could trust me and encouraged them to speak their minds in a respectful manner. Now I was seeing the fruit of that seed. Izidol and Fortunate spoke with assurance as well as respect. I could not have been more proud.

After lunch, we continued eastward. I deliberately passed through Masaka and Rakai so they would see the area most devastated by the AIDS epidemic.

"There are orphans everywhere," Fortunate said, face pressed to the side window.

We stopped at the equator next. Izidol and Fortunate had their picture taken with one foot in the northern hemisphere and the other in the southern hemisphere.

"This is zero longitude," Izidol said.

"No, latitude," Fortunate said.

Izidol pursed his lips. "No, I think it is longitude."

"Latitude," Lydia said. "Longitude goes from pole to pole, remember?"

"Where are the circles of Capricorn and Cancer?" Izidol asked.

"They are very far from here," Lydia said. "The world is a big place."

Later, Lydia pointed out the lines on a map hanging in one of the gift shops. Fortunate took paper from her pocket.

"Director," she asked. "Do you have a pencil?"

I had suggested before the trip that they maintain a written record of their experiences. This would be similar to the journal the students had created to hold pictures of their parents, letters, and other keepsakes. A record of this journey would be something they could look back on the rest of their lives.

"I have pens in the car," I said.

After purchasing *gonja* and bottled water, I pulled back onto the road again. We passed fish stands, now abandoned for the day, and miles of shrub-covered land. Traffic grew more congested the nearer we came to Kampala. Buses and trucks rumbled past and taxis cut in and out. Amid this chaos, people walked along the roadside with jerry cans, bunches of green bananas, and baskets balanced on their heads.

"There are students," Izidol said, pointing at dozens of students in green uniforms strolling along the opposite side of the highway.

"They walk to school too," Izidol said.

"Yes," Emma said. "Like in the village."

"Why do they not ride in all these buses and cars?"

"All these people are—"

"What is that?" Fortunate said. Ahead, Kampala's skyscrapers stood starkly against the darkening sky.

"Downtown Kampala," I said. "You will see buildings taller than you ever imagined."

I remembered being overwhelmed the day I arrived in New York City. Not only were the buildings taller than any in Kampala, it was freezing cold and there was snow on the ground. Izidol and Fortunate would no doubt experience similar shock when they visited Parliament, the State House, the Bank of Uganda, and the Uganda National Examination Board the next day.

Darkness fell while we crossed the city to Emma's house. Electric lights blinked on, and the city transformed from dusty, traffic-laden sprawl to a headdress of sparkling jewels. I dropped Fortunate and the women at Emma's house, where they would spend the night.

Izidol was quiet as we continued to Makerere University. At first I thought he was asleep, but later found that he was gazing out the window at all those colorful lights.

"It is a lot to see in one night," I said, turning onto the university drive.

"I will need more paper," Izidol said. "There is so much to write. More than a composition!"

I nodded. Izidol was already a good student. After this journey he would work even harder to become a doctor. I wished again I could have brought all the primary-four students. What a thrill it would be to see all thirty working on journal entries, asking questions, and buzzing excitedly among themselves.

At least we were able to provide two students with an experience that would change their lives. When they returned they would tell their stories to the others. Anecdotes are not the same as experience, but they often inspire. And inspiration is the blood of human existence. Without it we are empty.

CHAPTER 29

THE BRIGADIER

After a busy day in the city, the cool shade of the Kampala ban-quet site was a welcome relief. Faida, Christine, and I arrived early. A white tent had been erected on a manicured lawn separat-ing one of the local Catholic churches from its dining hall. A dozen people had already gathered among the white plastic chairs arranged in rows before a cloth-covered table. A second table covered by red-checkered cloths had been set with plates, silverware, and food warmers just beyond the tent.

"This is very nice," Faida said. "I hope we have many people attend."

"So do I."

Fund-raisers were essential for Nyaka School's existence. When David Bremer, Otto Ray, and Allen Pease sponsored the first Nyaka benefit, they raised more than two thousand dollars. The most recent banquet sponsored by their new organization, Indiana Friends of Nyaka, had close to one hundred people in attendance. Sarah Cochran and Karen Like had joined the fund-raising team and it was a wonderful success.

As I walked, I remembered David's words at that banquet.

"Last year we began this process. A process to save lives." As he spoke his eyes scanned the room, connecting with each person individually. "The measure of a human being is not what he accumulates for himself or herself, but what he gives away, what she gives away."

At my table in the audience, Allen Pease nodded in agreement.

"We are here to change the world," David said, voice gaining volume, "one child at a time. There is no room for failure. We will not say no. We will redouble our effort. We will strengthen our arms. We will lift up those who are hurting. We will dust off those who have fallen down."

"We WILL . . . NOT . . . fail!" Now he thundered. I could not imagine anyone looking away.

Then, more quietly, "We will turn this world upside down and make it better. We will do it one child at a time, one village at a time, one country at a time, and we will begin with our own community as well. We will change the world.

"We WILL . . . NOT . . . fail!"

The Bloomington banquet had inspired me and others associated with the project. The Kampala event was no less important.

"Welcome!" Sempa ran up to greet me. He looked very dignified in vest, tie, and black leather shoes that nearly outshone his smile. "I am glad you could come."

I laughed. "I would not miss it. How many were invited this year?"

"More than a hundred people," he said. We strolled along the gravel drive. Other vehicles pulled in behind us, crunching stone. "We hope to have a minimum of fifty attend."

"That will be a good turnout," I said. I must thank Sempa,

Emma, and Danson Kamugisha as well as our student coordinator, Rwaboona Milton, for their hard work planning the event. The previous year Sam Mugisha and Sempa had done the bulk of the work, and we had held the event at a hotel. This year, we booked a less-expensive venue and were offering a free meal with the hope it would encourage attendees to pledge more support.

"You will sit up front," Sempa said as we entered the tent. He pointed to the table decorated with the white cloth and flowers.

"I would rather sit with the audience," I said.

People entered in small groups and couples. All wore formal attire, women in professional dresses or long gowns, men in suits. Chairs filled with people connected to me in one way or another. There were friends, and friends of friends. Some I had grown up with in Nyakagyezi, some I had met in secondary and high school, others I had met at Makerere University. Some were people I supported as students, who now had good jobs, were married, and had families of their own.

I continued to be amazed at how much local support we received. I had discovered that effective fund-raising comes from face-to-face encounters. It is a matter of trust and accountability. Maybe that is why so much of our United States funding came from churches where pastors were able to vouch for our program.

I saw that Lydia had arrived with Izidol and Fortunate; they sat quietly near the back of the tent. The children wore their purple uniforms and seemed a little stunned. I made my way over to them and squatted.

"Are you nervous?" I asked.

Fortunate nodded. Izidol seemed lost in thought.

"They have had a busy day," Lydia said. "We toured Makerere University, and saw the Parliament building and many other landmarks in the city."

"The hospital," Izidol whispered. "It was so big. There are many, many sick people."

Fortunate took a deep breath. "Must we say something?"

"Everything will be fine," I said. "Just remember, all these people are friends of Nyaka. They believe in you. They are your family too."

Fortunate frowned.

"They are your cousins from the city," I said. "It does not matter what you say. Just thank them for their support."

"May I have your attention," Sempa said from the head table. "I welcome you all to the Nyaka dinner and wish you a wonderful evening. Let us introduce ourselves so that we know each other as we share our meal.

"I am Sempa Baker, and I live and work here in Kampala. I have been a volunteer with Nyaka School since its opening. Please, stand and introduce yourselves."

One by one, attendees stood, some reluctantly blurting out names so fast no one could hear them, others taking time to say where they lived or announce their professions. I was glad to see so many friends: Sempa's wife, Marjorie; Promise and his wife, Cate; Emma and her husband, Polly; and Wilfred, Stanley, and Freda's daughter Gloria Mutesi. My nephew Stephen had arrived too, and was video-recording the event.

"Thank you," Sempa said after the introductions. "Now, we will have brief remarks from our organizers. When my stomach growls, it will be time to stop."

Laughter erupted.

After Rwaboona Milton and Danson gave short welcoming statements, Lydia and the students were introduced.

"I thank everyone for their support," Lydia said softly. Fortunate stood stiffly beside her, staring at her new black shoes. Izidol fidgeted with the edge of his shirt.

"We have good children," Lydia said. "First we were suffering much because we had no help. But now, thanks to you, the children know how to sing and to play. Thank you very much."

Lydia put her hand on Fortunate's shoulder and whispered to her.

Fortunate looked up, eyes darting.

"Thank you very much," she said in clear English. "We now have uniforms and new shoes."

After a short pause, Izidol stepped forward and stared straight ahead.

"I thank you for letting me go to school," he said. "Today I saw big hospitals. There are many sick people who need doctors. Thank you for helping me become a doctor."

By the time I was introduced, information swirled in my mind. I thanked everyone and outlined our goals for the future. I also made it clear that my work was voluntary and I did this for love of the children.

Since so many of these people were originally from Kanungu District, I recounted some of the hardships the children faced and reminded the audience that many of these orphans had no one to love and guide them.

"We are the ones with a choice," I said. "We can ignore the problem and let these children become victims of neglect and abuse, or we can save them, one child at a time. *We* are the ones who must rescue our community. *We* are the ones who have the opportunity to save these children. God has given us this chance and we must make the most of it."

Danson came forward from a front-row seat.

"Before we help ourselves to the fine food that is being served here tonight, I would like to pledge one year's service to audit Nyaka's books."

The audience applauded.

"Please," Danson said, smiling. "There is hot food at the buffet table."

Some people lined up for food while others mingled. A few late-comers arrived, including a heavy man who walked with a limp.

"Who is that?" I asked Danson.

He shrugged. "Some military man Promise knows."

As the night wore on, people helped themselves to the food and ordered drinks. Christine and Faida were particularly animated that evening, catching up on news from friends they had not seen in a while. Faida was happier than I had seen her since her divorce.

Stanley stood from his seat, and raised his hand. The crowd quieted.

"Each time I visit Nyaka, the boys are playing soccer," he said. "To identify teams, one group takes off their shirts. But when it comes time to compete with other schools, what will happen? They cannot play without shirts."

The boys called their team Nyaka Starz. It was a name that meant that the sky was the limit. Their mission was not only to win but to show teamwork. They were taught to care about one another and show the rest of the world that unity and working together starts with children when they are young. Consequently, the Nyaka boys were the most well behaved and admired team in the area.

"Since I do not want to see them without uniforms," Stanley said, "I will donate uniforms for the team!"

Applause shook the tent poles.

I noticed the military man again sitting with a group of men who had arranged their chairs in a circle near Stanley. His plate over-flowed with food, but he seemed uninterested in Stanley's contri-bution.

Wilfred, who worked for Mango, a mobile phone company, stood next. "I will provide the school with a cell phone and complete ser-vice for the first six months."

The crowd erupted again. A group of women who had not yet eaten made their way to the buffet. I saw Sempa near the food and wandered over to him.

"Good news," Sempa said. "Gloria passed me a piece of paper just now. It says she and her husband will buy books for the school."

"That is wonderful," I said, still eyeing the military man. He downed a glass of beer and returned to his food. "Do you know who that man is with Promise?"

"They call him the Brigadier," Sempa said. "He was a paymaster in the Ugandan Army. I think Promise invited him."

"He is certainly eating his share of the food," I said, trying to control my irritation.

"We already have more contributions than last year."

As if hearing our conversation, the military man rose clumsily to his feet.

"I came late and I apologize," he said. "But I have no idea what this Nyaka is all about. Maybe someone can tell us and then I will make my pledge."

I fought my anger. This man had arrived just in time for free food and had a few drinks and *now* he was asking about Nyaka?

"This is for the students," Sempa whispered in my ear like a guardian angel. "Go talk to him."

I prayed as I walked across the tent. *Please help me deal with this man.* I reached the circle of chairs and Promise gave me his seat.

"I am afraid because you arrived late, I cannot give you all the details," I said, controlling my voice. "But I will give you a summary of what Nyaka is all about."

I proceeded to explain my involvement in the school and what had been accomplished since its opening.

"Is that so?" the Brigadier said. "Thank you." He stood from his seat and meandered through the crowd.

"Who is this friend of yours?" I asked Promise, standing so that he could have his seat back. "Has he come just for the food and drink?"

"You will see," he said.

The Brigadier had found Lydia and the children and was nodding as they spoke.

"I would like to pledge," the Brigadier shouted. "These children tell me they need sweaters because the mornings are chilly and when it rains they get cold. I promise a sweater for every Nyaka student! I will pay half tonight and the other half when I visit the school."

The cost for the sweaters was $300 and he gave $150 that night.

While the audience applauded and Fortunate covered her mouth in surprise, I chided myself. What gave me the right to judge this man, to make unfounded assumptions about his intentions? I was reminded again of the verse in Matthew: "Inasmuch as ye have done it unto one of the least of these my brethren, ye have done it unto me."

"I am sorry," I whispered. "I should never question Your ways."

A new energy filled me. I thanked the Brigadier for his generosity and invited him to visit the school and tell the children about his army experiences. I sought out the least familiar faces in the crowd and thanked each personally for choosing to attend our banquet. I gave people phone numbers and contacts for future donations.

When the food was gone, Sempa clapped his hands.

"Please, let me have your attention one final time," he said. "You are all invited to next year's dinner. We encourage you not only to bring friends but also to find corporate sponsors. How many companies are represented here tonight? USAID, Transparency International, the Ugandan Ministry of Finance, the Pan Africa Insurance Company, Hotel Equatorial, Barclays Bank." Sempa scanned the crowd. "And there are private practices as well: GroFin, the World Food Program, Uganda Telecom. If each of us does our part, we will double or triple our support for the school next year. Remember, Nyaka serves less than ten percent of the orphaned children in Kanungu District. Think of what we will accomplish with more funding."

The event concluded with handshakes and hugs. I said good-bye to friends new and old. *Come back soon. Have a safe trip. Take our love and wishes to Beronda and Nicolas.*

Afterward, I walked Lydia, Izidol, and Fortunate to their vehicle. I could not have been more proud of them had I been their biological father. It was a joy to see these children talking with people they had never met about their lives and the school. Seeing children their age holding their heads high and speaking English clearly, especially with strangers, was a rare sight. Nyaka had empowered them.

Faida and Christine joined us.

"We will see you back at the Inn," Faida said.

"I will be there—"

"Where is Twesi?" Stanley called out. "He has not left yet has he?"

Faida took my hand.

"Twesi!" Stanley said. "Come. This is our last night together."

"I will see you later," I said, giving my sisters each a hug.

Promise's circle of chairs had become a drinking circle for old friends.

"We must celebrate," Wilfred said, lifting a glass of golden beer.

I raised my Fanta soda. *Yes,* I thought, *this is my time of celebration.*

I strolled between chairs, promising myself I would not stay long, but this was a promise I would not keep. Despite the geographic distance that separated us, these men were my closest confidants. They had supported Nyaka when it was merely a dream, and I knew they would be there for me anytime. I pulled a chair to the circle and sat.

Wilfred drank deeply from his beer. I sipped my soda, thanking

God for this companionship. I had devoted my life to Nyaka, sometimes to the point of obsessive distraction. These men reminded me
there were deeper calls than duty and social responsibility. Friend-
ship requires more than an eloquent speech and glossy Power-
Point presentations. To be a friend is to deserve the trust and love of
another person. To have friends is priceless beyond measure. These
men reminded me to be true to my values, to deserve rather than
demand things from life.

CHAPTER 30

ONE MORE GRAVE

It was a cool Michigan morning, but the sun's warm light bathed the kitchen as I cooked eggs. Beronda had already left for work, and I was in charge of getting Nicolas ready for preschool before leaving for my own job.

"Nicolas," I said. "Your breakfast is ready."

I glanced at my watch. Uganda was eight hours ahead of us, almost five in the afternoon. I had time to call and check on my family and the school.

"Nicolas!" I slid scrambled eggs from the pan onto a plate, poured a glass of milk, and set a plate and glass on the bar in the kitchen.

"I can't find my Bionicle," Nicolas said. He ran into the room and climbed onto a stool.

"We will find it later," I said. He took his Bionicle action figure with him everywhere. I had no doubt it was still in his bed. "Now eat your breakfast."

While Nicolas moved food around his plate, I dialed Christine's number and waited for the call to be routed. Her phone began to ring.

"Hello," Christine said.

"Hello!" I said.

"Oh, Twesi," Christine said. "I am so glad you called."

"What has happened?"

"One of the students."

"Scovia?" My heart sank.

There was a pause. "She has died."

I watched my healthy son lift a forkful of eggs to his mouth like a steam shovel, remembering Scovia's tired face and fragile body.

"God's will," I said. "He has ended her suffering." Inside I was screaming, *Why this child? She did nothing to deserve an early death. Why have You snuffed out her light so soon?*

"It is unfair," Christine said. "No child should have to die in this way."

"I know," I said. A third of untreated pregnant women infected with HIV pass the infection on to their babies. Neverapine reduces the transmission of HIV from mother to child to 1 percent. But at a dollar a dose, it is too expensive for village mothers. "When did she pass?"

"Three days ago."

In the past decade, death marches had become daily occurrences in villages across the country. Neighborhood burial associations helped purchase coffins, organized labor to dig, and hired men to carry the body home by stretcher. Patients were commonly carried to and from hospitals by stretcher as well, but one could tell a death march as it approached. The men were silent, eyes downcast. Women followed behind, crying or wailing.

"Did we help?" I asked. I remembered the nurse complaining the mortuary was so full they must pile bodies one atop the other. The thought of Scovia being stacked like firewood revolted me.

"Do not worry, Brother. Taata hired a truck to bring her home."

"Taata?" I was surprised, but not shocked. Although he never spoke of his sorrow, he understood the pain of losing children to AIDS. He knew this was something the school must do.

"Faida contacted the burial association," Christine said. "We purchased the coffin and white burial cloth."

"And the uniform?" I asked.

"We paid the tailor to make a new one quickly."

"Good." I remembered working on the uniform's badge with Beronda. We had ended up choosing a simple design showing two children standing beneath a house roof, a symbol of our commitment to protect and provide for the children of Nyakagyezi who no longer had parents. A commitment I had been unable to keep in this case. My chest ached with that thought. In my mind, I understood I should not feel responsible for Scovia's death, but I could not help myself.

I sighed, trying to ease the pressure inside me before Nicolas would see me crying. No matter how diligent we were, we could not protect every child. It was an unreasonable expectation. Still, my heart ached.

"What about the funeral?" I said, keeping my voice steady. "Has it taken place?" Usually a burial was delayed until family could arrive from distant areas, but Scovia had only two close relatives, her *mukaaka* and an aunt who lived nearby.

"Yesterday," Christine said. "We gave the students and staff the day off so they could attend." Scovia did not have many relatives, but she did have the Nyaka family to grieve her passing. We also had five interns working at the school, four from the United States and one from Norway. She would have had people from across the globe wishing her farewell. That offered me some solace, at least.

I imagined their hour-long trek between banana plantations to Scovia's house. They would arrive at a simple dwelling nestled within a grove of trees. There would be no fancy arrangements, no undertaker, no lavish floral displays, no limousine to carry the body to a manicured graveyard. A simple wooden coffin in the sitting room would hold Scovia's body. I envisioned her peacefully asleep in her new purple uniform, hands folded atop her chest. My throat clenched.

"Maama wants to speak with you," Christine said. A scratching noise marred the connection.

"*Agandi*, Twesi," Maama said. "How are Beronda and Nicolas? Are they well?"

"They are fine, Maama."

"It is a sad time," she said. "Many neighbors and friends came to Scovia's funeral. The students made a wreath of orange and yellow flowers. She was buried alongside her parents."

I remembered Frank's funeral. Hers would have been like that, men from the village bearing the closed coffin from the house through a shadowy banana orchard to Scovia's final resting place, an unadorned family plot, rich brown soil piled next to a five-by-three-foot hole. Her aunts, uncles, and cousins would be buried there too, grave mounds marked by pieces of wood or nothing at all.

"The choir sang such beautiful songs," Maama said. "Everywhere, tears flowed."

I said a silent prayer for Scovia, but she did not require my help to enter God's Kingdom. She had accepted Jesus Christ as her savior and the angels in heaven awaited her. Prayers were for my own comfort now.

"Who is that?" Nicolas said.

"Mukaaka. Do you want to say hello?"

Nicolas nodded and I gave him the phone.

"*Agandi*, Mukaaka," he said.

I kissed the top of his head, thankful that Nicolas was not required to witness the deaths our students experienced in their short lives. Mothers, fathers, aunts, uncles. More deaths than any child should be exposed to. It was enough to test my faith sometimes. Perhaps that is God's purpose or perhaps not, but in a world gone dark with tragedy, faith is a beacon.

While Nicolas tried to speak to his grandmother in Rukiga, I thought of Ecclesiastes: "To everything there is a season and a time to every purpose under heaven; a time to be born, and a time to die; a time to plant and a time to reap; a time to kill, and a time to heal." . . . Tears came into my eyes. I remembered lowering Frank and Mbabazi's coffins into the ground.

Earth to earth, I thought.

Moist earth filtering through my fingers onto their wooden coffins. The sudden force of that sound, a final drumbeat for the living.

Ashes to ashes. Dust to dust.

In fits and starts I heard Nicolas relating the tale of his missing Bionicle to his grandmother.

I mouthed the Lord's Prayer.

"Our Father, who art in heaven . . ."

Every day in Uganda, fourteen hundred mothers pass HIV on to their newborns.

"Hallowed be thy name . . ."

Fourteen hundred deaths.

"Thy kingdom come . . ."

Fourteen hundred graves.

"Thy will be done . . ."

Red earth drummed onto fourteen hundred coffins.

"On earth as it is in heaven."

If only I could do more.

"Bye-bye, Mukaaka," Nicolas said. He handed the phone back to me. "When are we going to visit? Mukaaka says we should come soon."

I hugged Nicolas and kissed his head. "We have to wait until Christmas break."

"I want to go now," he said.

"So do I." I lifted the phone. "Maama?"

"I miss my grandson," she said. "When are you and Beronda coming to visit?"

"We have to work, Maama." It would be months until we saw her again, and I worried her fragile health would fail. She could not live forever. "We will visit as soon as we can."

By the time I said my good-byes, Nicolas had found his Bionicle and was waiting near the front door with his backpack.

"I'm ready for school," he said.

I looked at my watch. If I was to get to work on time, we must leave quickly. I thought about calling Beronda to give her the sad news, but she had a busy day ahead of her. I would save it for the evening. By then, maybe some of the pain in my own heart would subside.

CHAPTER 31

A GATHERING OF GRANNIES

Almost a year had passed since my return from Uganda, and I was out of the United States once again. Only this time I did not go to Africa, and I did not go alone. It was a sunny August day in Toronto, and I was in the city with Beronda and Nicolas to participate in a unique celebration: the Grandmothers' Gathering.

A few days earlier, I had received an e-mail from Sempa, relaying news from Christine regarding the school inspection. The inspectors had come and done their job, but they refused to approve the school's makeshift kitchen and also would not pass us because we did not have a trash pit. I knew they continued to hope for a bribe. Other schools had worse kitchens, but I would not cooperate with corruption. Indiana Friends of Nyaka was planning to raise the funds for a new kitchen at their next banquet, and we could soon begin construction.

I was again waiting for the Stephen Lewis Foundation grant to be renewed. We were so grateful for their aid, but I wished we were more self-sufficient and didn't have to rely on them so heavily.

While we waited at the airport for our guests to arrive, I found myself becoming as fidgety as Nicolas. Each time he ran from his seat to the windows to point out an arriving plane I felt the urge to run with him.

"When are they coming?" Nicolas said.

"Soon," Beronda said, though their plane was late.

"Is Mukaaka coming?" Nicolas climbed onto the seat behind me and peeked over my shoulder.

"No," Beronda said. "But your Aunt Christine will be here. She is bringing two grannies, Freda and Leonarda."

"There they are," Nicolas said, pointing out a group of older women in colorful dresses and head wraps.

"No, that is not them," I said. "Christine and Freda have their hair cut short like Mama's." In all, a hundred grandmothers would arrive from Africa for the event, so we had already seen many grannies being greeted by the volunteers.

The Grandmothers' Gathering was a precursor to the 2006 International Grannies Conference and was hosted by the Stephen Lewis Foundation to bring together grandmothers from Africa and Canada in order to build a solidarity movement. Grandmothers and facilitators from Foundation-supported projects in eleven countries of sub-Saharan Africa would be given a forum to speak about their experiences living with the HIV/AIDS epidemic. Canadian grandmothers would take their stories across the country to raise awareness of the African plight, and bring in funding to help.

Nyaka had been invited to bring two grannies and one coordinator to the event. It had been a difficult decision to select our granny representatives. We could have brought the grandmother who supported the most orphans, but it was just as important that the woman speak English. So in the end, we chose Freda, who had been instrumental in getting the school started, and Leonarda Ndazororera.

Leonarda was on the local management committee for Nyaka School. A retired teacher who understood the importance of education, she had taken three of the school's orphans into her home when she was sixty-six years of age. Without doubt, she was one of the most caring people I knew. She and her husband, who had paid for the bricks to get the Nyaka building project started and sat in as an adviser to the Nyaka management committee, remained big supporters.

"There they are!" Nicolas said.

Three familiar figures trudged down the concourse: Freda, in her tie-dyed purple and burgundy dress, looked tired but determined; Leonarda wore a black and gold dress, a bright red scarf about her neck. Christine brought up the rear, carrying two soft-sided travel bags. All three were smartly dressed for their American debut.

"Twesigye!" Freda called out.

Their exhaustion fell away and they nearly ran toward us. Nicolas jumped up and down with excitement.

"Even if we die now," Freda said, taking me in her arms, "we have seen so much and enjoyed the world."

I chuckled. They had been inside only airplanes and airports. "You have not seen anything yet."

"The teachers send you greetings," Freda said, "and the students."

"Maama and Taata send their blessings," Christine added.

"And I have letters from the students," Freda said, reaching for her bag.

"We have plenty of time for that," I said. After waiting for two hours in the airport, I wanted to get them to their rooms at Ryerson University, where they would be staying for the next week. They needed to check in and collect their information packets and stipends.

On the ride to the dormitory, we talked about their flights and the stopover in Amsterdam, and caught up on family news, but all conversation stopped when we parked in front of the building. The multistory white and tan structure towered above surrounding trees. Leonarda did not say anything, but her forehead wrinkled.

She looked even more concerned when they checked in and found they were staying on the eleventh floor.

Elevators became their first challenge. Christine showed them the buttons and how they worked, but as we ascended, I got the feeling the grannies were praying for their lives. There was a collective sigh when the doors opened and they exited into the linoleum hallway.

Their rooms were small, with a single bed in each and shared bathrooms and showers, but the Stephen Lewis Foundation had provided each of them with a welcome basket of fruits, bread, tea, and coffee. The window offered a spectacular view of downtown Toronto and its skyscrapers, but neither Freda nor Leonarda got close enough to it to see.

"Staying in this building is like living on the edge of the *enengo*," Leonarda said.

The first evening we had planned on taking the grannies out to dinner, but Freda and Leonarda were too nervous. They had been given $360 Canadian for expenses, and were having problems figuring out the exchange rate. When they finally realized they held more money than they had ever carried before, it became overwhelming. They decided to stay the first night in their rooms and eat the fruit and bread in their baskets. Not wanting to push too hard, we left them to rest.

"Do you wish to stay and sleep?" I asked Christine, assuming she might also be tired.

"I will sleep when I get back to Uganda," she said.

We walked down Parliament Avenue to a restaurant called the House. After dinner, we returned to a small home in town that

Brendan, a friend of the Foundation, had loaned us. Christine related news about my parents and the school. We talked late into the night, then escorted Christine back to her dorm.

When I arrived the next morning, I found Freda and Leonarda a bit more relaxed. They were ready to tour, but Christine looked irritated.

"I had to help them with everything," she said. "They were afraid to leave their room without me. I had to bring them down to breakfast and then back to the room to change clothes. They will not even use the elevator buttons."

"It will take them time to get used to things," I said. Christine was younger and had experience traveling in Kampala. "This is a shock for them."

We drove around the downtown area that morning, visiting the harbor, the CN Tower, and Chinatown.

After an afternoon nap, the grannies were ready for dinner with Stephen Lewis. The event was held in one of the dorm cafeterias. Women formed a rainbow of bright oranges and yellows and reds, waiting in line at the buffet. The grannies were happy to have "real food" instead of sandwiches, but they were amused by the salad.

"How can people stay healthy in this country eating raw food?" Leonarda asked. "People are not like *embuzi,* sheep, and *ente,* eating their greens raw."

In Uganda, especially in the villages, water and soil contaminated with bacteria from animal and human waste made it unsafe to eat raw food. Tradition dictated cooking everything but fruit.

"They eat not only raw vegetables," I said, "but also raw meat."

"Raw meat?" Freda gaped at her plate and gingerly stabbed her beef.

"In Japanese restaurants they eat sushi," I explained. "It is raw fish eaten alone or wrapped in rice."

Others sitting nearby must have thought I was telling good jokes, because the grannies erupted in such laughter that tears came to their eyes.

Stephen Lewis was introduced and applauded for his work as an envoy for the United Nations and creator of the Foundation and the Grannies program. The grannies turned their attention from food to the sophisticated-looking gentleman with glasses and graying hair, a colorful blue shirt, and a gray suit standing at the podium. When he welcomed the group to Toronto, Freda and Leonarda grinned like teenage girls smitten with a boy. Many Lewis Foundation recipients met Stephen when he visited program sites, but Nyaka was a difficult location to reach, and his busy schedule had kept him away so far.

That did not mean the Foundation had not visited Nyaka. Because they normally assist small grassroots organizations, it is important that they verify every program they support. Each year a consultant arrives to assess the project. Nyaka would never have attracted funding if our first consultant, Lucy Steinitz, had not made the long trip from Kampala to see the school. It required hours to visit her other projects; to get to Nyaka and back took days. But Lucy found the trip worth her effort. I think she fell in love with our children the moment she arrived.

Friday morning brought the official opening of the event. The grannies were transported in school buses from their dorms to an auditorium at George Brown College. There, I basked in the electric anticipation of three hundred grandmothers, two hundred from Canada and one hundred from the African countries of Kenya, Malawi, Mozambique, Namibia, Rwanda, South Africa, Swaziland, Tanzania, Uganda, Zambia, and Zimbabwe.

The women quieted as Stephen Lewis began his address.

"I am so happy to welcome you here today," he said. "It is difficult to believe we have managed to bring you all together." He thanked his daughter Ilana Landsberg-Lewis for organizing the event and the many volunteers for helping. Ilana had told us earlier that everything had been donated to the program: rooms, souvenir T-shirts, paper, books, and tickets. The support these grannies received was truly overwhelming.

"I am not here to take up your time with a speech," Stephen said. "It is you who deserve the credit. You are the experts. It is you who have been through so much. This event is to make your voices heard."

Next, Angelique Kidjo, a small woman with short cropped blond hair and a wonderful smile, came forward. A native of Benin and a UNICEF goodwill ambassador, she was intimately aware of the plight of the African grannies.

"*Ashe e maman, ashe e maman afirika. Maman afirika,*" she sang.

The crowd erupted, singing and clapping along with her. As she sang of Africa, of its heart and its strength, women stood and danced in the aisles. Grandmothers from opposite sides of the earth took hands and joined with one another, transcending differences of language, culture, and history. At that moment, they were all the same; women who shared a love for their children and their grandchildren, women who cared for one another, women who wanted to end the suffering, women whose voices would be heard.

When the singing ended, those voices *were* heard, loud and clear.

A South African granny told of losing two daughters and a grandson to AIDS and her efforts to care for her remaining grandson who was HIV positive. Another woman, from Zambia, spoke of directly caring for eight orphans and helping to look after sixty others at a children's center. An HIV-positive grandmother from Uganda told how she worked in a stone quarry and did beadwork to support twenty-eight dependents. A South African woman related the tragic story of her son, who had poured gasoline on his body and set himself afire when he learned he was HIV positive.

The Canadian grannies asked questions of the African women, amazed they could survive amid such poverty and loss. They wanted to know how they could provide more help. The African grannies wanted to know more about establishing and sustaining projects that would continue to care for their grandchildren when they were gone. There was much give-and-take between attendees. Each side had its own expectations and fears, but in the end they realized they shared a common goal. Governments could pass laws, write legislation, and send money that never reached them or only covered certain care, but these women held the power to make their own future. One way or another, the grandmothers were going to save Africa's orphaned children.

Listening to their stories I realized how blessed the Nyaka grannies already were. With the school there, they need not worry about their grandchildren's health and future support. They had arrived at the conference with more advantages than many of the other women. They did not have to ask the Canadian grannies for more assistance, and did not have to bring handicrafts to sell at the event to raise money. Even though I worried about the school every day and felt I was not doing enough, through this conference I saw how much progress we had made in Nyakagyezi. It filled me with pride, but also sadness that so much more needed to be done.

At the closing ceremonies Stephen Lewis and other United Nations dignitaries spoke. The women listened intently, some with tears in their eyes, most with heads held high, revitalized with a sense of mission. I knew their voices would continue to be heard. This was only the beginning.

Multicolored bead necklaces made by a Ugandan woman were handed out to everyone at the end of the event as a confirmation of support and unity. Each granny placed a necklace around the neck of her neighbor. I placed a necklace on Christine, feeling somber that the two-day event had passed so quickly, but hopeful that it marked the beginning of great change.

That change began on Sunday with a wave of women, music, and song thundering through the streets of Toronto. "We are marching in the light of hope," three hundred grandmothers chanted.

Flags and banners flashed.

Freda, Leonarda, Christine, and I flowed with the parade. Voices lifted skyward. Drumbeats echoed through the air, carrying a message of unity. Some grannies wore traditional dresses and colorful head wraps while others wore the T-shirts they had been given at the conference. The Canadian grannies came with running shoes and canes and walkers.

All the while, crowds cheered us onward and we felt as if nothing could defeat us.

The march ended at the CBC's Toronto headquarters. Inside the atrium, decorated with posters and banners, we gathered around a stage where Alicia Keys offered her support.

"Grandmothers," she said, "are the silent victims of the AIDS pandemic in Africa as they bury their own children and then begin parenting their grandchildren. I have a grandmother of my own and she's one of the most important women in my life. I admire you greatly and I support you so much."

Elton John sent a videotaped message promising his support in the United Kingdom.

Then two women, one from Africa and one from Canada, came forward to read the Toronto Statement.

Jo-Anne Page from Toronto said, "We demand the ear of the powerful; these words are for the conference and the twenty-five thousand delegates. Grandmothers are worth listening to. We demand to be heard."

Joyce Gichuna from Kenya continued, "Each of our stories is different, each of our experiences is unique, and yet we are here as representatives of countless women who share our tragedy; for every grandmother here today, there are fifty, sixty, seventy thousand at home. We have needs today, needs for the short-term and needs that will never go away. It is our solemn duty to the millions of grandmothers whose voices have never been heard that gives us the courage to raise those needs to demands—on their behalf, and on behalf of the children in their care."

After the reading, Stephen Lewis took the podium.

"I never imagined that there would be such a profound uniting of forces, the forces of the African grandmothers and the forces of the Canadian grandmothers." He added that he hoped the movement would grow to encompass grandmothers from around the world.

Other women came forward to make statements, sing songs, and present gifts. I had made arrangements for Freda and Leonarda to make a statement, but when it was their turn and they approached the microphone, Leonarda was overtaken by stage fright.

Freda was more comfortable speaking in Rukiga, so I translated for her.

"As Jesus came to the world to save us, Stephen Lewis has opened his heart to Africa and saved the children and the grannies. He is our savior, and on behalf of all the grannies here, in Uganda, and in all of Africa who did not come, I would like to thank the Foundation, Ilana, and its director, Stephen Lewis, our savior."

Applause rang through the building and Freda stepped back from the microphone with a look of serenity on her face I had never seen before. This was a momentous occasion in her life. As a mother who had raised nine children, a teacher who had inspired thousands in her thirty-plus years of teaching, and a volunteer who was now helping AIDS orphans reach their potential, her voice had become the voice of thousands of others, bringing AIDS awareness to the world. It was a moment none of us would forget.

Over the next couple of days, we toured more of the city and visited the local mall, where the grannies shopped for clothing and gifts. They both bought wedding rings to replace the wrinkled copper ones they wore. Freda complained how much land had been paved over to park cars when it should have been used for agriculture.

As we drove back to the airport on their final day, they bubbled over with excitement. They would have loved to stay longer, but were also eager to see their families and children.

"This experience will live close to my heart forever," Leonarda said.

My heart too, I thought, glancing into the rearview mirror. Nicolas had fallen asleep, nestled next to Christine. Freda and Leonarda glowed with such faith and expectation that I was sure God had reached down and touched them. I know He had touched me. I still had to worry about finding funding for the school, but with our Stephen Lewis Foundation grant, our generous Kampala supporters, the Global Fund for Children, and Indiana Friends of Nyaka raising more money each year, my optimistic spirit was rejuvenated.

CHAPTER 32

GRADUATION DAY

Graduation morning at Nyaka AIDS Orphans School December 2008 was blessed with sunny skies and overflowing with excitement. I gazed through the doorway to the school's new kitchen, watching Faida direct food preparation. She had nearly twenty people working for her catering company today. Men and women prepared meat, bananas, beans, ground nuts, and assorted vegetables for the celebration.

Fires burned hot in all three hearths, bringing large saucepans to boil. Two *ente* purchased by a generous New Mexican donor had been slaughtered the evening before. Some of the beef still hung from hooks. Much had already been cubed to be added to the soup pot. Other pieces were roasting, filling the kitchen with a meaty aroma.

"Good morning, Twesi," Faida said. "Have you come to help?"

"Cooking is woman's work," I teased, squeezing her shoulder.

"Because men are too lazy," she said.

I laughed, but my mood turned serious.

"It seems like only yesterday we were digging trenches for a two-room school," I said. "Now look at this big facility."

"You are indeed a man of miracles, Brother," Faida said. "I am so proud of you. But today I need someone to wrap the *matooke.*"

A man lowered a bag of potatoes to the cement floor.

"Or to cut potatoes," she added.

"Sorry, Sister." I hugged her gently. "You are a capable woman and will do a good job bossing all these workers. But you know, I am the *director,* and I have much work to attend to."

Faida grinned. "We have enough food to feed all Nyakagyezi today."

"Good," I said. "I hope they all come to see what our students have accomplished."

Outside, the children had already gathered in the school yard near the building, creating a sea of white with their new Nyaka T-shirts. Graduates huddled in a group, looking excited and anxious. I knew how they felt. Moving on to secondary school was a time to be free of home and at the same time miss one's family. I was confident they would all do well. All, except one.

I thought of Hannington as I walked across the lawn and mounted the steps to the sidewalk abutting the classrooms. Hannington had struggled with school from the very start, and we suspected he would not pass exams required to continue on to secondary school.

"Do you like school?" I had asked him during one of my visits to the village. Oftentimes, dislike of school led to poor attention and test scores.

"Oh, yes," he said. "I have many friends, friends I will have for life."

"Your test scores have been very low," I said.

"I know," he said, looking down. "I study hard and pay attention in class, but when I sit for an exam, I forget everything. But I will not give up, Director!"

Worry gnawed at me. Many of the students had big dreams

of being doctors and lawyers. I did not want to see Hannington disappointed.

"So, what do you want to do when you finish school?" I asked.

"I want to be a driver and mechanic," he said. It seems he had told all his friends that one day he would be the school's van driver, transporting sick people and students. He knew his limitations, but was determined to get a job and become a responsible citizen.

Relieved, I had smiled and patted his shoulder. "That is a good profession," I said. "We need more good mechanics in the village."

Stepping into the shadow of the school roof's overhang, I checked my tie to make sure it was straight. *No child will be forgotten,* I thought. If Hannington wished, we would send him to technical school to learn to be a master mechanic. Ironically, if he succeded he would finish his training and begin earning money before our doctors and lawyers even graduated from college.

At nine o'clock sharp, headmaster Stephen Kagaba welcomed me, and told the teachers and students to assemble in their class groups. People from America, including our international board chair, Robert Auld, Chris Singer, my new assistant in Michigan, and several volunteers joined us on the sidewalk while the children formed lines on the grass. Grannies and guardians waited in the shade of a tree in the yard beyond the students.

"I would like to see the graduates in my office," Headmaster Stephen said with a serious look.

The graduates looked worried as they filed past me into the headmaster's office. A few doubting grannies had spread rumors that there was not enough money to pay secondary-school tuition, and the students probably thought they were going to receive bad news.

When Maureen, one of the quieter girls, gave me a questioning glance, I held back a smile, for I knew they were in for a surprise.

Screaming erupted from the office, and those of us standing on the sidewalk moved to the window. Inside, graduates jumped up and down, laughing and dancing. Headmaster Stephen had a stack of graduation gowns on his desk and was holding up a blue cap.

"I think they like their surprise," Rob Auld said. The students would graduate in style thanks to a donation from a middle school in Rob's hometown of Aspen, Colorado.

"They are very happy," I said. "We cannot thank you enough for all that you have done." Rob and his wife, Carol, had become Nyaka supporters only two years before, but in that time they had been ardent fund-raisers, obtaining enough donations to build a second school, Kutamba, in a neighboring district.

Students streamed out of the office waving their graduation gowns and cheering. They gave me a group hug. It was difficult to believe these were the shy, undernourished children who barely reached my knee in 2003. Now they were confident, taller than me, educated, and ready to move on with their lives.

Headmaster Stephen emerged last showing a wide smile. He clapped his hands once to command everyone's attention. The graduates quickly donned their gowns and caps and formed two neat lines alongside the younger students.

"Good morning, children," Headmaster Stephen said.

"Good morning, sir."

"How are you?"

"We are well!" their voices echoed in the cool morning air.

"Are you winners?"

"We are winners!" they shouted. I found myself grinning. Bruno had grown into a fine young man. Emmanuel flashed his big white teeth, and Suzan, who had ridden on my lap to the Independence Day Parade, was now one of the first-year students. *We are all winners,* I thought. Seeing these children succeed was the biggest victory of my life.

After Headmaster Stephen's introduction, I stepped forward and thanked the teachers, volunteers, staff, the Nyakagyezi community, and our family around the world for their support.

"Please," I said to the younger students. "Turn and look at our graduates. They have suffered just like all of you." Olivia's father died when she was nine years old. Moreen lost both parents when she was six. Denis lived with his *mukaaka*. But now they were reaching for the stars. Onesmus and Izidol would be doctors, and Anita and Brenda would become teachers. Irene would study law.

"Do you see them?" I asked.

"Yes, sir!" they said in unison.

"Do you like what they are wearing?"

"Yes, sir!" Emmanuel's voice overpowered all the others.

"Do you want to be like them?"

"Yes, sir!"

"What do you need to do?"

"To study hard!" they shouted.

"In a few hours Professor Mondo Kagonyera will be here to award the graduation certificates. And someday soon, all of you will graduate with a cap and gown and move on to secondary school. Your dreams *will* come true."

The students erupted in cheers. I saw the glint of a tear in Mr. Agaba's eye.

"It is time for the parade," Headmaster Stephen said. With help from the teachers, the students formed a long line across the school yard, three abreast. Two of the taller boys were given the task of holding the Nyaka banner announcing the first graduation ceremony. They were followed by Nyaka students, Kutamba students, and guardians.

Guests joined us in the yard, some arriving from the street entrance, others walking up from the guest house or arriving through the banana plantation along the rear of the school. I was happy to see friends from Kampala: Sempa Baker and his family and staff;

Stanley; Emma Mugisha; our school chairperson, Dennis Mukasa; Frank's wife, Edith; and others.

I looked through the growing crowd for Nicolas's inquisitive eyes. He had made himself at home the moment we arrived. That morning, he had been busy with his cousin Sam, playing and checking on the livestock I had purchased for Nicolas the previous year. I spotted him with the third-year students and waved. He ran up to me and gave me a big hug.

"I have picked out the sheep," he said. "It is at Mukaaka's house."

"Good," I said as we walked to the parade line. Nicolas had already become a philanthropist, giving one of his sheep to a family in need each year. "We will decide which family gets the sheep after the graduation."

"Okay." Nicolas ran back to be with the younger students.

Wilfred, my longtime friend and our master of ceremonies, joined me. He shook my hand and stood back to look at my suit. "I must say, you do look like a director today."

Most of the time I wore casual clothing when I visited. "I could not let you outshine me today," I said.

Wilfred laughed. "No one can outshine you today, Twesi. Let the doubters eat their words."

Before I could respond, drums sounded and the children began singing the Nyaka School song.

"Everyone march!" Headmaster Stephen shouted.

The staff tried to keep everyone stepping in unison as we left the school yard. Excitement mounted on our way up the hill to Zeituni Church for a blessing. By the time we neared the church, everyone walked to their own drumbeat.

Wilfred moved to the front of the procession. I strolled beside Derick, thinking back to the eight-year-old boy who had arrived at Nyaka with his grandfather. If not for Nyaka, he would be tending goats in the field today with no plans for the future. Now he was on his way to becoming a major general in the army. Hellen walked ahead of us. She had dropped out of school at age nine when her parents died and her uncle could not afford the school fees. Now she planned to be a teacher at Nyaka School.

"It is a joyous day," my friend Stanley said, moving alongside me. "You should be proud of all you have accomplished here."

"I was only the catalyst," I said. "I could never have done this without the help of so many people."

"Including your father?"

I looked back. The hedge-lined road was entirely filled with white shirts, a wave of hope moving over the countryside.

"Taata and I still do not agree," I said.

"He complains you do not speak to him," Stanley said.

"He complains about everything."

"He is still your father."

"I know," I said. I had a living father, which was something none of our students could claim. As annoyed as I was with him, I had to admit I would never have accomplished very much without him. His iron-fisted stubbornness had shaped me as surely as Maama's loving arms.

"We will find common ground," I said. "Someday."

After the blessing, we marched to Kambuga, where we were met by a band playing trumpets and drums. People ran from their houses and lined the roadway to get a look at our graduates. Some of the town's children followed us on foot or bikes. Hundreds of people joined us on our return march to the school.

Three open-sided white tents decorated with orange and purple balloons and streamers had been erected on the basketball court near the road. Country-western and Ugandan music played over the public-address system. The graduates sat beneath one tent on white plastic chairs in front of the grannies. Younger students sat on benches in the open yard. My family, visitors, board members, teachers, and other local officials found seats in the other tents.

"Welcome everyone, to Nyaka AIDS Orphans School's first graduation," Wilfred said over the PA.

I sat between Professor Mondo and Rob Auld, while Wilfred introduced church officials who led us in prayers. The ceremony continued with introductions and words of thanks to board members, teachers, and many other people. The Nyakagyezi Grannies Group gave gifts to administrators and teachers. The choir sang and awards were given to top students in each class.

"And now," Wilfred said. "I would like to introduce the founder and director of Nyaka School, Mr. Twesigye Jackson."

I stood and scanned the crowd, throat tightening. How could I possibly tell these people what was in my heart? I was so proud of our students and what they had accomplished. I was so grateful to everyone who had helped us that no *thank-you* would be enough. Instead, I began with the story of Frank's death.

"When my brother died," I said, "I promised to take care of his son and daughters."

Stephen stood across the court filming me. Seeing my nephew, I wanted to cry with joy.

"But what of the children with no uncle?" My voice cracked and I swallowed hard. "Who will take care of them? I asked myself."

The crowd went silent.

"It was that day I decided I must help. So with the dedication of many people here and across the world, Nyaka AIDS Orphans School was built for you."

Maama and Taata were seated in the shade behind me. When I turned, Maama smiled, and I remembered what she'd said earlier in the day. "I am so proud of you and I know God is just getting started." I could barely choke back my tears to continue speaking.

"The Rotarian motto is 'Service Above Self,'" I said. "As a Christian I am called to be a servant. I am your servant."

I focused on the graduates. "You must become servants also. You must provide examples for the younger students. This day is not the end of your association with Nyaka; it is the beginning of another journey. I promise to support you until you finish your education, no matter what happens."

The audience applauded.

"Nyaka will always be your home," I said.

After my speech, graduates came forward to receive their certificates. When their names were called, I gave the students their certificates of completion and Rob presented them with a calculator. Three graduates gave short speeches of thanks.

Letters of congratulation were read from one of our most ardent supporters, Harriet Lewis, as well as Lucy Steinitz. Rob Auld spoke to the students about pride in one's self and one's community. Professor Mondo gave a rousing speech about the importance of community and education. After Mondo's speech, Wilfred welcomed everyone to stay for the feast.

With indescribable pride, I watched our twenty-two graduates stroll to the buffet table. They had witnessed the deaths of parents much too early in their young lives. Some had suffered neglect and abandonment, others simple poverty. Yet they were standing here with the promise of a good life and future before them. This day made up for all our grieving; it was a celebration of success.

"Congratulations," Sempa said, taking my hand and shaking it hard. "We have made it."

"Yes," I said. Not only had we just graduated our first class, our clean water system had been expanded, and we had our own educational radio program broadcasting from Rukungiri, and the Grannies Project. Our three-acre farm allowed us to grow maize, potatoes, and vegetables, and a grant from the Blue Lupin Foundation was funding the first public library in western Uganda. But there was much more to be done.

"You do not look convinced," Sempa said.

I chuckled. "Well, you know how I am. Now I am inspired to write more grants and make more phone calls. We have raised enough money to send all our students to secondary school this year only. We need more endowments. We need more schools in more villages, and better health care. If we could get the public schools to offer two meals a day—"

Sempa raised his hands between us. "Enough," he said. "Let us get this one graduation finished before we decide to educate the entire district."

I laughed and wrapped my arm around his shoulder. "You are right."

"Come," he said. "Let us fill our bellies with this good food."

I looked up the slope. A line stretched all the way from serving tables near the kitchen to the guest house, across the yard and down to the tents. Students and guests waited patiently for heaping plates of hot food and bottles of soda.

I thought of the line outside my parents' house each Christmas.

You do what you can, Frank's voice whispered.

I blinked back tears, imagining Frank smiling down on us, Mbabazi and little Gaddafi at his side. I saw Scovia in her new uniform sitting with the graduates, sipping milk and eating *mugaati* bread.

I *have* done what I can, Frank. And there is more that I will do.

AFTERWORD

I have been to the Nyaka AIDS Orphans School only twice, each time for just a short visit, but my memories of Nyaka inspire me every day.

Both professionally and personally, for the past thirty years I have sought to care for as well as to build the inner strength and emotional resilience of orphans and other vulnerable children in Africa and the United States. Yet the Nyaka AIDS Orphans School showed me a whole new way to do this work. Nyaka's concept is to create a holistic center that starts with a school but extends far beyond a formal primary education to include agriculture and nutrition, cultural programs, life skills, psychosocial supports, health care, and a home away from home. Local materials and people are employed: Nyaka is very much integrated into the rural life of southwestern Uganda.

Clearly this is not a minimalist approach: one dream at Nyaka is to take these children—one orphan per foster household initially—and support them all the way through secondary school and tertiary or vocational studies so that they can come back to support their own families and provide new leadership for their community and their country. To imagine this requires a huge leap of faith: after all, these children are among the poorest of the poor; almost none has a bed to sleep on; most are malnourished; and all have already lost at least one parent to HIV/AIDS.

When you come to Nyaka, however, this dream no longer seems far-fetched. That's because Nyaka is what dreams are made of. So much of what seemed impossible a few years ago has already come true.

I initially came to Nyaka in 2004 to assess the school for possible funding by the Stephen Lewis Foundation (www .stephenlewisfoundation.org). About eighteen months later, I returned to review its progress. On both occasions I spent time with the parents of Twesigye Jackson Kaguri—Nyaka's founder and director—and marveled at the elderly couple's dignity, warmth, and good humor. Since my visits, I have gladly directed students, friends, and individual donors to Nyaka, and have provided the school with professional resources on HIV/AIDS-prevention education, communication skills, and home-based care.

Nyaka introduced me to some amazing teachers, administrators and volunteers, grandmothers, and, above all, to Twesigye Jackson Kaguri himself, who interweaves his own life story in this book with that of the Nyaka AIDS Orphans School.

A freak accident when he was very young taught Twesigye Jackson to see suffering not as a punishment but as a lesson. Although he has faced the lessons of suffering many times in his life, each loss seems to motivate this man to work even harder for the sake of Nyaka's children and the future they represent. Moreover, Twesigye Jackson now fosters an even bigger idea to create more Nyakas elsewhere in Uganda—oases of learning and leadership that will gradually change the face of Africa and the world for the better.

Nyaka showed me that it is possible to achieve positive, sustainable change on very little money, so long as you have an unwavering vision, an abiding faith, and a near-infinite dose of love.

Nyaka also introduced me to Bruno, the fourteen-year-old boy you met in these pages. When I asked Bruno what aspect of his life was most difficult for him as a child living alone, he answered without hesitation, "When I wake up in the middle of the night."

"And what do you do then?" I asked, my heart breaking.

Bruno answered without hesitation. "I recite my homework for Nyaka in my head. That makes me feel better."

Whenever I feel discouraged in my own life, I now think of Bruno and the other Nyaka children. Rather than sadness or self-pity, these children evoke courage, insight, joy, and optimism. Their laughter is contagious. Each one is a testimony to the invincibility of the human spirit.

Although the Nyaka AIDS Orphans School upholds a Christian philosophy, I have noted with pleasure that the chairperson of the Guardians and Teachers Association, Habib Museka, is a Muslim. The management committee has members of all religious groups. Thanks to an arts and drama program, everyone learns to appreciate others' cultural traditions. Thus, when I was asked during my first visit to share a cultural song of my own, I taught everyone a simple two-word ditty in Hebrew entitled "Shabbat Shalom" (Sabbath Peace). During my second visit the students and teachers were still singing the song. It has now become part of Nyaka's regular repertoire.

When I first came to Nyaka, I wondered about the wisdom of separating orphaned children into their own school, rather than investing the same amount of money into the existing public education for all children. But I've since learned that the latter approach would have missed the central point of Nyaka's core philosophy.

Nyaka was created with the understanding that the impact of the HIV/AIDS pandemic is so pervasive in sub-Saharan Africa that we must approach child care and education in a new way. A holistic response is needed, one that listens to the children themselves and learns from their ideas and coping strategies. But this cannot be done in classrooms of sixty or seventy students or more, the situation in most government schools in rural Uganda. Rather, in order to meaningfully assist these orphans and build their resilience—that is, in order to recognize and strengthen their resources, skills, and endurance—these children require settings where teachers can work with them on a one-on-one and small-group basis.

In addition to guaranteeing a high-quality education to its pupils year after year, Nyaka School strives to create an environment that helps children build that inner resilience—their ability to understand and cope with adverse events, such as the death of one or both parents. Nyaka achieves this by providing a close and secure relationship with adults, ensuring strong peer relationships, growing and distributing wholesome food, giving out sufficient clothing, offering basic medical services, and fostering close links with each child's extended family and cultural community.

Nyaka didn't just happen. Without the vision, energy, and single-minded dedication of Twesigye Jackson Kaguri, the children of Nyaka would be destined to live with shattered dreams, malnutrition, illiteracy, and continued cycles of poverty. Thus, Nyaka is also proof that one person can still make a hugely positive difference in this world. And as Twesigye Jackson will be the first to tell you: the potential to do the same lies within all of us.

In Africa, we are sometimes reminded that if we want to see how bright the stars of the universe really are, then we must wait until the sky is darkest. We must go outside on a clear moonless night, when at first it seems that we can't see anything at all. That is how things first felt under the weight of the AIDS pandemic; when it seemed that everyone was dying and the future looked bleak and totally dark. But as time passes and we stare harder, gradually we begin to see more and more tiny stars glimmer through the blackness. It is on a moonless night that the stars seem brighter than ever.

So it is in Africa today: these stars are the world's children, who give us hope, and among them are the bright and shining faces of the Nyaka AIDS Orphans School.

Lucy Y. Steinitz, Ph.D.[*]
Regional Technical Advisor for Vulnerable Children and Families
(Africa)
Family Health International
Windhoek, Namibia

---

[*] The views expressed here are my own and do not necessarily represent the views of Family Health International.

AFTERWORD TO THE
PAPERBACK EDITION

THE BEST IS YET TO COME

I first learned about the Nyaka AIDS Orphans School and its founder, Twesigye Jackson Kaguri, through my graduate studies at the University of Arkansas Clinton School of Public Service (UACS). I had been searching for an organization to partner with for an international public service project. Whether by luck or a simple twist of fate, I came across Nyaka's Web site. Little did I know that only six months later, I would be making the very same trek down the steep *enengo* that Jackson describes in the opening chapters of this book.

I consider myself to be part of today's generation of young people committed to making a difference. My experiences in AmeriCorps and Teach for America strengthened my belief that quality education is the means by which we will break the cycles of poverty and inequity that exist in our world today. I chose to pursue my Master of Public Service degree at UACS because I was intrigued by former president Clinton's vision of a global leadership program, and I wanted to learn more about creating meaningful social change in real-world educational settings.

In my search to find an international project, I became inspired by the idea that a school that could transform and uplift an entire community through the education of its most vulnerable children. In the months leading up to my journey to southwestern Uganda, I had many conversations and e-mail exchanges with Nyaka's staff, board members, and with Jackson himself. We developed a project for my three-month visit, which was to gather information about Nyaka's education and community development programs and present it in a comprehensive model plan for use by other people around the world hoping to set up or expand a similar school.

In late May 2009, I boarded a plane at Boston's Logan Airport and traveled to one of the world's most impoverished regions. In August, I returned to the United States after having had some of the most rich and meaningful experiences of my life. It is a privilege to share some of these with the readers of this book.

Early in my trip, Teacher Agaba invited me to join him at one of Nyaka's Anti-AIDS Choir's performances. Words cannot adequately describe my emotions when I first heard the beautiful sounds of the children's voices, singing in unison the heartbreaking lyrics, "Every now and then, we are shedding tears. AIDS is killing our people." The members of Nyaka's Anti-AIDS Choir represent only a small fraction of the estimated two million Ugandan children who have lost one or both parents to the disease. While some adults avoid discussions about HIV/AIDS, Nyaka encourages its students to address the issue with grace and composure, for they know that education is the only way to escape the disease and its detrimental effects.

I also had the opportunity to meet a number of beneficiaries of Nyaka's Grannies Project. *Mukaaka* Hannah told us that she was probably sixty-five or seventy years old, though she could not be sure. If she were in the United States, Hannah might be enjoying her retirement. In rural Uganda, she faces the difficult task of caring for and raising ten children, all of whom are under age ten. Eight of the children are her biological grandchildren; the two others have no one else to care for them. HIV/AIDS and other factors have taken their toll on Hannah and her family. Hannah's house is smaller than the average school classroom, and even though it is a fairly sturdy structure, its roof leaks. On rainy nights, Hannah and her family crowd in one corner of the house to keep dry. No one complains, though.

With the support of the Grannies Project, things have improved for Hannah and her family. On the day that I visited, she proudly showed me large cabbage plants growing in her garden and the newly constructed pit latrine structure near her house. She also has a new kitchen, complete with a fuel-saving stove, which replaced the three stones she had previously used to cook food. To some, Hannah's living conditions are still depressing, yet she is grateful for all the opportunities she has been granted. Nyaka's Grannies Projects is successful because it mobilizes and empowers groups of women to help themselves. Together, they are making progress.

The students at Nyaka represent hope for Uganda's future. In their young lives, they have faced hardships that many of us cannot even comprehend, yet they are still children who like to laugh, play games, and learn. Emmanuel, now a P-6 student, is one of the children I had the privilege of meeting and teaching while I stayed at Nyaka.

One Sunday morning, Emmanuel accompanied Jackson's father, *Shwenkuru* (grandfather), and me to a church service. The thought of Shwenkuru, Emmanuel, and me traipsing across the hills and through the banana plantations still makes me smile today; we were an unlikely trio. We eventually reached the church and stayed there for several hours. Shwenkuru eventually suggested, through Emmanuel, that I go home for lunch. Emmanuel and I set off for the school, leaving Shwenkuru to bask in the limelight of being in the front row with his friends. Walking back, I had the chance to talk with Emmanuel about his life.

At his young age, Emmanuel has already lost both of his parents and the grandmother who took him in following their deaths. Today, he lives with another grandmother (not his own) and children who are not his biological brothers and sisters. Even though he would love to turn his passion for football (soccer) into a profession, he knows that he would probably need to be in a reserve camp by now in order to make it to the Premiere League. He explained to me that he is determined to focus on his studies and become a doctor. Emmanuel speaks English very well and stands near the top of his class. He has always had the ability to do great things, but with the support of Nyaka, he will also have the opportunities to do so.

As we neared the school, I felt my stomach growl. I knew that I had a meal of beans and *matooke* waiting for me at Nyaka's guesthouse. At this late hour, I did not know if the same was true for Emmanuel. Before parting ways, I suggested that we walk up the hill to one of the village stores so that I could treat him to a snack for helping me that day. When we got there, Emmanuel got a grape Miranda soda and I got a Mountain Dew. Together, we sat on a bench outside the store, shared a bunch of small, sweet bananas, and talked some more.

When it was time to leave, I thanked Emmanuel again for his help. He turned to me and said, "Surely, you're doing a good thing, Madame." At the time, I did not think to ask if he was referring to me buying the snack or teaching him how to write friendly letters in class or just visiting his school. Whatever the reason, his words stopped me in midstride, made me smile, and have stuck with me since. I could have gone anywhere in the world that summer; Emmanuel's words assured me that I went to the right place.

By August, I completed my project and said my tearful (though I hope not permanent) good-byes to the students and staff of Nyaka. Since then, the school has expanded to include the addition of a farm and a public library, the first of its kind in southwestern Uganda. At least one other organization has used the Nyaka model to start its own community-based school in neighboring Kenya. In December 2009, the school's leadership and staff celebrated the graduation of its second group of students, all of whom passed their exams, making them eligible to attend secondary school. All of these milestones suggest, as Jackson often likes to say, that "the best is yet to come" for Nyaka.

Ali Turro
Little Rock, Arkansas
November 2010

GLOSSARY

agandi—How are you?

akaro—a ball of ground millet paste

akeibo—a small papyrus basket with a lid used to serve *akaro*

asikali—guard

batembeyi—teenage hucksters

boda boda—a commercial motor bike for public transportation like
 a taxi

busuuti—the traditional women's dress worn on special occasions

ebishansha—dried banana leaves

embuzi—goat

Enda ezaara mwiiru na muhima—an old Rukiga adage meaning: In
 a family you get all sorts of people.

enengo—a rugged sharp ridge

ente—cow

gomesi—women's traditional national dress with a square neckline,
 full skirt, and sash

gonja—roasted plantain

kaa kiini—Lie down!

kabalagala—small sweet banana

Keije/Buhooro/Buhorogye—Rukiga expressions of excitement in greeting a guest you have not seen for a long time.

maama—mother

matooke—steamed green bananas

muchomo—roasted chicken on a stick

mugaati—yeast bread

mukaaka—grandmother

Mukama akurinde okuhisya obuturirebana—May the Lord protect you and keep you safe until we meet again.

muzungu—humble name for a white person

Nigye—I am fine.

Nimarungi—I am fine.

Nkakugambira—I told you so!

Nkuyambeki?—May I help you?

obudongo—cement used to build mud daub buildings

panga—machete

Ruhanga wangye—Oh my God!

shamba—garden field

shwenkuru—grandfather

slim—slang for AIDS

taata—father

waringa—scarecrow

wazungu—Swahili term for white people

Webale—Thank you.

Webale kwiija—Thank you for coming. You are welcome.

Yetegyereze—Watch out!

ACKNOWLEDGMENTS

This book could never have been written without my family and the wonderful mentors and teachers who prayed for me, inspired me, believed in me, and encouraged me to work hard and to strive for a better life: my maternal grandmother, who provided spiritual light in my darkest days; Maama and Taata, who saw to it that I received an education; my brother, Frank, who showed me the meaning of "Good Samaritan"; my sister Mbabazi and teacher Freda Byaburakirya, who became second mothers; Professor Mondo Kagonyera, who was a hero and role model for many of us in the village; my sisters Faida and Christine, who support me at every turn; Beronda, who became my most radiant source for inspiration and love; and my son, Nicolas, a true gift from God.

Thanks to Emma Mugisha for supplying blueprints to Nyaka's unique community plan. Thanks to Lucy Steinitz and Ilana Landsberg-Lewis from the Stephen Lewis Foundation for recognizing our school's potential and becoming invaluable supporters for the cause. And thanks to Maya Ajemera of the Global Fund for

Children for being the first U.S.-based foundation to support Nyaka and for their continuing assistance.

There are not enough pages in this book to adequately express my gratitude to the many people, churches, organizations, and Friends of Nyaka groups in Uganda and across the world that helped bring this project to fruition. You know who you are and the children thank you every day in their prayers.

I would also like to thank our current and past board members, volunteers, staff, and community supporters. Without them Nyaka School would not be the flourishing success it is today. I send my love to them.

Special thanks to Susan Linville for her tireless work in bringing this book to life, and Steve Ramey for his help along the way. I owe a debt of gratitude to our agent, Caitlin Deinard Blasdel, for her most excellent advice in revising the original manuscript and for finding the perfect publisher. Her counsel was greatly appreciated. I am happy to say that Viking Penguin has indeed been the perfect publisher, and I want to thank everyone there for all their care and support, especially Clare Ferraro, Nancy Sheppard, Carolyn Coleburn, Yen Cheong, Amanda Brower, and the best sales force in the business.

Finally, I thank Carolyn Carlson at Viking Penguin for her incredible enthusiasm and sharp editorial eye. This was truly a match made in heaven.

And to those of you who read this book and are moved to help make this world a better place, I thank you most of all.

HELP MAKE A DIFFERENCE
"FOR OUR CHILDREN'S SAKE"

1. Visit www.nyakaschool.org or www.thepriceofstones.com for more information, book reviews, events, and ideas.

2. Become a friend of the Nyaka AIDS Foundation on Facebook—or become Jackson Kaguri's friend there. You can also follow Jackson on Twitter at twitter.com/twejaka

3. Recommend *The Price of Stones* to a friend; colleague; book club; women's group; your church, synagogue, or mosque; civic group; Rotary, Kiwanis, Lions, Farmers, Elks, or other club; or any group interested in education, literacy, cross-cultural issues, Uganda, HIV/AIDS prevention, or alleviating poverty. Help spread the word-of-mouth by offering to lead a discussion of the book at your house of worship, library, or book club.

4. Propose *The Price of Stones* for suggested reading at a school or university near you.

5. Check to see if *The Price of Stones* is in your local library. If not, either donate a copy or suggest to your librarian that the book be

added to the collection. Ask your friends or family in other states to do this also. Or check to see if the book is in the library of your church, synagogue, or mosque; if not, donate a copy or recommend the book to your librarian.

6. Encourage your local independent or chain bookstore to carry this book if you don't see it on the shelves.

7. Write a book review of *The Price of Stones* for Amazon, Barnes & Noble, Borders, or a blog. Your comments will help bring awareness to this (or any) book.

8. Ask the book editor of your local newspaper or radio station to consider letting you review the book. Or review the book for the newsletter or Web site of a civic or religious organization you belong to.

9. If you want to support our efforts to promote education, you can make a tax-deductible contribution to our nonprofit organization. Donate through our Web site or through the Global Giving Fund. Donate once or become a Monthly Sustaining Donor. To give via check, please write to:

> Nyaka AIDS Orphans Project
> P O BOX 339
> East Lansing, MI 48826

10. Form a Friends of Nyaka Group or join one in your area. Our Friends Groups help spread our message. Check our Web site to learn how you can start your own group in your community or on your college campus.

11. Invite Twesigye Jackson Kaguri to speak at your house of worship, library, or civic organization—and bring lots of friends to hear him!

12. Volunteer at the Nyaka School or do an internship there. Past volunteers, interns, and mission groups from churches have helped with teaching; tutoring; building and road construction; health education, especially HIV/AIDS prevention; medical care; agriculture; business and marketing; and counseling. Whatever your talents are, you will have the opportunity to serve these children, and you will also have the experience of a lifetime as you learn from them and the community they live in.

13. Knit or crochet a Comfort Doll that will be given to the school's children, to help provide students with psychosocial support, trauma counseling, and bereavement care. For instructions, visit our Web site.

14. Your child may want to become a Young Hero for Nyaka. Some Young Heroes have gathered books, collected relatives' pocket change, and dedicated birthday money for donation.

15. Please direct media or book inquiries to info@nyakaschool.org, info@thepriceofstones.com, or call (517) 402-2787, or write us at the address above.